JAMES HASKELL
RUCK ME

I'VE WRITTEN ANOTHER BOOK

HarperCollins*Publishers*

BY THE SAME AUTHOR

What a Flanker

HarperCollins*Publishers*
1 London Bridge Street
London SE1 9GF

www.harpercollins.co.uk

HarperCollins*Publishers*
1st Floor, Watermarque Building, Ringsend Road
Dublin 4, Ireland

First published by HarperCollins*Publishers* 2021

1 3 5 7 9 10 8 6 4 2

© James Haskell 2021

James Haskell asserts the moral right to
be identified as the author of this work

A catalogue record of this book is
available from the British Library

HB ISBN 978-0-00-847222-1
PB ISBN 978-0-00-847223-8

Printed and bound in the UK using 100%
renewable electricity at CPI Group (UK) Ltd

MIX
Paper from
responsible sources
FSC™ C007454

This book is produced from independently certified FSC™ paper
to ensure responsible forest management.

For more information visit: www.harpercollins.co.uk/green

'I would rather be ashes than dust! I would rather that my spark should burn out in a brilliant blaze than it should be stifled by dry-rot. I would rather be a superb meteor, every atom of me in magnificent glow, than a sleepy and permanent planet. The proper function of man is to live, not to exist. I shall not waste my days in trying to prolong them. I shall use my time.'

Jack London

CONTENTS

FOREWORD

Why another book? I imagine they asked Tolstoy the same question after the publication of *War and Peace*, and Dickens after writing *Great Expectations*. Well, let's just say my first book *What a Flanker* raised more questions than it answered (and it has absolutely nothing to do with the fact that it sold more copies than expected and the publishers offered me better money to write this one).

Who is James Haskell? Why do people think he's a dickhead (even his wife)? Why do some people no longer think he's a dickhead? What is a dickhead, anyway? What was it about his typical childhood – the summers in Rangoon, the luge lessons, the making of meat helmets in the spring – that made him the man he has become? Was it his humble schooling that made him the reserved, unassuming adult Haskell we see today? Was it the fluffy world of rugby union that made him the very model of a modern man?

To answer these questions – and others like, 'What percentage of the jokes I come out with over dinner are shit?' and, 'Why do I spend my time arguing with trolls and trolls' wives on Instagram when I could be having a cup of tea and a Hobnob with an actual mate in real life?' and, 'Do I really have the mind of a serial killer?' – I have taken a trip through the foothills, the peaks and the canyons of my life, from the cradle to digging in a quarry in a JCB.

Along the way, I have spoken to some of the most important people I know – my mother, my wife, schoolmates, teachers, ex-teammates, ex-coaches, business partners, Kevin the security guard in Waitrose (though he didn't make the cut) – in an attempt to make more sense of me. Why the intense shyness in public? Why the almost feminine sensitivity? Why the pathological hatred of confrontation? On reflection, I have to say that most of them had no idea what they were talking about, and at times I wonder if they weren't in fact recounting the life of someone else entirely, but they gave it a good crack, bless them. To be honest, my publishers wouldn't let me extend the deadline for this book by interviewing some actual Haskell aficionados or in fact people who appeared to like me.

So join me on an epic odyssey of discovery like no other – a Haskovery™, if you will. You will laugh, you will weep, you might still think I'm a dickhead at the end of it. Whatever you think, I will keep bouncing back and most definitely have the last laugh.

1

I, DICKHEAD

PAUL DORAN-JONES, BEST FRIEND & ENGLAND TEAMMATE:
'Why do people think James is going to be a dickhead?
Because he is.'

OLLIE PHILLIPS, STADE FRANÇAIS TEAMMATE:
'It's true, when people find out I'm mates with Hask,
they'll roll their eyes and say, "Isn't he a dickhead?" And
I think some of his Stade Français teammates thought he
was a dickhead at the beginning. Fair enough, to be
honest.

'Hask is an expressive person who wins people over
with his brashness and crass wit. Or at least that's
normally his approach in England. But he didn't speak
French, apart from rude words. So when he first walked
into the changing room and some of his teammates
started shouting, "Fucking 'ell, it's 'askell! Fucking rosbif,
it's the little English gay!" he started calling them all
wankers and telling them to suck his cock (suce ma bite,
as every naughty schoolboy will know). Most people in
that situation would be shy and timid, but he went the
other way completely. What kind of person walks into

*their first day of work in a foreign country and starts
abusing his colleagues? James Haskell, that's who.*

*'Remember, he'd just left Wasps, his childhood club,
and this was the first time he'd played abroad. He'd taken
a big risk by moving to Stade, because most people
thought it would put his England career in jeopardy.
He'd just broken up with his first long-term missus. His
life was pretty complicated. But he didn't seem to give a
shit. And once his teammates got over the shock of this
massive English bloke turning up every morning and
slagging them all off, they learned to love him. He won
their respect by training hard, being the most professional
member of the team and delivering in games. It was clear
that he really wanted the club to do well. And they soon
began to see past the brashness and realise that he was
actually a really good lad. Soon, if Hask wasn't abusing
them, they'd be disappointed. That was part of his
charm.'*

Thanks, lads. What a way to start this book off. Two of your
best mates confirming what most people suspected, that I am
a bit of a dickhead. But, to be fair, I dragged them into this.
And as Jules said to Vincent in *Pulp Fiction*, 'If my answers
frighten you, then you should cease asking scary questions.'

More on my time in France a bit later, but what readers need
to know for now is that I've never really fitted in and always
been a bit of a wrong 'un, at least in some people's eyes. Back
in school, I was never particularly popular. I divided opinion,
was probably liked and disliked in equal measure. I know
what you're thinking: Marmite. I should have that word chiselled into my headstone: 'HERE LIES JAMES "MARMITE"
HASKELL – THEY LOVED HIM OR HATED HIM.'

I'd describe myself as 'anti-cool', especially at Wellington College, which I joined when I was 13. I had good friends, but I was never one of those kids who was liked by everyone, from the geeks and the alternative kids to the jocks. Plenty of my current friends were those super-cool kids liked by everyone, invited to all the parties – that was certainly not me. Now, I finally know my value and spend time with people who enjoy my company. But when you're at school, it doesn't work like that. You're thrown into the mix and it's sink or swim. I was outspoken, had a sharp tongue, which some people couldn't hack. If someone had a go at me, I never really had the self-restraint not to give it back, whether they were older or younger. That can make things a little difficult for you when you are young. Saying that, some people still can't hack it now.

For most of my teenage years, there was nothing cool about me. I don't mean that in a let's be humble way; I was honestly like Carlton from *The Fresh Prince of Bel-Air*. Until I was 15, my mum laid my clothes out for me to wear to places and they were not cool clothes. They were jeans with the pleats ironed in and jumpers that more often than not matched my younger brother's. If you saw me back in the day you would have earmarked me as someone who was going to be a permanent virgin. My mum would also encourage me to comb my hair into a side-parting so I looked like one of Bill Gates's mates. I had no concept of fashion (many, including my wife Chloe, would argue that fashion is a concept I'm still to wrap my head around). I never read magazines or knew what cool was. The standard stuff that all the other kids had – Stüssy tops, Naf Naf jackets, the T-shirts that changed colour when they warmed up and jeans that didn't make you look like a paedophile – I missed out on. I didn't even realise I was that uncool, I just had very little self-awareness.

When I needed new shoes for example, I was whisked straight off to Clarks to get the most basic shoes known to man, the only highlight of the trip being you got to put your feet in that electric measuring device, which was definitely the best part about the trip as the shoes looked correctional at best. Sadly, after about age 10 my feet were too big for the machine, so I had them manually measured by some old harridan who hated me.

My shoe game was rubbish but made even worse by me having clown feet at an early age. If I did spot someone wearing cool shoes I'd say to my mum, 'Could I have them, please, please, Mum?' and she would say, 'No, you're getting these Dunlop trainers instead, it's what the school recommends.' So for most of my life, all I rocked with was a pair of Green Flashes. The irony is that they are now actually cool to wear and I am wearing what's not cool.

I wasn't into music, like most teenagers. I certainly didn't buy the *NME*, listen to the latest indie bands or go to gigs. I was, to use an old-fashioned phrase, a bit of a square.

When I first arrived at Wellington, I tried smoking and drinking with the cool kids, but I knocked all that on the head when I started taking rugby seriously. Wellington traditionally had a reputation as a top rugby school, but back then the new headmaster was what you might call a progressive, in that he thought the school needed to step away from its old ways and become a much more academic force rather than a place for meathead rugby players. Instead of keeping what was good about the school, he decided that focusing on athletic pursuits was a bit vulgar, so he would underplay that side of things while overplaying everything else. He was constantly trying to deflect from sport to more niche pursuits, presumably to be more inclusive and not upset the Dungeons & Dragons players and the origamists. Wellington back in the day was not the highly regarded academic force it is today. It was only under the stewardship of the great Anthony Seldon that it was transformed from a middle-of-the-road public school to one of the best schools in the country. The very fact they let me in all those years ago should tell you everything.

To give you an example of this emphasis away from sport, we used to have full school assemblies with all 800 students including staff every Monday morning, in which the then headmaster got the various team captains to talk about their latest results – the captain of the a cappella team, the captain of the mime team, the captain of the basket-weaving team. Basically, any other sport or club that the school was not known for was asked to give a quick match report, and if there was any time left over they might let the rugby captain say a word or two, but more often than not the headmaster would say that's all we have time for and we can hear about the rugby team next time.

Down the years Wellington had become a bit like an American college where the primary school sports team (rugby in our case, American football in the USA) sort of did what it liked as long as it won. Jonty Driver, the headmaster in my first year, was proper old school and loved his sport. If you could play rugby you got away with anything. A lot of the teachers hated that, so when the new head came in it caused a bit of a revolt, which passed down to the pupils. No longer were the rugby players afforded any leniencies or special privileges; in fact it went the other way. Nerds, rebels and liberals were in, jocks were out.

Surprisingly I was quite academic. Yes, I got up to mischief, but it wasn't really jock stuff, it was just what most boys got up to, whatever kind of school they went to. It's not like we were standing around in corridors in lettered varsity jackets, pushing nerds into lockers or flushing a chess kid's head down the toilet. It was just common-or-garden mucking about, like throwing water balloons out of windows on each other, tripping each other up, smashing books out of kids' hands – or my favourite, which took place when leaving the dining room. We would fill plastic cups up with water and then turn them upside down on our trays, thus sticking them in place due to the water and air seal. We would then put them on a conveyer belt that would disappear through a hatch into the kitchen. You would wait outside as some unwitting kitchen staff would, without thinking, yank the cup off the tray to put it into the bin and get soaked. You would then hear this scream and a 'Fuck you, you little pricks!' and more often than not this irate pot-washer would come storming out to find the culprits, as we ran off laughing as if it was the greatest thing ever. To be fair, it does sound like a dick thing to do, but they fell for it every single day, so at some point you had to ask yourself who was really to blame.

PAUL DORAN-JONES:

'Not a jock? That's utter bullshit. James paints this picture of himself as a self-effacing schoolboy, quiet, a bit of an intellectual. Some of that rings true, in that he was articulate, studious and brighter than some people gave him credit for. But he was also larger than life, even called himself "The B-NOC" – "The Big Name on Campus". He was a man-sized unit at the age of 15, already a rugby god. He had his own personal trainer, for Christ's sake!

'The only time James would tone down his jockness was when he was trying to create an in with one of the girls, in which case he'd suddenly turn into Oz from

American Pie, *the lacrosse star who joins the school choir in a bid to get laid. The reason James liked – and still likes – to make out he wasn't a jock, and was really a sensitive soul, is to further his cause in life …'*

Okay, so Dozzer thinks I was a jock. He might be right, up to a point. I don't ever remember calling myself BNOC, but I do remember Dozzer describing himself as the BLT on more than one occasion. (In case you haven't read *What a Flanker*, BLT stands for Big, Lean and Tanned.) So it was the BNOC and BLT doing bits with the ladies. With a duo like that, it's a wonder we didn't have our own TV show. If I am Oz, then Dozzer is Finch from *American Pie*: he'd hit you with some sophisticated chat and then bang your mum.

Actually, now is probably a good time to tell you about the first time I met Dozzer, or Paul as he's known these days, because he'll be popping up a lot in this book (usually to contradict me, as has already become apparent).

Having not really given much of a shit about rugby for many years, once I realised I was pretty good at it and could maybe become a professional player, I took it far too seriously. Playing for Wellington's first XV seemed like the greatest thing a boy could possibly do, so pre-seasons had a very intense vibe. That was the time to put your stake in the ground, make a position your own. Even though the headmaster may have tried to detract from the rugby team, all the coolest and most popular people in school during my first couple of years were in the rugby team. The whole school would turn out for a game, chant and dress up. These guys were heroes and certainly the people I was inspired to be like. So, when it was our time to try out for the first XV as members of the lower sixth, we were all fired up. This was our big moment.

Picture the scene: all these young bucks, myself included, and the previous years' players now the senior statesmen, all getting our boots on by the side of the pitch. There was nervous energy in the air, the odd bit of chat, but also that overriding atmosphere of fear that you always have before a trial or a big session. What did the coach have planned? Would we do well? Would we make the cut? This was make it or break it time, at least in our small-minded world. Ken Hopkins was the king, the man to impress. He was the architect of so many unbeaten seasons, a legend on the school coaching circuit who had harvested some of the best talent in the country. He was the man we all needed to impress. This Welsh wizard could make you a star – or not.

I never spoke to Ken for my first three years at school. I was too scared. He had an aura about him. Everyone knew he was Wellington College's first XV coach, and one of the most successful ever. He used to just give you a nod, never a smile, when you passed him, and walk on. But as I got to know him, I realised that Hoppy was a lovely and very funny man. He was also Dozzer's housemaster, which I think is why he retired not long after we left. Poor bloke.

Going back to that day when we were trialling for the first XV, just as we were about to step onto the hallowed Wellington turf for the first time this fat, rosy-cheeked kid, with big traps, appeared out of nowhere to join the party. To make matters worse, he was late and was brazenly wearing another school's kit, which was a cardinal sin on the public-school circuit. He sidled up and was about to say hello when Ken stopped him before he could utter a word and said, 'Dosser, you are late, mate, give me five laps of the field!'

Incidentally, Ken always called him 'Dosser' instead of 'Dozzer', though I think he really wanted to call him 'Tosser' but remembered he was a teacher and not in the Valleys anymore. Anyway, not the ideal way to start pre-season for old Dozzer. There were instant murmurs like, 'Who the fuck was that kid? Did you see the size of him?' One kid chimed in that he looked like a Portaloo with legs. (When I say kid, I think that may have been me.) Others were thinking, 'How dare this kid rock up in the last two years of school and try and get in to the team, *our* team? A team we had waited four years to play for.' Well, that's what I was thinking anyway and I am pretty sure everyone else was too.

This kid, who turned out to be none other than Paul Claude Arbuthnot Lawrence Doran Jones, aka Dozzer (okay, there is no Claude Arbuthnot in his name, but the prick said I called myself BNOC so he can deal with it), was plodding around the pitch with the speed of a small, slightly damaged tug boat, he had a surly demeanour, still had all his own hair and may or may not have heard some of the abuse I was directing at him, like the big posh lout that I was.

Unsurprisingly, Dozzer didn't take too kindly to this rather hostile welcome, and we didn't really speak for a while. Just a lot of cold looks and pretending each other wasn't there. Dozzer is such a personable bloke that he soon ingratiated himself with some of the other lads, but we only really clicked after a kid from the upper sixth started on us both on a staircase up to my dormitory. If I remember rightly, Dozzer, who never likes to take shit off anyone, was having none of this kid's rubbish and was certainly not going to take his books to his room for him or make him any buttered toast, and did not like being called a dick. So Doz did what Doz does and pushed this guy, the guy bravely swung at Dozzer (I say bravely, as Doz was shorter but about five times wider and this senior kid looked like a keen member of the Wellington Warhammer club), and even though we were not mates at that time, the brotherhood of rugby united us and we replied with a few crisp body shots before shoving him down the stairs. The bully had chosen the wrong people to mess with. Someone may have then picked up his books and other accoutrements and lobbed them down on top of him for good measure. After that, we bowled off up the stairs, our chests inflated, confidence soaring, and a look passed between us that said, 'You're all right, actually.' By the time this kid's Transformers pencil case had ricocheted off his crumpled body, Doz and I were firm friends. We went off and shared an illegal beer, and have been thick as thieves ever since.

Becoming friends with Dozzer was very much like *I'm Alan Partridge* when Alan befriends Dan in Michael's petrol station, they bond over 'Lexi', the Japanese Mercedes, and begin finishing each other's sentences. It was quite clear to me that Dozzer was a fantastic man. Sometimes after a home game for the school, we'd go to a pub around the corner called The Wellington. I've no idea why they served us because they must have known we came from the school, but we'd have a few pints and come back steaming. Like when Alan met Dan, it was almost an epiphany: I'd suddenly found someone who got all my little nuanced jokes and references that other people didn't get, and vice versa. Sometimes, we'd laugh so much we had Kenco coming out of our nostrils. Other times I'd find myself repeatedly shouting Dozzer's name – 'Dozzer! Dozzer! Dozzer! Dozzer!' It was odd when he was with girls, he could never hear me. I was always desperate to get his attention. And, of course, we both turned out to be 'sex people', which you will know from *What a Flanker*, but more on that later.

I was a meathead if we are being honest, and *Ruck Me* is all about telling the truth (well, as much truth as the lawyers and my wife will let me tell). Me and Dozzer did once lock a mate in a trunk and pretend we were going to drop him down numerous flights of stairs, which being fair to him were pretty high up and would have caused some sort of injury. Again, I will flag this up before you label me a complete prat: who would get into a trunk willingly after being asked to by me or Doz? A muppet, that's who.

He must have known when we said, 'Listen, we are just going to shut the lid for a second,' that something was going to happen. But every day is a school day, and for this kid it was a much-needed lesson in who to trust and who not to. Better he learned it from us than someone with really bad intentions.

Of course, we clearly didn't push him down the stairs but we walked him around the room for a while, pretending to go through doors, along corridors and finally put him up on a desk in the same room. Of course, being dark and disorientating, he had no idea where he was. When we said, 'Be careful, you are on the edge of the stairs, you better come out slowly … we are unlocking the lid,' he didn't listen to our advice and opened the lid with one aggressive flourish and proceeded to tip the trunk off the desk onto the floor, which was a fall of around three feet. However, in his confused state he thought he was at the top of thirty flights of stairs. So when he went arse over tit, he thought his short, privileged life was over.

If I close my eyes now, I can still hear his scream. I imagine that after years of therapy he can probably manage in a confined space now, or perhaps not. Obviously he snitched, so I had to answer to a charge of bullying from my housemaster, a rather officious man of the cloth. Apparently, saying the simpleton got into the trunk willingly and that we didn't actually push him down the stairs didn't wash as a valid excuse for our behaviour.

There's no way I was a classic jock, as in American high school movies, because I was simply never hip enough. The fact I use the word 'hip' goes to prove that.

In the movies, jocks have hot chicks dripping off them at parties, where they're all drinking Rolling Rock out of those red plastic cups. I didn't even get invited to parties. I was standing outside parties with the kid who ate the glue. Even the nerds were cooler than me. Movie jocks are allowed to get away with things others aren't and are respected for their sporting talent, but most people thought I took rugby far too seriously, especially the girls. I'd be working with my personal trainer and people would be looking at me as if I was mad. They were no doubt thinking, 'He's already training three times a week with the rugby team. Why is he doing extras? Who does he think he is?' When I developed abs, I thought it might bag me some lady action. You always see the jocks take their tops off and there isn't a dry pair of knickers in the house. Now admittedly, I had the abs but not the boat race to match, which I will concede. The old 'body like *Baywatch* and face like *Crimewatch*' problem.

Instead of loving the abs, the girls took one look at them and said, 'That's disgusting. It looks like you're made of plastic.' They found the boys who drank, smoked, smelt of body odour and knew all about the latest bands while affecting a lack of interest in anything else much more attractive.

Okay, so here's the most jock think I ever did. Wellington's first XV pitch was called 'Big Side', and rugby players like me regarded it as hallowed ground. However, the cool kids used to smoke on it and leave their fag butts, cigarette packets and other crap all over the place. They knew they were besmirching holy turf and that it would wind the rugby players up. Sure enough, one night a few of us rugby lads marched down there;

we waited silently in the dark like members of the SAS; some of us may even have been wearing balaclavas, which I can neither confirm nor deny. We then waited for all these miscreants to convene, and like a precision air strike we all came flying in and dump tackled the lot of them. Some tried to run. Big mistake.

Imagine one moment having a fag, sipping on your can of Fanta, when one of your mates who was standing next to you a second ago is suddenly upended like a bin bag without warning. You panic, you run, you think, 'What the fuck's happening?' It's fight or flight. You find yourself flying through the still dark night racked with fear, when bang, someone axes you from behind in the dark, stuffs your head in the floor and shouts, 'Get the fuck off Big Side!'

Once they had dusted themselves down and some of them had stopped crying and saying we'd wrecked their Stüssy hoodie or torn their Ed Hardy jeans, they were told collectively never to set foot on Big Side again. As we walked off, we were whooping and hollering and high-fiving like over-excited Americans. And when I look back, I think, 'Oh my God, what an utter loser I was. What *was* I thinking?' I cringe so hard just writing these words. No wonder people thought I was an arsehole.

But not fitting in never really bothered me. In fact, not fitting in as a kid has its advantages. If you're one of the popular kids who finds life a breeze, I'd imagine you can get complacent. That's why, looking back, I'm glad I wasn't. If you're a bit different, and feel like you're not quite good enough, you become determined to prove your worth in whatever way possible. Proving people wrong and using negativity were huge driving forces for me.

* * *

For years, people would say to me, 'I thought you were a wanker, but you're actually all right.' That went through the roof after my previous book, *What a Flanker*, was released. Suddenly, loads of people were sending me messages on social media, telling me they thought I was a prick before they read it. Now to be honest, it was really humbling to get so many nice responses; in fact I was blown away by how many people bought and loved the book and ended up changing their opinion of me. I would read the comments that said how much they disliked me but had changed their opinion after reading the book and think, 'Honestly, where did you get the idea that I was a prick from? How small-minded do you have to be to take a dislike to someone because of the team they play for or something you read about them?' But when I thought about it a bit more, I understood why. People form opinions about you from the small snapshots you show them – I'm no different. We all see things online or in the papers and go, 'Oh God, so-and-so is such a nightmare,' or 'What a plonker.' So it's not surprising that people see me taking my shirt off on social media while effing and blinding and being a bit of a lad on podcasts, or read about me having a row with someone online, and think, 'This guy is an idiot.'

JAMIE JOSEPH, FORMER HIGHLANDERS HEAD COACH:
'I never had any misgivings about signing Hask. He'd had a few off-field problems at the 2011 World Cup, but I spoke to his England coach Martin Johnson and he assured me that Hask was a good bloke. I also got on the blower to a couple of guys he played with in Japan, Tamati Ellison and Ma'a Nonu, and they both loved him. They gave me glowing reports of his work ethic, as well as his character. They said he was different, a bit quirky,

brought a bit of fun to the place, and I like players with a bit of personality.

'I couldn't believe my luck. It was hard to get quality players that far down south, and now this England international had become available. That just didn't happen. It still doesn't happen now. I remember thinking, "Wow, he really wants to come and play in Dunedin?" We had an inexperienced team, were looking to build, and Hask fitted the mould perfectly. Plus, he was quite happy to come and play for bugger all. That's what sealed it for me, because I knew he was coming for the experience, and not for the money.

'My first impression of Hask was that he knew how to handle a coach. I'd ask him a simple question and he'd give me a minute-long answer. I'd smile at him, as if to say, "Come on buddy, I'm not stupid …" But we immediately got on really well. And once he got comfortable within the team, the true James Haskell came out. Hask always talked too much and did not stop telling tales about his time in France and Japan.

'One team meeting, I referred to him as Gulliver, as in Gulliver's Travels. I was having a little dig, I suppose, saying, "Mate, I know you've been around, but you're in New Zealand now and it's time to front up." He got the Gulliver reference straightaway, because he's a smart bloke, and had a little giggle about it. But after the meeting, which was quite a serious one, one of the other players said to me, "Jamie, who's Gulliver?"

'I tell that story to illustrate that Hask was operating at a different level to most of his teammates. I got his humour, understood that it was all in good spirits and never malicious. I used to sit at the front of the bus, *having a bit of a giggle. But if you don't get Hask's humour, which a lot of the Kiwis didn't, you just think he's constantly taking the piss, trying to do you down. That's why some of the Kiwi boys got a bit sick of him. I could see that from their body language and the looks on their faces: "Here goes Haskell again ..." Sometimes Hask needed to be reminded that he was maybe getting a bit a too much, but it never got to the point where he became intolerable.*

'And when Hask put his rugby boots on, he was very professional. In fact, he was the most professional player in the team. There's no doubt that Hask's presence inspired a lot of guys. He was also a great coach's aid because he understood and believed in everything we were trying to do. On top of that, he was smart enough to be able to articulate that to some of the younger players, who maybe weren't confident enough to ask questions.

'It's safe to say Hask was wired a bit differently to most, which appealed to me. He could have stayed in England and become Wasps' most capped player of all time, but he wanted more from life. Some coaches are too focused on getting guys with the perfect "character". But having "character" doesn't mean you are a character. Characters, like Hask, aren't normal. But they're often the people who make the difference in a team.'

When I joined the Highlanders in 2011, I was used to a cut-throat changing-room environment with Wasps and England, very intense and brutal at times. Nothing was off limits; imagine a Ricky Gervais Golden Globes speech, but harsher. With this background, it meant I could never quite get the levels right in New Zealand. I quickly worked out I needed to dial things down a bit, but people were still constantly saying to me, 'Mate, you can't say that.' I was used to people saying to me, 'Hask, do you ever shut the fuck up?' But I don't think a teammate had ever told me I literally *couldn't* say something. It was quite a shock to the system.

The Highlanders boys were particularly quiet, so I was the noisiest person they'd ever met, bar none. But I was never going to be shy and retiring – I was away from my family, living on my own in Seilala Mapusua's house in the middle of nowhere, so I needed an outlet. By the time I got into the changing room every morning, I was gagging to talk to people – 'Hello! Hello! James Haskell is here! Loud stories! Loud stories! Can we be friends?!' I had to be like that, otherwise it would have been awful. But some of my teammates had never left New Zealand, apart from playing games in Australia or South Africa. They had quite narrow horizons, so couldn't get a handle on me.

I'd tell them about the time I did a naked photoshoot on a rooftop in Paris while painted gold, and they'd look at me like I'd been beamed down from another planet – the planet Dickhead. I'd fly through the door of the changing room and start gobbing off about DJing or shooting or some other weird shit I happened to be up to outside of rugby, and they'd visibly shrink away from me. Most of them had never met anyone like me, full stop. And if they had, that poor unfortunate was probably locked up in a madhouse.

Like most new teammates, they probably thought I was going to be a thick English meathead who didn't know what he was talking about. But I'd obviously been around the block a few times before I arrived at the Highlanders, so would give Jamie a whole paragraph when he was used to his players giving him a couple of words. I remember chatting to Jamie after training once, and noticing the other lads looking at me as if to say, 'What the hell is he talking about now?' I was probably asking questions about rugby – I was always asking questions about rugby in New Zealand, trying to learn their approach to the sport, because I wanted to get better. I was also nervous because I felt I had a lot to prove. Remember, I was on the other side of the world with no family, no friends, on terrible money in a place that would make Swansea look like Las Vegas; on top of that I was in the heartlands of rugby. All I had seen before were Sky Sports highlights of Super Rugby teams playing a brand of rugby I was not sure I could cope with. I was also giving up playing for England by being over there, so I wanted and needed to get better to make it worthwhile.

It's lovely to hear that Jamie felt I brought so much to his team. That's all I ever wanted to do. Jamie was one of the best coaches I worked with in my career: he was shrewd, charismatic and very intelligent. Some of his pre-game talks still live with me now. Playing for the Highlanders was one of the biggest highlights of my career, and I learned so much about myself and definitely came back a much more rounded person. I wanted to stay another year and not go back to Wasps, but unfortunately I had already signed my contract. Luckily everything worked out in the end.

Right, back to France then. There's quite a lot to tell you. Ollie Phillips describes the time we spent together in Paris playing for Stade Français as the best two years of his life. That's beautiful to hear – his wife might think differently, but knowing Ollie some details have probably not been recounted. We certainly shared some amazing memories, although I couldn't have been easy to live with at times. I dragged that poor boy into some ridiculous scrapes, like the time a French woman nicked my parking space.

We lived in a very smart part of Paris, the 17th arrondissement, and were surround by restaurants, so when returning from training, tired and exhausted from yet more French madness, I would often go out to eat at a local bistro. The only issue was parking, which could be a nightmare. So on one occasion when I found a space that was blocked by a lorry being loaded by some builders, I put my indicator on and waited for the space for about 15 minutes. Now my French was limited, but the old nod of the head to the foreman and the pointing of a finger to the space and the okay sign in return were enough to give me the confidence that this space was mine and mine only. But just as the builders' lorry pulled away and I was starting to reverse, this woman shot in front of me, skimming my rear bumper. She was in this little rascal, drop-top French number. I pulled up next to her, wound my window down and started calmly saying, 'Pardon, madame, je suis désolé, cette space pour moi,' but she ignored me completely, so I tried again, saying, 'Pardon, madame.' But still she blanked me, so I got out the car and said in calm, polite English, 'I am sorry but this is my space. I have been waiting for 15 minutes please.' She just gave me a dismissive Gallic shrug. That's when the red mist descended. I was actually so angry I didn't know what to do. I was hopping from foot to foot, all manner of dark thoughts going through my head. Do I chase her down the road and spear tackle her into the ground? Do I push her shoebox of a car out the space? Do I tip it over, do I pull the door off? During this whole time the builders, who had been watching with some amusement, caught my eye and quickly got on with whatever it was they were doing or suddenly pretending to be doing. I was so incensed. I had tried to be calm, I had done the right thing, I had even tried French, albeit crap French. The woman had just pretended I wasn't there.

I drove back to our house, and when Ollie returned from training I was sitting in the dark of the living room with a hoodie covering my face.

'Hask, what the fuck are you doing?' he asked.

'We're going on a mission,' I replied. 'That fucking bitch ...'

He couldn't get an explanation out of me, because I was so angry – better described as a black rage rather than a red mist. All I could say to him was, 'That fucking bitch ...' over and over again, before marching into the kitchen and grabbing some eggs, flour and a bottle of salad cream. Ollie kept saying calm down, calm down.

I was adamant that revenge would be mine. So I made Ollie get a hoodie on and follow me on foot back to the woman's parked car. I needed him for moral support; either that, or if by some miracle the woman returned, and she knew kung fu and kicked the fuck out of me, Ollie could step in and help save my life.

We found the car in no time at all, and without warning I lobbed four eggs at the car windscreen followed by the bag of flour. Ollie was open-mouthed, as were some of the builders. I sounded like Muttley from *Wacky Races*, angrily muttering to myself, 'Fucking bitch, my space ...' until it became an incoherent ramble of 'rasa, frasa, rasa, frasa'. I was spitting feathers, but just as I was about to walk off my mood somewhat lightened: I noticed that she had not put her window up properly. It was then that I played my master-stroke in poking the end of the plastic salad dressing nozzle into this crack, and by the power of all the gods I squeezed that bottle hard with all my might. The inside of her car resembled a decorator's radio by the time I had finished.

With that we were off into the afternoon sun. This attack had taken no more than 30 seconds, but it was enough to shock Ollie, and start him panicking about being involved in a crime. To top it all off, it was a crime that he still did not fully understand. All was revealed later over a *plat du jour* at another restaurant well away from the devastation.

Looking back, it was quite an extreme reaction (not dissimilar to the time my French teammate refused to do rock, paper, scissors for the big bed in our shared room, so I removed the main slats from his bed while he showered and threw them out of the window and he ended up knackering his back and having to pull out of the game the following day). But that's just how my mind works – if you behave unreasonably and fuck me over, then I won't let you get away with it. And you might think twice about doing it again. In reality, I normally end up fucking myself over and having to read about it in the papers, and actually lose out more than if I had just let things slide.

Yes, Ollie's correct that I'd walk into the changing room and start swearing at everyone. But – and this a key point – it was a two-way affair. I'd put one foot through the door and Pascal Papé would start shouting, 'Fucking 'ell, it's 'askell! Fucking *rosbif*!' And then two or three of them would pipe up, calling me the little English gay, a son of a bitch, or something else wonderfully rude phrased in French. I'd start swearing back at them and Pierre Rabadan, who was very suave and utterly adorable (he once dated a Bond girl, but that's another story for another day), would put his arm around me and say, 'Hey, little bitch, how are you today?' And I'd tell him to fuck off, and that he was *très vieux* (very old) and to calm down, and we'd all have a laugh about it. I did have to be a little careful, as Pierre once did a shit in another player's boot in revenge for something, and the player put his foot into it just before he was going out for the warm-up. It was always light-hearted, but with a watch-your-back mentality. The French players loved a stitch-up and an aggressive practical joke, and things could escalate from there. I don't tend to get into those sorts of battles as they can get very messy very quickly.

I'm not saying it wasn't a bit odd, telling them all to suck their dicks as a morning greeting, but the main reason it happened was because I didn't speak much French and couldn't have a proper conversation with them. It wasn't quite the way it was painted by Ollie, that I was a violent English lout on holiday serving it up to some Frenchies. They realised I only knew some of the bad words to start with and loved getting a reaction from me. It was always fun and never serious.

Ollie says that when I first turned up at Stade, some of the players must have thought I was a complete idiot. But I won their respect through how hard I worked for the team. As I described in *What a Flanker*, they used to call me 'La Machine', because I always wanted to do more. I used to say to them, 'Some of you boys should try it, instead of going home bang on the dot every day.' And while I regret not mastering their language, I did try. During pre-season, I'd have French lessons for three or four hours a day after training. Anyone who's been through pre-season knows you are knackered, plus it was boiling hot in summer, so you are battered, bruised and tired of being asked, '*Où est la piscine?*' when you would rather have your feet up.

The lessons would start straight after training, and because I hadn't found time to eat I'd be falling asleep at my desk, like a kid in double maths last thing. I tried to remedy this by making an afternoon snack during the actual lessons, but the French teacher got most perturbed when I started buttering a baguette and arranging the fromage and jambon in it, while Ollie was making a salad complete with homemade vinaigrette. I will admit even I was shocked when Ollie pulled out a small portable stove to flambé his crêpes. Me and Ollie stopped going in the end. But while I hobbled on like Del Boy – 'Bonnet de douche, Pascal, bonnet de douche …' – Ollie bought some French learning tapes and became fluent in a few weeks. I'm not even kidding, he just nailed it and was invited out to soirées and dinner parties in the country, while I sat at home in my Spiderman PJs waiting up for him like an angry partner – 'Where have you been? Why do you smell of cheap perfume? Is that lipstick on your collar?' – before flouncing up to bed and slamming the door.

Apparently, telling everyone 'ferme ta gueule' (shut the fuck up) does not get you invited out on the town. It's a huge regret that I did not borrow those bloody tapes and nail it like Ollie. Don't feel too sorry for me, though; I still had a whale of a time, and while Ollie was serenading French women, it's amazing how many English girls want to come to Paris for the weekend and be taken up the Eiffel Tower.

Luckily, most of the French lads had at least a smattering of English, so we did manage to bond. Some of my favourite moments were post-training lunches, when we'd all pile in to a little bistro and have steak frites and a plateau de fruits de mer, with giant prawns, crab and lobster. After we had finished eating, we'd all start smashing back espressos, lighting up fags and telling stories. And while I didn't understand most of what they said, I still found it funny, and guys like Pierre, Benjamin Kayser and Ollie would always patiently translate for me. I loved these moments because the history of Stade Français as a club was wild and this particular team was jam-packed with characters. In fact, I'd say it was probably the most colourful changing room I ever set foot in. We won fuck all while I was there, but at least everyone had a jolly old time.

There was Dimitri Szarzewski, the most beautiful rugby player I'd ever seen, who'd sit there combing his long, flowing locks, fix you with his piercing blue eyes and treat you to a mysterious smile. There was Pascal Papé, who was completely insane and spent most of his time shouting *'rosbif!'* at me and laughing. There was a second-row, who shall remain nameless, who was like the village idiot. He'd been there so long, he thought he was the best thing since sliced bread, while everybody else thought he was a pain in the backside and should have been offloaded years ago. There was the Argentine contingent, including the legendary duo Juan Manuel Leguizamón and Rodrigo Roncero. Rodrigo looked like an angry old badger but was one of the nicest people going. There was the great Sergio Parisse, one of the best men and players I worked with. He'd smoke like a chimney before and after every training session with our scrum-half Julien Dupuy. Those boys never went out until three o'clock in the morning, three hours after I was usually in bed. So when they invited you for a night out you needed to make sure you had a couple of days off after or a really good excuse.

There is a great story about Julien, when he played for Leicester Tigers and got subbed off near the end of a European final. The game ran into extra time and then a goal-kicking challenge to decide who would win. Julien is a great goal-kicker, but when the coaches went looking for him to take a kick he was nowhere to be found. Most players when they are taken off sit in the stand, but upon further enquiry Julien was gone. A search party was sent out, and he was found in the changing room in his shorts, having a fag while talking on his phone. He hadn't been watching the game and thought he was done for the day. The coach went ballistic, so Julien stubbed out the fag, grabbed his boots and top, ran out the tunnel and kicked his penalty with his laces undone. I would like to say that's unique to Julien, but it's typical of the French way of doing things and similar stuff happened at Stade all the time.

There was the owner Max Guazzini, who'd stroll into the shower area post-game and make jokes with the lads. Max is openly gay and very flamboyant, so once I was showing off and pointed at myself naked and shouted to Max, 'What do you think?' He just laughed and said it was too small and walked off. That certainly took the wind out of my sails.

Then you throw me into this mix of wonderful people, the weird English guy who swore at people and worked too hard for people's liking, and Ollie, who scored tries for fun but looked like an accountant. It was a wild place, full of people pulling in different directions, but I would not have changed it for the world.

OLLIE PHILLIPS:

'My life in Paris would have been very different had Hask not been there with me. And I'm so grateful that he was. Life is for living and we lived it – what a ride. Barely a day went by without Hask creating a new story. Like the time he was on the Metro, coming home from training, and a woman was being harassed by some drunk bloke. Hask got up, stood over this bloke and shouted, "Arrête! Arrête!" But after he'd sat back down, the bloke started harassing this woman again, touching her up and making her very uncomfortable. So Hask got up, grabbed this bloke by the back of his shirt and his trousers and shouted, "Open the fucking door!" to this little French man standing in front of it. The shocked man lifted the

lever, the door opened and Hask threw the bloke out like an angry heavy in a movie. The man sailed through the air and came crashing down. Hask then lobbed his bag onto the platform after him. The woman was half in shock, half in awe. Most of the carriage applauded him, others clutched their belongings tighter, and that was Hask all over.

'It's like Hask was constantly creating content, so that he had stories to tell. That's why he always needed to be front and centre, and probably why he often overreacted. Like the time he attacked that woman's car, after she nicked his parking space. This was 2009–10, so social media had only just taken off. But Hask was one of the first sportspeople to understand its power.

'We recorded a series of videos in Carrefour, such as him rugby tackling me into a stack of bog roll, or me standing on a forklift truck, him pressing a button and me disappearing straight through the roof. He would drive me around, park up next to a person and go, "Can I get you this from the top shelf?" Hask would then raise me up too fast, to the complete surprise of the member of the public. We also did a skit where I pretended I was a little kid whose dream was to play for Stade Français, crawling around on my hands and knees, and Hask pretended to be Jimmy Savile: "Now then, now then, Ollie, come and sit on Uncle Jimmy's knee …" Let's be very clear, this was while he was a national treasure and not the most despicable human being going. However, the club still got upset as I am not sure they understood what was going on with us speaking English. The video looked a bit creepy and they said we were bringing their name into disrepute because I was wearing Stade

*Français boxer shorts, and made us take the video down.
Three months later, the Jimmy Savile scandal then
actually erupted. Thank God for those boxer shorts ...'*

Me and Ollie had a magical time in Paris together. We had so
much fun, we were constantly roaring with laughter. One
night, the whole squad was at a party at a restaurant called
Bagatelle, which was in the middle of the Bois de Boulogne. As
I remember it, Ollie was dating a girl from the Crazy Horse
nightclub in Paris, which is famous for its nude cabaret (when
I say 'nude', I mean beautiful, almost perfect women striking
poses, rather than pole dancing, legs akimbo and fivers in a
pint pot – which is how he sold it to me the first time we got
invited down, and I was mildly disappointed if I'm honest).
Ollie arrived in Paris somewhat naïve about women but soon
had his eyes opened to the full range of possibilities.

That would have been fine, and completely understandable,
if he hadn't kept telling women he loved them. One day, I'd be
having dinner with Ollie, his parents and the love of his life,
the next he'd walk into a bar with a different woman on his
arm. But they were all delightful and they were all besotted
with him, despite the fact he looked about 30 years older than
he was. However, the transformation from a person with Early
Learning Centre chat when it came to the ladies to genuine
Parisian Lothario was pretty impressive.

Back to the Bagatelle. Whenever we went out as a squad in
Paris, things got very loose, very quickly. And on this occasion,
free vodka was flowing and I was somewhat the worse for
wear. Also present were my mum and dad and a famous choreographer from the Crazy Horse who had brought along a bevy
of his cast to join the lads. I'm sure Ollie was behind all this.
His name escapes me, but this guy was decked out in a leather

trench coat and a red beret. He was also very taken with me, and I've still got a photo on my wall of the two of us sharing a kiss. I am not sure how this happened and there were definitely no tongues (I am not that much of a whore on a first date). What makes the photo even better is I'm actually wearing his beret. After our kiss, all he kept saying was how soft my lips were and he told Ollie that he thought I really meant the kiss. I can assure you I did not. I will kiss anyone, given half the chance.

As a quick aside, this same choreographer contacted me some years after leaving Paris and asked me if I would like to appear in an art house film. I have made it very clear time and time again that I have a great actor inside me bursting to get out, given the opportunity. Sadly, I have never had the chance. So I thought this could be my big break and bring me one step closer to Hollywood. I enquired about more details as to what was expected of me. They sent me a brief and basically it involved me appearing naked with a famous pornstar called Katsuni (professionals will remember her from back in the day) and doing all sorts of things, basically sex followed by her urinating on me. Now it may surprise you but I did take longer than necessary to say no to this mad scheme. Katsuni was fit (and what's a bit of wee among friends?), but it was like I could see into the future and knew that if I ever did that art house video it would never die. YouTube was just starting to be a thing and you will recall all the scraps I've had with the press. Imagine how much they would have loved dragging out this porno every time I fucked up. Plus I'm not even sure my mum could have got me out of that one, but as you read on you will see she had a good go at pretty much everything else I have ever done.

Back to the actual story, and having extricated myself from this man's passionate embrace (and there was a lot of passion coming from his side), I decided to pick up Ollie's squeeze for the evening. In my mind, she was a dancer and I was Patrick Swayze, so let's show how it's done. However, my first attempted lift ended with her dropping like a sack of bricks onto the hard ground. To get the picture, imagine someone being lifted and dropped on their head in a line-out. Thankfully, this girl wasn't hurt too badly, but I was absolutely mortified. I mean she was sobbing and looking up at me saying, 'Why, why, why would you do that to me?!' I apologised profusely but she did not like me and neither did all her hot dancer mates. I had set back Anglo-French relations once again. However, professional rugby players are tremendous opportunists where women are concerned, and while I was sitting in the corner feeling embarrassed and Ollie was attempting to apologise for the behaviour of his dickhead English mate, one of the French guys swept in, gave her a shoulder to cry on, and ended up taking her home.

Me and Ollie were given little cars to run around in as part of our Stade contracts, and we treated them like fairground dodgems. We'd do handbrake turns on cobbled roundabouts in the rain, and one time I even tried to drift my car around the Arc de Triomphe, but that went badly and ended up with me having a little chat with a gendarme. Sometimes, we would try these tricks and end up doing a complete 360-degree spin on a quiet Parisian roundabout and carry on driving, like a couple of 18-year-olds on a lads' holiday. My luck ran out when one day I was in the arse end of nowhere trying to find a UPS depot. I realised a second too late that I had missed a turn and thought fuck it, so attempted a handbrake turn, but the car didn't really do anything except slide straight into the kerb at high speed. There was a huge bang, airbag out. I thought *merde*, got out and found that the wheel had completely buckled under the car.

While I sat there trying to work out where I was, what the number for the French AA was and what the fuck I was going to say to our team manager, I came across the answer. I would tell them that I had swerved so as not to hit a dog. I mean, who would hit a dog deliberately? It seemed the perfect alibi.

Anyway, cutting a long story short, I got rescued four hours later and was given a replacement car the next day. I thought they had bought the story until about two weeks later when I got called into the office by a very sceptical team manager. He said the garage had been on the phone to say I had destroyed the car. It was a write-off, the first time a Stade player had done this. The chassis was so buckled it was beyond repair. It also turns out they had misunderstood my story and thought I said I had hit a dog, hence the damage to the car. 'You hit a dog? Really? What was it, a St Bernard?' I had to cut out the car play after that. I had no lives left and no more excuses would wash. I was a marked man.

We came across some real characters during my time in Paris. There was the mysterious male massage therapist we hired called Charlie, who had been locked up in Saudi Arabia by a sheik who made him massage him twice a day, every day. They took his passport and everything. If you have read *What a Flanker* you will understand that the reason we had to get a massage therapist at all was that trying to get any treatment at a French club is tricky to say the least, and if you do it's usually some machine-based madness. Also, if you walk into a massage place in Paris you often get more than you bargain for, so we thought it better to bring matters in-house.

We also had this mad cleaner who I caught having a shower and who appeared to be stealing our food. I tried to fire her (I waited until she'd put her clothes back on, of course), but she just kept coming back. She kept trying to blackmail me, saying that I had paid her cash or something like that. I am not sure what it was, but I knew she was trying it on. Basically, she was told in no uncertain terms to pack up and hop it.

Everything about our time in Paris was off the wall, a lot looser than in England. When we were supposed to play a Heineken Cup game against Ulster in Brussels, it was part of the owner's big plan to take the Stade Français brand on the road. This was mid-winter and there were snow warnings, but we all travelled to Belgium as usual. We arrived to find they hadn't even put covers on the pitch or have any undersoil heating. We had a great time going around the Christmas markets, though. I knew full well this game was never happening. It was freezing and now snowing. Saturday came round, and lo and behold the match was called off. Due to Heineken Cup rules, we had 48 hours to play the game or forfeit. We were duly rounded up and put on a Eurostar back to Paris, where they'd had the biggest snowfall in years. We were due to play the game on the Monday now, but I couldn't see how, as our Stade pitch was covered in 12 inches of snow and was in a worse state than the Brussels pitch. We went to the stadium on Sunday to do a team run and all our players not involved were out on the pitch beforehand trying to clear the snow and ice with shovels, like a scene from the 1950s. All the locals came out to help and bizarrely they managed to achieve the impossible, and we played on the Monday and won.

There were other crazy times too. Before another game against Ulster in Belfast, I think the return leg of the snow fixture, we were all out on a morning walk pre-game, talking about how we wanted to play and the key areas of focus, when our manager suddenly stripped off and jumped naked into the freezing river in town, just for a laugh. I looked at Ollie and said, 'What the hell is going on here?' I said that to him a lot.

CHLOE MADELEY, JAMES'S WIFE:

'*James is a walking, talking contradiction. He is so intelligent and so self-aware in some respects, but he doesn't seem to know where the boundaries lie. But that's hardly surprising. His parents were strict when he was growing up, he went to an all-boys' boarding school, he joined Wasps when he was still at Wellington College. All his life, he's been subject to the discipline of parents, teachers and coaches. But he's also been immersed in a very masculine, laddish environment. I reckon that must have messed with his perception of what is socially acceptable in the grand scheme of things.*

'*I'm always saying to James, "You guys literally bully each other. Things you wouldn't say to your worst enemy, you'll say while everyone is laughing and clapping." I've heard it, and I'll be thinking, "This is awful." But to them it's completely normal. James is a grown man, but if that's the environment you've been in for your whole life it's very difficult to suddenly snap out of it. James is a very complicated, interesting man, and I find it fascinating watching him operate. But now he doesn't have parents, teachers or coaches around, he needs someone else to keep him in check. Namely me.*

'*When I started seeing James, I found it very upsetting that all these people thought he was an idiot. I knew it happened to famous people, because I'd been around celebrity all my life, being the daughter of Richard and Judy. But it was difficult to take when it was the man I loved. People assumed James was an entitled, arrogant twat. And they'd be vehement about it, even if they'd never met him. The criticism from rugby fans was bad enough, but when it came from former players it was particularly difficult to take.*

'*During the 2015 World Cup, Neil Back, who won the tournament with England in 2003, wrote a scathing article about James, just because he took a GoPro to the opening ceremony and first game against Fiji. I wouldn't mind but he wasn't even in the match squad; all he did was walk around and did some filming. It was a huge occasion and he rightly wanted to have some memories. Neil Back was one of James's rugby heroes, someone he grew up watching and wanted to emulate, and now he was being annihilated by him in public. Neil Back had painted a caricature of James that was deeply unfair. But because rugby fans respected Neil Back, many of them would have taken what he said about James at face value.*

'*Don't get me wrong, I understand why James might not be some people's cup of tea. He can be very outspoken and loves the fact he's in great shape. When you're always taking selfies with your shirt off, you're going to rub people up the wrong way. But he gave absolutely everything when it came to his rugby, put everything on the line and messed up his body year after year.*

'*Before leaving Wasps for the second time, he literally begged them to let him play for free. He reminded them they were his boyhood club, said he was desperate to retire there. But they weren't interested and told him where to go. Meanwhile, it was all over the press that James was demanding too much money for someone who was old and creaking. James didn't want to say anything, and Wasps fans only learned the truth when I spoke about it on social media. And, to be fair to them, they gave him a great send-off.*

'Then when James joined Northampton, because he was desperate to remain in contention for England, their fans were all asking, "Why are we paying marquee money for a guy who's past his best?" The fact was, James was on an academy player's wage. We couldn't even get a mortgage because his income was so low. It was heart-breaking to see all these lies being spread about him. Meanwhile, James was so nervous about joining Northampton that he almost didn't go through with it. Poor guy, all he wanted to do was keep playing. He was a good man who had given his all for every club he'd played for and his country. He had so much integrity as a rugby player, emptied himself every time he walked onto a pitch. That's all that should matter, not his social media persona. But because of people like Neil Back painting inaccurate pictures of him, making out he was everything that was wrong with English rugby, he repeatedly got shat all over.'

Chloe got very passionate and upset about how I was treated and the incorrect assumptions people made about me. I understand why. When I was a kid, all I wanted to be was Neil Back, and Chloe knew that. But I shouldn't have been surprised when he wrote that article about me. The first time I met him, when I was doing a charity event at the Natural History Museum, which was a *Zoolander*-themed fashion show for Joe Worsley's testimonial, he blanked me after Joe introduced us. To be honest, he turned into a bit of a strange chap after retiring. Just have a look at his Twitter, it's like he is clinging on and trying so hard not to be forgotten: 'Look, look, remember me? I was a big noise in 2003.' All he does is reply with odd stuff to players and say contradictory things. To be fair, one of his former teammates did tell me he is a difficult nightmare, but a difficult nightmare you would want on your team.

Neil recently posted something on social media in response to an interview that Dylan Hartley and I did about how damaged our bodies were post-rugby. Backy's response to this was to list all the games he'd played during his 17-year career, all the things he'd won and tries he'd scored; he even included his drop goal for England. (When someone challenged him on a back row getting a drop goal for England, and if it was really true, in 0.02 seconds he had posted the newspaper article and score sheet from the game, almost like he had them to hand just waiting for this moment. It would take me about an hour to fish out any evidence I even played rugby, let alone scored a try.) The point of the tweet was that he had done all this and he didn't have any aches and pains in retirement. So basically, rugby didn't have a problem, me and Dylan were soft and all the hard work we were trying to put in regarding player welfare was irrelevant.

I was sent his response by one of his former teammates as I don't follow him. I thought on reading it, 'Neil, what are you talking about? For every one of you who got out of rugby with their bodies and faculties intact, there are hundreds of others who can barely walk and are feeling the effects of too many bangs on the head.' He's so out of touch, barely on the same planet as everyone else in modern rugby. What was even more sad was all the old-school prats who replied to his tweet with 'Bravo!' and 'Rugby has gone soft,' etc. There are former players, people who Neil played with, suffering from early-onset dementia and here's Neil boasting about the fact that he's all right, Jack.

Chloe once had a social media spat with former England scrum-half Matt Dawson, after the 2016 Test series against Australia. I can't remember the details, but I think he wrote an article or posted a tweet saying who should be player of the tournament and listed all these names and didn't mention me, despite the fact I was actually named player of the series. So Chloe went on Twitter and said to him, 'What about James Haskell?' He said a few things he shouldn't have, basically along the lines of Chloe was a WAG and should pipe down. Saying that to Chloe is going to only get one reaction and it all ended up being a bit fractious. I didn't care that Matt Dawson had overlooked me, I didn't see the article or tweet and Matt doesn't choose the winner. I know it wasn't personal in any way, but Chloe was always flagging stuff up that people had or hadn't said about me. And people would be quite horrible at times, saying to her face, 'So-and-so doesn't like James, so-and-so thinks he's a dickhead.' She obviously found that hard. I mean, who wouldn't?

On a serious note, being constantly misunderstood does take its toll, so that even you start believing you're the person other people think you are: in my case, not much more than a meathead, a cartoon version of myself. It was only recently that I had a bit of an epiphany. I thought to myself, 'I've written six books, I'm a DJ, I've made music, I am part of one of the biggest sports podcasts in the world, *The Good, The Bad & The Rugby*, I've had untold businesses. Why do I care what anyone else thinks of me?' It's easier said than done, but to be honest my focus has been and will always be about being the best version of myself. The rest is irrelevant.

SUSIE HASKELL, JAMES'S MUM:
'Yes, it does hurt me when I hear people being horrible about James. If some of the keyboard warriors who write nasty things about James met me in the flesh, they'd back off big time. And I have tackled some of the

haters. One England game at Twickenham, we were having a picnic in the car park and someone was being vile about James: "He missed that tackle, he dropped that pass, he should never play for England again because he's bloody useless ..." I'm very small, but I went straight up to this man and gave him a real blast – I was walking forwards the whole time, while he was walking backwards. The bigger they are, the harder they fall. I told him he ought to go to Specsavers, because things didn't happen the way he said they did. And you don't get to play for England unless you have talent.

'After the game, James joined us in the car park and a couple of people told him I'd had a real go at someone. James replied, "She may look small and sweet, but don't ever mess with my mother." And he was right. There was no way I was going to let that man trash my son and get away with it.

'After another game, during which one of James's teammates tried to make a monkey out of him, I walked straight up to this teammate and said, in a very loud voice, "If you do that to my son again, you'll have me to contend with." James's then girlfriend was mortified and said to me, "Oh my God, why did you say that?" I replied, "Because he was being a bully." Then there was James's first game for Wasps against Montferrand in France. Someone swung a punch at Lawrence Dallaglio, all hell broke loose and James got hit in the side of the face. I stormed through the metal railings and started shouting, "Get off my boy!" I got told off for that, but I thought it was all a bit unfair. Whatever scrapes my son gets into, I'll protect him. I know he's got into a fair few during his life, but I'll stand up for him every single time.'

For such a small woman, my mum has got a big bark. Most of the time, she's very sweet and serene, but she can be very fiery, especially when she's got a few drinks inside her. One time I did something wrong, probably had a fight with my brother or didn't do what my mum asked, and my mum marched into the TV room, pulled my PlayStation out of the wall socket and chucked it into a field opposite the house. When I shot my best mate, she took my BB gun and tossed it into a bush. She just didn't take any shit, and you knew when it was getting serious when she got her finger out and started waggling it in your face and swearing. My friend Nick Sanders came over once, when we were ten or eleven, and was supposed to stay the night. It was a rainy winter's evening, but we decided to dress up in camo gear and balaclavas and hide outside the house with guns, me in a ditch and Nick in an upturned wheelie bin. When my mum got home from work, we jumped out in front of her car just as she pulled in and scared the shit out of her. I'd never seen her so angry, she was screaming her head off. She bundled us both into her car and drove Nick straight home. She then made me knock on the door and explain why Nick would not be staying because he'd terrified my mum. Picture the scene: I am still in camo gear head to foot with proper army issue face paint bought from an army surplus store, with tear streaks down my face like a broken-hearted woman with streaked mascara, mumbling this incoherent apology while Nick's shocked parents looked on. To be fair to my old dear, she must have thought she was Shergar about to be kidnapped by the IRA.

It took me quite a long time to grow up and stop being a dickhead, which is the case with a lot of kids who attend all-boys' schools before going straight into a rugby career. Looking back, I cringe at some of the things I did when I was well into my twenties and already playing for England.

During one England camp at Pennyhill Park, I popped round to see my mate in Richmond. This mate was after my own heart, massively into anything laddish, such as walkie-talkies, guns and the like. So we were messing about in his bedroom, pointing his BB gun out of the window, when we spotted a gardener a couple of doors down, bending over with his arse crack out. That was like a red rag to a bull. My mate ran upstairs with his walkie-talkie to get a better view, and he had on these close protection-style headsets with sleeve mics and earpieces. I lined up his BB gun, which of course had this mega red dot sight. I was on the radio telling him what I was seeing, and he was relaying the details back. Think of every sniper movie you have seen, but better. *American Sniper* would have been proud of the way we were operating.

I had the shot and asked if it was a green light to take it. He replied, 'The green light is given for lethal force. Put him down!' I squeezed the trigger and this BB curled in the wind (I had factored for this) and hit the gardener right on the backside – it honestly dipped into his butt crack. It was an unbelievable shot, bang on the money, and we thought it was the funniest thing ever. Sam, my mate, radioed, 'Target down!', I was on the floor pissing myself. So I decided to do it again. The gardener had not moved from his position, but was rubbing his arse furiously. Again I radioed permission to shoot, and it was duly given. This time the BB curled and hit his bald head. Bingo, the money shot. Again we ducked down and were in hysterics. You would think we would have stopped there, but once we had caught our breath we peeked up and out to see what was happening, But when I went back for a third shot, the bloke had gone. I was just wondering what could have happened to him when we heard a knock on the front door.

What I forgot to tell you is that my mate still lived with his parents – and his mum was home. So I was suddenly back to being a child again, running around in a panic, thinking, 'Fuck, fuck, what am I going to do? I'm a 25-year-old man and I need to escape!'

A not dissimilar thing happened when I was learning to drive and crashed my Fiat Panda while doing handbrake turns down my parents' gravel drive. I had a full car (I say car, but it was a 900cc shoebox that had a plunger to put it in 4x4 mode and I had to drive with the window open to fit into it) with the usual suspects: Paul Doran-Jones, Thom Evans, Stuart Mackie and myself. That is a lot of weight for a tiny car. I took the slight bend a little too fast, pulled the handbrake and we started drifting beautifully around the corner, until I overcorrected back the other way and we careered, albeit slowly, into a bush and a little raised kerb. My mate Stuart, who was strapped into the front seat, jolted forward, and because the car was so small he hit the window with his head, smashing it to smithereens (it was the original non-safety glass from about 1955), just as my mum was pulling into the driveway behind us. She slowly drove past, shaking her head with a look that could kill.

Anyway, I digress. Back to the BB gun story. We were hiding in the bedroom and we heard this gardener talking to my mate's mum. Let's go with the distinguished Mrs Patterson from *Kevin & Perry Go Large*: imagine me being Perry and my mate being Kevin. So the gardener is telling her he thought he'd been shot, and he suspected that it had come from her house. And because Mrs Patterson knew her son owned a BB gun, she immediately knew it was us. She called us down with a shrill scream. I said to my mate, 'I am not going down, she can't make me,' but before the last words had come out of my mouth, my mate had scarpered, knowing intimately that his mum was not to be messed with. As we came down the stairs, the gardener was there and so was the angriest mum I have ever seen.

Mum: 'Did you shoot this man?'

I looked at the floor and said nothing.

My mate Sam: 'Erm, yes … we … James may have done it.'

There was a slight quiver of emotion in his voice, and you could hear and see his lip wobble.

Mum: 'Well, you need to apologise now.'

Me: 'Hi mate, erm, I am really sorry for shooting you. We thought it was a joke. Sorry if it hurt you.' I could feel myself going red; the heat coming off me could have fried eggs.

Gardener: 'Aren't you James Haskell, the rugby player?'

I was thinking shall I tell him no, or that I always get that from people, but the fact Sam had called me James meant I was a bit stuffed. So I said, 'Yes, mate, it's me.'

Gardener: 'Oh, right, I am a big England fan.'

Silence as we looked at each other. What next? What could I say? 'Great, does that make it better or worse that I shot you? Want me to sign your bruised arse and head?' Then again, maybe not.

He broke the silence to say that he wouldn't have noticed he had been shot until the second one. He thought the first was a bee sting, until he saw a little yellow pellet on the floor after it had bounced off his head.

I said sorry again, and he seemed happy and left.

As the door shut, I knew this was only the beginning of the drama. I tried to intercept the forthcoming by apologising to Mrs Patterson profusely, but I couldn't look her in the eye. That was the most embarrassed I've ever been. And there's a lot of competition. And after an agonising silence, which probably only lasted about three seconds but felt like three hours, she finally screamed at me, 'You're a bloody England rugby player, what were you thinking? How dare you do that!' She then turned to Sam and said, 'As for you, that's it, it's time you moved out. I'm going to phone your father.' With that she stormed off, slamming the door behind her.

After being released and knowing that perhaps shooting people had not been the best plan ever, I drove straight to a local florist and bought her a big bouquet of flowers. I also bought her a card. Which, if I am honest, I thought was the perfect chance to say sorry but also take the piss a bit. Being frank, reader, I found the whole thing hilarious and another chance to take some chat back to the lads in camp. Yes, it was embarrassing to have a four-foot mum bollocking you, and slightly concerning to be recognised as an England player by your victim, but what a story for post-training the next day. So I channelled my inner Perry, and on the card I wrote: 'Dear Mrs Patterson, I'm so sorry for shooting the gardener. I don't know what came over me; I know I have let myself down and my parents. I've probably watched too many war films and played too many video games which have warped my young, impressionable mind. I will be seeking help immediately to remedy these shortcomings. Yours sincerely, James.' I gave Sam's mum the flowers and card, then burnt it back down the M3, wondering if I was going to read about this in the *Daily Mail* the next day.

I am told by Sam that Mrs Patterson still has that card. She shows it to visitors, before launching into the story of how an England and British Lions rugby player once shot a gardener in the arse from her son's bedroom window.

2

FLY IF I WANT TO

SUSIE HASKELL:

'As a child, James was very loving, very cheeky, very bright and full of energy. He was much larger than the average child and developed much quicker. When I joined a mothers and toddlers group, he could sit up while all the other children were flopping around. We took him to swimming lessons when he was ten months old, he stood up and started walking when he was eleven months, he was doing gymnastics and riding bikes at the age of three. My husband and I were getting very agitated because James just had so much energy and there wasn't much more a lad could do. Then I spotted an advert in the local newspaper: "Mums, do you want your Saturday mornings back? Bring your children to Maidenhead Rugby Club."

'James was only four, and I initially missed the small print that said the minimum age was six. But that didn't put me off. When we arrived at the club that first morning, I said to James, "If anybody asks you how old you are, just say you're six." He looked up at me with his angelic face and replied, "No, Mummy, that's telling fibs."

I tried to explain the situation, but he wasn't having any of it. Fortunately, I had some Rowntree's Fruit Gums in my pocket, so I gave him a green one, his favourite colour, and that kept him quiet. Nobody questioned his age anyway because he was so big. And I'll never forget the first time James got the ball: he ran like hell, knocked everyone flying like skittles and put the ball down. I started cheering and this irritating man said, in a very posh voice, "Oh no, he's scored at the wrong end." I didn't know anything about rugby, but James soon learned which end was the right one. The rest is history.

'Whatever my husband and I asked James to do, he'd do. Whatever was on offer, he embraced it. He was interested in everything, and always wanted to please my husband and me. I taught him to have no fear of anything, explained that he could fly if he wanted to. I've always been a positive person, and I told James to aim for the stars. Which is why he always has.'

I don't remember my mum telling me I could fly if I wanted to, but it does sound like something she'd have said. If me or my brother wanted to try something, my parents would do everything to make it possible. They might let us know they couldn't really afford it, that it would be a struggle, that they'd have to work even harder than they were already (that was them reminding us that it was us Haskells against the world). But they'd always deliver.

I was a nightmare, a hyperactive kid. I'd play army and carry out missions on the neighbour's house, armed with a BB gun, my face covered in professional camouflage paint. I was obsessed with bonfires and digging. At our first house, all I wanted to do was do the gardening and digging. I would go out into the garden and sit on my plastic JCB and pretend that I was doing roadworks. I graduated quickly from plastic spades to taking my dad's metal ones from the shed. My favourite spot was to dig under one particular tree in the garden. I would dig and dig, and after about six months my dad came rushing out one Saturday to tell me to stop it and look what I had bloody done. I had dug so many times on one side of this tree and cut through so many of the roots that the tree had started to lean to one side. You only really noticed it when you drove up the road or when you looked at it from a distance, which I never did. It became so bad that eventually my dad had to get someone in to chop it down. I'd follow the gardener around all day in my plastic tractor. If a builder was doing some work, I'd be one of those annoying kids who'd stand behind him all day, asking if there was anything I could do to help. My parents probably signed me up for everything just to get me out of my mum's hair, for the sake of her sanity.

Even if I wasn't interested in something, my mum and dad would persuade me to give it a go. I remember saying, 'But I don't like it,' and my dad replying, 'But how do you know? Give it a try and then make a decision.' At school, I appeared in lots of plays. I took acting, ballet and tap lessons at a theatre school. I think my mum saw me as the next child superstar, like Shirley Temple or Macauley Culkin. Chloe reckons I looked like an alien as a little kid, but my mum seemed to think that I was the best-looking child in the world. Imagine my shock when I didn't get all the girls.

I made it to the last two for a Heinz Baked Beans advert but blew the opportunity, big time. I was supposed to look at the food on my plate and say, 'There's the boat [the sausage], there's the sea [the beans].' But I just wouldn't do as I was told. I kept saying to the director, 'But that sausage doesn't look like a boat.' And it didn't matter how many times the director told me that's just what I had to say, I wouldn't go along with it. As far as I was concerned, if the sausage didn't look like a boat, I wasn't going to pretend that it did.

Mind you, my brother blew an even bigger chance at stardom. He could have been in a John Goodman movie, and all he had to do was sit in front of a xylophone and whack the thing for a couple of minutes. The whole family were so excited, but when it came to the final audition he refused to play ball and hid under a table instead. My dad was fuming, thinking he'd just seen a Hollywood career – and millions of quid – go up in smoke. And you want to know the worst part? The little prick played the xylophone all the way home.

While I gave almost everything a go, I was totally disorganised. I bumbled from one thing to the next, not really knowing why I was there or what I was supposed to be doing. My childhood is just a haze of activities, schoolwork and no awareness of anything else. One year, I decided to learn how to play the drums. But I didn't turn up for a single lesson, because firstly I always forgot I had them, and secondly I didn't know when or where the lessons were being held or how to find out. Someone did show me, but I forgot I had them or to check when I had them. Eventually, the drums teacher just gave up on me. I also remember staring out of the window during a dance class and waving at some guy, who on seeing me duly gave me the middle finger. I didn't know what it meant at the time, but he did it with a half-smile, so I thought it must be good. I was soon doing it to everyone in the room. I was like a young Homer Simpson, distracted by almost everything. When I got in the car, I flicked my mum the bird as well. She went mad and was like, 'Who showed you that? It's very rude, James, stop that at once.' Of course, I kept doing it when she wasn't looking. When she next looked up, I was doing it to everyone and anyone, and she bollocked me again. I claimed that I was just counting my fingers but starting from the middle, which seemed like a valid excuse. She did not buy any of it.

On reflection, I would say that my parents were pretty strict with us; there was a lot of discipline in the house. When I was insolent, I was placed in a burlap bag and beaten with reeds. Pretty standard stuff, really. And if I didn't eat my vegetables, I'd be made to sit at the table until I did. If I got up from the table without asking my parents' permission, they would drag me back and make me sit down for another five minutes, which seemed like an extra hour. They would set the oven timer as a way of knowing when the time was up, so when the alarm went we were free. For a kid who couldn't sit still, that was hellish. I also remember my dad trying to teach me to tie my shoelaces and learn capital cities for school, and him getting more and more irritated because I couldn't focus for more than a few seconds or remember anything. When I desperately wanted a BB gun, my dad drew 20 BB guns on a sheet of paper and crossed one off every time I got a capital city wrong. To be fair, he was just trying to improve my powers of concentration and using the old carrot and stick trick. I did still get the BB gun in the end.

Nick Sanders, my old-school pal, was the complete opposite to me: scrupulously polite, really religious and quiet as a mouse. But he was a good friend who introduced me to the wonder of books. I remember him saying, 'You need to read this,' before handing me a copy of Alistair MacLean's *Where Eagles Dare*. We would share a dormitory together and I think the school basically put him in with me to keep me from going all Just William on the place. He was basically my friend and carer. I am pretty sure he gave me the book to read because he wanted some peace and quiet and to shut me up and calm me down. Reading that book was an epiphany. I vividly recall sitting on my bed, with my nose stuck between the pages, and thinking, 'Oh. My. God. It's like creating a movie in your head.' From that point on, books were like magic and reading became an addiction. I'd read every spare moment I had – during break times, before lights out – and soon I was reading a few books a week, no problem at all.

The book thing is weird, because it doesn't really fit in with the rest of my personality – the not being able to concentrate for long, the constant bouncing from one thing to the next – and it's something that people have never been able to get their heads around. Even when I left my prep school Papplewick to go to Wellington College, I took my reading habit with me. When I became a professional rugby player, teammates couldn't understand how that bloke who had just trained the house down, taken the piss out of everyone in the canteen and made a lot of noise about the podcast/song/range of supplements he was about to release, was now holed up in his hotel room reading or working. But I've got a lot to thank Nick for, because reading is my way of switching off from the world.

Because I wasn't really aware of anything beyond what I was doing at any given time, besides reading – whether that was playing army, digging holes or giving people the finger – I didn't develop much of a passion for rugby, or any sport, until I was in my teens. I'd play football with my dad in the garden and he'd get frustrated, because I wasn't very good. He'd try to teach me to kick properly – 'Use your instep instead of your toe!' – but I'd have no idea what he was talking about. Eventually, he'd stick me between the sticks and start pinging in goals from all over the place, like Competitive Dad from

The Fast Show. He'd sometimes say, 'The amount of money I've spent on your education and I could teach a sea lion to do what you can do.'

It's not as if my father was a relentlessly self-improving boulangerie owner who'd make outrageous claims about inventing the question mark or accuse chestnuts of being lazy. But he was a workaholic, there's no doubt about that. My mum would always get me to call him at the office, to see if I could persuade him to come home. Sometimes he did, but I remember spending a lot more time with her in the early days, although he never missed a school match, play, you name it – he was there to support me. That first time she took me to play mini-rugby at Maidenhead, I didn't really want to go, because it was cold and wet. And when I started playing, I found it quite intimidating and had no clue what I was supposed to be doing. I vividly remember getting the ball, running the length of the pitch, scoring under my own posts and a parent looking at me and saying, 'You silly boy.' But I still didn't understand what I'd done wrong. Before you laugh, there has been some progression as I now run into the posts, not over the wrong line.

I went back to Maidenhead when I was about 19, a couple of years after I started playing professionally, and some gruff old bloke said to me, 'I remember you, Haskell. You were such a little shit when you were younger.' At the time I thought, 'Fucking hell, what a welcome back that is.' But now I think, 'Blimey, imagine how bad I must have been.' I reckon I was like Mitch Murphy from *Home Alone*, the annoying kid from across the street who doesn't stop asking weird questions: 'Do these vans get good gas mileage? How fast does this thing go? Does it have automatic transmission? Does it have four-wheel drive?' To which the van owner replies, 'Look, I told you before, kid, don't bother me. Now beat it!' Come to think of it, I do vaguely remember a lot of people saying to my mum, 'Isn't your boy a proper little character.' Which was a polite way of saying, 'He's an annoying prick, I wish he'd fuck off and never come back.'

But it's not as if I stopped being a whirlwind when I went to Wellington College. In fact, I was doing more things than ever, maximising every opportunity. As my dad used to say, 'If someone asks if you want to do something, always say yes. Go along, have a look and see what becomes of it.'

I wasn't even slightly religious, but still ended up doing Bible studies. I'd like to pretend that I was into it for the right reasons, but I wasn't. I was fully cognisant that if you said X you would get Y. The great Ricky Gervais did a skit about how people get kids into religion, which went something like this:

ADULT: 'Do you believe in Jesus?'
KID: 'Yep.'
ADULT: 'Good. Here's a can of Coke. Do you believe in God?'
KID: 'Yep.'
ADULT: 'Excellent. You can go quad-biking.'

That was what it was like on religious retreats, which I first started going on with Nick. They were basically mega-activity camps but even better, as we all know the church is well funded. When on these camps the equation was a simple one.

PRIEST: 'Have you said your prayers, James?'

I'd tell him that I had of course thanked God, and not to forget the Holy Spirit and the other one.

PRIEST: 'I think you mean Jesus, James.'

'Yes, that's right, Jebus (sic).'

PRIEST: 'In that case, you can go orienteering tomorrow.'

When I got to Wellington, it was more about the free food. I'd sit in a prayer circle for an hour, shaking so hard with laughter that people thought I was getting emotional, before being rewarded with piles of sandwiches, doughnuts and biscuits – all stuff that wasn't normally available at Wellington. Once, I grabbed about ten biscuits and another much younger kid grabbed my arm and told me to share them, and to remember Jesus and the feeding of the five thousand. How dare this first-former stop me grazing my way through the custard creams? Forgetting momentarily where I was, I told this younger kid that if he didn't get his fucking hands off me, they were going to find him upside down in a wheelie bin and no god in the world could help him. He told me not to swear in the presence of God and I told him that God wasn't in the room. As soon as I said that, I thought, 'Maybe this isn't for me. Even if there is a God, I really shouldn't be pretending to worship him for the sake of a few custard creams.'

KEN HOPKINS, JAMES'S SCHOOL RUGBY COACH:
'I was in charge of the first XV when James was playing for me, and what a huge contribution he made to Wellington rugby. From the very beginning, it was obvious he was a star. And not just one of the best players, but also one of the great personalities.
'I was fortunate in that we had a galaxy of talent – Paul Doran-Jones, Thom and Max Evans, who both

went on to play for Scotland; Tom Williams, who had a long career with Harlequins; Adrian Jarvis, who played for quite a few Premiership clubs; Kai Horstmann, who played for Worcester and Exeter – but James stood out even in that company, he was a man among boys.

'He was 6 ft 3 in., 16 stone and quick, an intimidating, frightening sight for the opposition. I'll never forget one try he scored – he took a pop pass on his own 22 and the opposition melted away, allowing James to score under the posts. But he wasn't just an outstanding rugby player, he was also a huge presence off the pitch. I'll never forget James's speech at an end of season dinner. He was quite magnificent, unbelievably articulate, and everyone was in awe. Even then, people were calling him 'FEC' – future England captain.

'We were very ahead of our time, almost like a professional team. We trained Monday, Tuesday, Thursday and Friday and played on the Saturday. But James would still do extra training on his own. He even had a personal trainer who'd turn up at five o'clock. Most kids at that age are chasing girls and getting into drinking – quite rightly – but James had tunnel vision. He was the first pupil I came across who was 100 per cent committed and knew exactly what he was going to achieve, which was to become a professional rugby player at the highest possible level.

'That might suggest James was all about himself, but that wasn't the case. He was an inspiration to others, always upbeat and great fun to be around. And he was very loyal. One weekend, he was playing for England Under-18s on the Saturday and we had a big sevens tournament in Wales on the Sunday. I didn't expect him

to play in the sevens tournament, but he said to me, "Mr Hopkins, I'll be there. Don't you worry." And sure enough, he turned up on the Sunday morning – fresh, keen and ready for action – having played for England and travelled all the way from London to Brecon.'

Besides all the more physical sports like rugby, football, hockey, tennis, field gun and Combined Cadet Force activities, I also represented Wellington at chess. I wasn't what you would call a chess prodigy; I knew how to play it but not to any great level. Now I think about it, I am not sure how the hell I ended up playing a school match for the team, but I did. I saw it as a chance to prove that I was more than just a meathead. So I got a few proper chessheads in my house to teach me some opening moves and ended up winning, fair and square. Unfortunately, everyone was convinced I'd only beaten this kid because he'd been intimidated by my size and thought I was going to snap his fingers off if I lost.

Then there were my appearances in Wellington's field gun team. Field gun is that thing they do, or used to do, at the Royal Tournament, when teams compete to transport a small cannon on wheels, and all its bits and pieces, over a series of obstacles in the shortest time. I did that three years in a row – on speech day, in front of 3,000 people – and wouldn't have had it any other way. Thinking about it, I reckon I was afraid of not doing things. That's what my mum and dad instilled in me, this terror of missing out and not making the most of life.

If I was sat on my Xbox for any amount of time, my dad would storm into my bedroom, like an SAS soldier during the Iranian Embassy siege, and start shouting at me: 'You're always on this bloody computer! Get up! Make life happen! Embrace and maximise every opportunity! Don't waste your life playing computer games!' I suppose a lot of kids would just tell their dad to piss off and carry on being lazy bastards, but I took that to heart. Now I run from pillar to post, on a constant path of self-discovery and self-improvement. Which has been detrimental at times and something Chloe is always going on at me about. Doing everything is not always the best policy. As I have got older, I have refined what I am interested in and what is worth saying yes to.

EDDIE JONES, ENGLAND HEAD COACH:

'I haven't worked with many players who were more single-minded and determined to succeed than James. He wasn't the most talented rugby player in the world, but he had that obsessive trait, which most successful people have.

'When I first started coaching him, he wasn't using that obsessive trait in the right way. But through the work he put in, and with guidance from others, that obsessiveness started revealing itself on the rugby field. When a player plays to his strengths, they can achieve great things. Everyone wants to be Lionel Messi, but if you've got the skills of John Terry, and don't try to be something you're not, there's no limit to how far you can go. In James's case, he became a really big part of the England rugby team's renaissance.

'I felt he needed some security because he'd been in and out of the England team. So I said to him, "You're gonna be in the team for the whole Six Nations, so you better front up." That was me telling him I thought he was an important player, but also challenging him to get better. And by getting him to concentrate on what he

could do – which was basically hit and carry hard – rather than what he couldn't, he did just that.

'That 2016 series against Australia was probably the high point of his career, where he got absolutely everything out of himself and became a strong leader of the England team. He was able to physically impose himself on the opposition and finished that tour with his big toe hanging off, which showed he couldn't have given anything more. He got a lot of respect for his performances on that tour, which I was pleased about, because he deserved it.

'Let's not forget that James also had the courage to go and play in New Zealand and Japan, which was very unusual for an English player. And since retiring from rugby, he's taken a lot of those lessons forward and is creating others successful careers for himself. There's a great lesson there, in that you never stop improving, if you're prepared to keep working.'

I have read a few self-help books, including Mark Manson's *The Subtle Art of Not Giving a F*ck*, which didn't really teach me much. When I was younger and more impressionable, I read *The Secret* by Rhonda Byrne, which claims that your thoughts can change your life directly. It tells you to visualise your desires and ask the universe for help, and I wrote down all the things I wanted in life, and even did drawings, but I don't recall the universe delivering much at the time. I think most people's personalities are hard-wired from an early age, by their parents and schooling and what not. Once you reach adulthood, you can make changes, but I'm not sure anyone can change themselves completely. I've always worked hard to improve myself, but if that trait isn't drilled into you in childhood, like it was drilled into me by my parents, it must be difficult to suddenly start being like that as an adult. I am not saying it's impossible, but it must be way harder.

Rather than trying to change who you are completely, I think it's better to try to learn how to deal with the way you are. Everyone can be more disciplined and more successful, whether that means trying harder to understand your partner's needs or learning to spot when you're disappearing down a rabbit hole. I think there is too much acceptance of mediocrity nowadays, too much whingeing and blaming other people for your failures. And there are an awful lot of chancers out there telling other people how to be more successful in life when they're not really successful themselves. The shops are full of books written by people who have become successful solely based on the fact they've written a book about how to be successful, which I think is quite ironic.

PAUL DORAN-JONES:

'One of the strange things about James is that he feels like he has to portray a certain version of himself, while also being frustrated that people don't realise there's more to him than that. He plays up to this caricature of himself, that he's a mutant who spends his life in the gym. But that's only part of the story. What people don't realise is that when he's in the gym he's probably listening to an audiobook or a song he's just produced.

'When we were young pros, we weren't really allowed to drink much. So our hobby was women. We'd go out on a lot of sober dates, and because we weren't going to get drunk and fall into bed with a woman, James would constantly be reading up on different strategies. He called it "the system". It would involve the technicalities of

lovemaking and oral gratification, so that he'd constantly be giving me advice and telling me things I should be reading on the internet to up my game. Whatever it is, he just gets so into it, so over the top. James can't just enjoy having sex, like most people; he has to be the best in the world at it.'

I can't believe Dozzer is telling people this stuff. It was not going to be an area I thought I would talk about in *Ruck Me*, but now he's mentioned it I suppose I have to run with it, or at least put it into some context. Let's be clear: I do not regard myself as a modern-day Don Juan. As you've probably already worked out by now, I can't just be average at things, I have to be as good as I can possibly be, or at least try to always be better. Whether I improve is for others to say. Take, for example, oral sex. I'm not going to lie to you, I quite enjoy performing oral sex. Who doesn't, if they are being honest? I'm not sure how we got onto the subject, but one very famous current England player told me recently in a conversation that he never does it and hates it. I did point out that if he doesn't do it for his lady some man will, and that he needs to grow up. I pride myself on my oral sex performances. And like any good performer, whether a musician, a stand-up comedian or a sportsperson, I was always keen to seek outside help, so that I might become a virtuoso in the field of cunnilingus. From what I have heard from many women, there are a lot of men out there who could do with some serious assistance, so before you turn off and think what a prat, read on and you might bring a smile to someone's face.

To this end, I got my hands on a book all about oral sex, *She Comes First*, by a bloke called Ian Kerner. Jesus, the pressure that man must feel whenever he disappears beneath the sheets – it's literally a whole book about going down on women. It contained a lot of bullshit about emotions (I guarantee someone will say that's your problem, James, emotion is half the battle), but also lots of priceless technical advice about how to raise your oral sex performances from perfectly acceptable to elite, adult entertainment level. It's like getting a black belt in muff management. I got very excited about this book, and I remember telling Dozzer all about it in hushed tones, as if I'd discovered the Holy Grail. And when I put the book's advice into practice, and realised it worked a treat, I started upskilling the rest of my sex techniques. People might be reading this and thinking I'm a bit weird, for taking sex so seriously. But, to me, it makes perfect sense: if you're going to be a sex person, why would you not want to be the best sex person you could possibly be?

I read that book just before heading to New Zealand to play for the Highlanders. I remember sitting around and talking about it with my teammates, and them sniggering and looking at me with deep suspicion, as if I'd lost my mind. I shouldn't have been surprised, because by the time most Kiwis hit middle age they're sprouting nose and ear hair at an alarming rate, so that they look half-human, half-shrub. Male grooming is strictly for ponces, or was at the time in deepest, darkest Dunedin, so the chances that any of my teammates had read a book on oral sex were slim to none.

But, lo and behold, over the next few days two or three of my teammates sought me out after training and said, 'Mate, how do I get hold of a copy of that book you were telling us about?' It was all very hush-hush, as if they were seeking entrance into some Satanic cult. I told them what it was called and that they could download it onto their iPhones or iPads using the Kindle app, so that no one would ever know they were reading it. And I kid you not, about a month later two of these blokes' partners approached me on two separate occasions and said something along the lines of, 'Thank you, just thank you,' and 'I can't thank you enough for your book recommendation … it's been well amazing.' That book changed the game in Dunedin, sex-wise. And whenever I'm feeling a bit low, I console myself with the thought that at least two women of that parish benefited from my hunger for improvement and willingness to share secrets.

As an even younger man, I spent a lot of time working on my pulling 'system'. I read the book *The Game*, about how to pick up women (no doubt considered highly problematic in today's more politically correct world). After reading *The Game*, among other things I started painting my toenails before going on holiday, so that girls would comment on them. As any reader of *The Game* will know, and for those who don't, this type of thing is called 'peacocking'. Of course some of my teammates went with the much quoted line, 'Haskell's gone gay,' when they saw my painted toenails. Even though I did point out that being gay has nothing to do with gender or painting your toenails, that didn't detract from the narrow-minded stereotyping that any man who exhibits any perceived feminine trait, such as wearing pink or painting his toenails, has to endure.

In Las Vegas one year, I nicked a big feather duster from a maid's trolley and spent all day dusting people down at a Hard Rock pool party. It's not like I was chasing people around with the duster, like in a Benny Hill sketch. Oh no, I was walking around the pool and going in the shallow water holding it. Women were literally bending down in front of me and asking me to dust their arses or breasts. That duster was the greatest pick-up tool I ever used, and led me to believe that Ken Dodd must have owned two sticks: a tickling stick to woo the ladies and a shitty stick to fight them off with.

I wasn't always so forward with women. Like most teenagers, I'd sit around staring at girls, chatting about how pretty they were and doing fuck all about it. That was all down to nerves and the fear of rejection and being embarrassed in front of your mates. But as I got older, I began to enjoy and embrace the fear. I began to view chatting up women as a process and a performance – subconsciously, I'd be saying to myself, 'Can you execute an introduction? Can you make her laugh? Can you spark a conversation?' It was almost like acting. In the end, me and Dozzer codified 'the system': if we were in a bar and you commented on how attractive someone was, you'd have to go and speak to them straightaway. So if Dozzer said to me, 'Man, that girl over there is fit,' I'd say, 'System', and he'd have to go over and say hello. The system was just about backing yourself in any situation, any time and place. A lot of the time it worked, like you wouldn't believe, and created some pretty amazing situations. But neither of us ever walked out of a bar wondering.

Let's be clear that none of this was about pestering women. It was mainly just walking up to them and politely saying hello. If they didn't want to be bothered, we'd immediately withdraw. But most women are quite happy to chat with a couple of polite blokes in a bar. In Vegas, we'd go up to a group of American girls in a casino and say, 'Hi ladies, sorry to disturb you. My name's James, this is Paul. This is our first visit to Vegas and we were wondering what we should do, any suggestions most welcome.' They'd spend the next five minutes telling us about all the best bars, nightclubs and pool parties. And usually before we'd said goodbye we'd have one or two of their numbers. The whole idea was that they didn't feel under any pressure because we made it clear from the start that we only wanted a bit of advice and that we were on a schedule, so there was no fear we would be following them around. But it often led to a bit more than that.

Dozzer has always enjoyed my competitive nature. But he's never been able to get his head around the animalistic intensity of my competitiveness and the lengths I'll go to. I think he finds it slightly unnerving. When I told him I was reading an oral sex manual, he shook his head and said, 'You can't do anything small, can you? You always have to be the fucking best.'

3

IF A SHARK STOPS SWIMMING

ALEX PAYNE, THE GOOD, THE BAD & THE RUGBY CO-HOST:
'I don't think Hask is searching for contentment, but
maybe he is searching for a purpose. Or maybe he just
has boundless energy that needs an outlet. Having built a
production company and podcast together, I'd love him
to focus on that a bit more. But there's no point trying to
constrain him, because it's impossible to dim his fire.

'Hask is street-smart, business savvy and comes up
with lots of good ideas. But it must be exhausting being
him, because he has this all-consuming "let's get into
this" attitude. He says yes time and time again, to things
that other people simply wouldn't consider doing. He
went and played in France when people were telling him
it might end his England career; he did a naked calendar
shoot on a rooftop in Paris when other people would
have said, "What are you even asking me to do?"; he
went and played for peanuts in Japan and New Zealand
when no one else from Europe was doing that.

'I often counter Hask's stories with the line, "I'd much
rather have a cup of tea and a Hobnob." But he can't be
like that. If there's an opportunity to experience

something new, and create new stories, he has to do it. "Why not? Let's do it ..." he'll say. That's the man he is: take up the challenge, ask questions later.'

I'm a restless soul, there's no doubt about that. I have been since I was a kid, when I was diagnosed with Attention Deficit Hyperactivity Disorder (ADHD), which is why my doctor put me on Ritalin. Before that, I just couldn't sit still and focus on anything. But after I started taking Ritalin, I started having moments of deep immersion. That's what saved my academic career, because I was able to cut myself off from everything else and concentrate on study and revision. Even now, I become very intense, almost manic, about whatever it is I'm doing, whether it's scribbling down reams of notes or writing books.

I always use the analogy that if a shark stops swimming it dies. Some of that is to do with my parents' situation when I was a kid, when they put themselves under a lot of financial pressure by putting me and my brother through public school. They had to work non-stop just to keep from going under, and that's my mentality. Stopping for just a few minutes feels unnatural and uncomfortable.

But I do have things that make me feel mindful, to use that modern term. The Covid-19 pandemic meant I didn't have a choice but to sit back and reflect on things, and it was quite nice to do so. And it didn't make me feel anxious, because I knew everyone else was doing the same and the world wasn't moving on without me. When I go on holiday, I'll lie by the pool and read all day. I'm voracious, I can read two or three books in a week. When Chloe can get me in the pool, we'll play catch. And after dinner, me and Chloe will sit on the balcony, where I might have a cigar, we'll just be chilling, reading and sipping on a whisky sour. But a holiday's a holiday, it's meant to be relaxing. When I'm at home, I find sitting on the sofa with my feet up just a waste of time. As far as I'm concerned, every second you spend watching TV is a second you could have spent doing something useful. I only really watch things when I eat, otherwise I am always working.

Clay pigeon shooting is a new hobby of mine which I find good for my head, because I'm not thinking about anything else while I'd doing it. I got into shooting almost by accident. I took one of my sponsors, GoPro, down to Honesberie, my local shooting school, to do some filming for a day-in-the-life-of sequence, and Nick Hollick the owner and instructor said to me, 'You know what? You could be pretty good at this if you wanted to be.' I was only doing it for a bit of fun, but I got a buzz from it. And I soon realised that it wasn't the actual shooting that was giving me the buzz, it was being taught something new and putting it into practice. Having not shot for about nine years, I was suddenly entering loads of competitions. Nick probably thinks I'm going to become a professional shooter, which I'm not sure will happen, but it's something I have definitely fallen in love with. But if I'm going to spend time doing it, I'm going to make sure I'm half-decent. What would be the point otherwise?

That ability to knuckle down and immerse myself in projects is a very useful trait, but it means I'm unable to switch off. It's almost like I can hear a clock ticking in my head and that I'm racing to fit things in before my time runs out. People sometimes equate restlessness with discontent, and I think there's an element of that about me. I'm always wondering, 'How do I quantify that what I'm doing is good? Is it financial? Is it happiness? Is it that I'm successful at it? Is it that I'm better than anyone else?'

I regret not savouring my successes in rugby, because I was always focused on the next training session, the next match, the next tournament, the next tour. But at least I had a clear idea of what success looked like. It was winning games, playing well, people saying nice things about me, getting picked for the next game. But in my new world – or worlds – it's not as clear. For example, when my song 'Make You Feel' was played on the radio, that was a good day for me, a stake in the ground. I made sure that I celebrated that success with a bottle of champagne and a dance around the kitchen. I had a similar reaction when *The Good, The Bad & The Rugby* got to number one in the world in the Apple podcast charts. But the intensity isn't the same as in rugby, and the feeling of contentment is far more fleeting. And so it's always on to the next thing, and the next thing after that, never wanting to rest on my laurels.

When my last book *What a Flanker* came out, I was apprehensive about how it would sell and how it would be received. I didn't really write it for the money (there's not a lot of money in books anyway), I wrote it because I wanted to entertain people. You leave yourself wide open to criticism when you write a book, so you feel quite vulnerable when it first comes out. But once it got a few good reviews in the media, I knew it was selling well and the feedback from the public started rolling in, I started promoting it with everything I had. Being a minor success suddenly wasn't good enough, it now had to be the most successful sports memoir of the year.

But that's when the definition of success becomes muddied. What if it hadn't sold as well but I was still being sent video after video of people reading the book and laughing their heads off? What if the media reviews had been terrible but people were still telling me that the book had changed their opinion of me, that they now realised I was a pretty good guy, rather than a dickhead? I suppose it's a case of looking inwards rather than outwards, of saying, 'If the public are saying nice things, surely that's enough. Be happy, you've done all right.' However, so many of the public don't know you, don't have the full picture. What is more important than the public is that my peers and people I looked up to love the book, which made it worthwhile. The opinion of those you respect, and who are at the top of that specific area you are working in, is all that matters. Everything else is background noise.

CHLOE MADELEY:

'James's dad used to say to him, "Every second you have free in a day is a second you could be working or learning something new." That message was hammered into him, so that now when James is sitting still, apparently doing nothing, he's actually working on a million different things.

'Sometimes James is so busy he forgets to eat. We'll be on holiday and he'll sit by the pool with his laptop open and his headphones on, for hours and hours. I'll ask him to come for a swim and he'll give me a dismissive wave. He puts a crazy amount of pressure on himself. He thinks that if he stops for a second, he's failing at life. He also thinks that if he's not the best, he might as well be last. I say to James all the time, "The irony is, by having that attitude, you're not making the most out of life, because you're never stopping to appreciate what you've achieved."

'When the most recent Lions squad was announced, James didn't want to know anything about it. When I reminded him, he said, "I'm going shooting. I really need

to get good if I'm going to compete ..." Instead of thinking, "Isn't it amazing that I played for the Lions?", all he could think about was the fact that he was no longer a top-class rugby player and still in contention for the Lions. The fact that he felt like a failure, simply because he'd retired, was heart-breaking.

'He was only supposed to be at the shooting school for two hours, but he was actually there for five. When he finally returned home, I sat him down and said to him, "Hey, I want you to know that you achieved so many great things in your rugby career. No one can ever take that Lions tour you went on away from you. You should be so proud of being part of that exclusive club." All he could say was, "I know, I know." But he just couldn't see my point.'

Another reason why I'm desperate to succeed in my current endeavours is because I don't want to be defined by rugby for the rest of my life. I don't want to be invited to things in ten years' time because I once played for England. In my head, I've already moved on from that, so that it's like it didn't happen. I look at some former players, people who retired 15 or 20 years ago, and all they talk about is rugby and it's all that defines them. The issue of something you did so long ago being the pinnacle of your career means you are very quickly forgotten and what was once something to be proud of becomes something you won't stop harping on about. Yes, you did X and Y, but what the hell were you doing after that? It always reaches the stage where people below a certain age don't even know you ('Hey, you played rugby?') and it all becomes very awkward.

I once attended a dinner at Harrow School and a former England player – one of the Underwood brothers, I forget which one – was invited to make the speech. He started the talk with the line, 'You will be all glad to know that my mother's not here,' and there followed utter silence, apart from one older duffer at the back who laughed. He had clearly been using the same line for the last 20 years, and none of the kids had any idea who he was. They had all missed the point that his mum used to be at every game, was a big character and famously starred in a cameo with her sons on TV when she fake-tackled Jonah Lomu in that spoof Adidas advert all those years ago. I only got the reference at the age of 24, so the rest had no chance. And that happens to everybody. It doesn't matter what you achieved, it eventually gets forgotten, unless you're Jonny Wilkinson, Dan Carter or Richie McCaw.

I was out shooting one day and this bloke came up to me and said, 'I know you, don't I?', like people sometimes do. (They also sidle up to me and say, 'Are you famous?', and then ask for a photograph, even though they don't really know who I am, other than some vague notion that I might be a Z-list celebrity. I'll be thinking, 'This is mad. Why would anyone want a photo of someone they've never even heard of?' I just can't get my head around it.) On this occasion, I replied, 'I don't know, do you?' He said it would come to him in a minute and he drifted off. He then came back and was like, 'I've got it. We did a shoot together a couple of years ago; you're that guy who designed those really powerful shotgun cartridges.'

I was like, 'You know what? Yes, that was me, good memory.' Not another word was uttered until someone else explained to this bloke who I actually was. He then scurried up to me in a panic, hugely embarrassed, and said, 'Shit, I'm so sorry, I didn't recognise you. You must have thought, what an idiot.' And I laughed and replied, 'Mate, don't worry about it, it's fine. I'm a nobody, I have no delusions of grandeur, why would you know me unless you like rugby?' In other words, what I did in the past shouldn't be a ticket to acceptance and respect in the present, just as past mistakes shouldn't make me a prick.

I don't mind revisiting my rugby career, at least for now, but if that's all you've got to talk about, it suggests your life pretty much ground to a halt in your thirties. If anyone bumps into me in ten years' time and I'm banging on about the tour to Australia in 2016, when I played a couple of good games, you have permission to shoot me. You can't be defined by what you did years earlier, you've got to keep evolving. It's nice to be respected, but you can't keep dining out on your past successes, because they've got no bearing on what's going to happen today or tomorrow. That's why I've never wanted to be a full-time rugby pundit, covering 40 games a season, because it would stop me DJing in Ibiza, doing public speaking, writing books, shooting. I'd even like to do a stage show or acting. I have always said if Vinnie Jones and The Rock can do it, surely I can. The one problem with *What a Flanker* is that it's made any speaking gig I do now more difficult, because it means I have to keep creating new stories. At a few of those events, people were finishing my bloody jokes. (And to think I'm about to make it ten times harder with the release of this book.)

I've never really liked talking about rugby in my social life. There's nothing to be gained from talking about rugby with people who don't really understand it. And I talk about it enough already on my podcasts and with my occasional punditry. I'm far more interested in other people's worlds and what makes them tick. But it isn't always easy to avoid the subject. I once turned up at a dinner, started tucking in to my starter and the bloke next to me asked, 'How much protein do you eat?' I said to him, 'Really, your opening line is "How much protein do you eat?"' Then I found out he was a banker and we started talking about that instead. But however much I try to talk to someone about what they do, they always keep bringing it back to my rugby – 'What's it like playing at Twickenham? Who was the hardest bloke you played against?' – and it's a bit much when you've been asked those questions a thousand times before. The funny thing is, I talked a bit about this in *What a Flanker* and that if you are a super keeno you are a nause. Not a day goes by that people don't come up, ask all the same silly questions and then go, 'Sorry for being a nause,' while poking me in the ribs and winking. Then at the other end of the spectrum are the people who are super respect-ful and ask politely for a photo, but then panic, saying, 'I know you hate this,' and 'Sorry to be a nause'; or worse, they don't ask, when you can see that they really want one. Let's do a role play to illustrate what is okay and what is not:

Asking me for a photo or autograph is a huge honour for me. I love it, have no problem with it at all and it's not nausey one bit.

Asking me what my favourite bushtucker trial was while I take a piss next to you in a urinal is nause central.

Asking me for a photo and then standing next to me with your phone in your hand telling me that you once knew Ben Kay and that you were going to play for England too but injury got in the way, without taking the photo, is nausey as fuck.

Standing next to me after a DJ set while I take photos with your friends and you repeatedly saying, 'You are shit, you were shit at rugby and now you are shit at DJing and Chris Robshaw is better than you,' all the while laughing and getting progressively louder the more I ignore you, is next-level nause and you should upper-cut yourself and throw yourself into the sea.

There are of course other situations that are hard to define. I was recently at Twickenham, watching the Champions Cup final in a special Heineken hospitality box, and this bloke turned around in the seats just in front of the box and said to me during the middle of the first half, 'It's my 30th birthday today. So can you answer some questions for me? I wondered what you thought of the Lions squad?' I was waiting to be fed and had been for hours, and will admit that I was slightly angry and thought he might be taking the piss, so after giving him a long, hard stare to see if he was joking or not, and with the former clearly not a possibility, I replied, 'Are you serious? I'm sitting here waiting for my pizza, which has just arrived, and you want to interview me about the Lions squad? Mate, you probably know more about it than I do.'

When his little face dropped and he said, 'Come on, answer my questions, it's my birthday, I won't get the chance again, it's now or never to ask them,' I realised I'd been a bit short and had made him feel a bit awkward, and he was not going to give up without a fight. So I humoured him with a few lines about players who should have been picked but weren't, while I stuffed my mouth with pizza and tried to watch the final. All I said was the sort of stuff any random bloke down the pub could have told him. I honestly didn't have an opinion about the Lions and frankly didn't care. When I was done and got up to go to the toilet, two lads came over and asked for a photo. I said, 'Yes, no problem,' we did the photo, and this bloke I'd just been talking to said upon my return, 'You were nicer to them than you were to me.' I felt so bad, and he'd made such a fuss, that I got the whole of the stand to sing 'Happy Birthday' to him, which he loved. That bloke was a nause, a horrendous nause, and will go to nause hell, but at least he had a nice time.

My favourite/not favourite line at dinners is, 'I played a bit of county-level rugby, probably could have made it if other things hadn't got in the way and I hadn't picked up a couple of injuries.' I have very little patience for that kind of stuff, far less than some of my fellow pros. Dylan Hartley is perceived as a bit of a bad boy, but he's actually an excellent networker, very charming to everyone, whatever they come out with. But I just can't be like that, I'm unable to let things slide. For a long time, if someone came up to me and said, 'You know my mate John, you met him eight years ago at a post-match do,' and I didn't know him (of course I didn't, how would I?), I'd bluntly say to them, 'What do you think, mate? How am I supposed to remember your mate from eight years ago?' which could be a bit awkward and they always looked crest-fallen. So now, I just lie instead. I'll say, 'Fucking hell, John boy! How is he? Good? I hope so. What a guy.' Or if someone says to me, 'Do you remember that time when such and such happened?', I'll say, 'God, yeah, that was amazing. How could I forget?' Or if someone thumps me on the back (which I hate), instead of threatening to stick fold them up like a travel map and take their soul, I'll smile and go, 'Aargh!', as if I'm in pain. They always then apologise, and we don't have any ensuing drama.

Sometimes, they're definitely getting me mixed up with someone else, usually Chris Robshaw, Tom Croft or Lawrence Dallaglio. The other day, a guy said to me, 'I remember sitting next to you on the plane home from Australia, after you won the World Cup in 2003. Your biceps were unbelievable then and they still are now.' First of all, there's no way Lawrence would have been sitting next to some random bloke on the way home from Australia, he would have been celebrating with his teammates. Second, I wasn't at the 2003 World Cup, I was watching it on TV in my mate's living room. Third, Lawrence is 12 years older than me and bald as a coot, so I spent a lot of time looking in the mirror after speaking to that bloke, thinking, 'Jesus, I really need to start looking after myself a bit better ... perhaps it's time to get that hair transplant after all.'

As Chloe often points out, recipes for personal success can also be recipes for personal undoing. If you don't stop and reflect every now and again and savour your successes, there's not much point in having those successes in the first place. My therapist gave me a great example. He had a client who was earning tens of millions of pounds a year, had an incredible lifestyle, including an incredible house. And this bloke's housekeeper phoned him one day and said, 'Thanks so much for letting me stay in your home, it's so beautiful. I'm sitting in your infinity pool right now.' This bloke thought, 'What the fuck?! I'm sleeping in this hotel, running around like a lunatic, trying to make more money, and my housekeeper is in the infinity pool, reaping the benefits of my labour.'

Too many people lose sight of why they're working so hard and trying to earn money, so that earning money becomes an end in itself. But I've learned that a lot of what I do is about the experience and the excitement, with the money as a bit of a bonus. That's why the health and fitness stuff has kind of fallen by the wayside for the moment, and shooting and digging are very much in vogue. There's no money in shooting and digging, unlike the health and fitness stuff, but I missed being coached and missed learning new skills.

I also believe that being successful is about creating time, rather than money. That's why when a guy got in touch and asked if I wanted to come and work for the investment bank Goldman Sachs, and that he could sort me out with an interview, I immediately said no. I couldn't work in an office, even if it meant earning millions of pounds a year. He couldn't believe that I didn't want to take the interview. In his world, that was what I should be doing and consider it a great honour, but for me it did not float my boat one bit.

Money is a big motivator in my life, but I also recognise that some things are more important than that. Immersing yourself in new cultures, testing yourself in new environments, there is nothing better. Playing in France ticked all those boxes, but I earned good money over there. Playing in New Zealand was purer, probably the purest rugby experience I ever had. No friends, no family, just totally immersed in rugby, in the sport's spiritual home, surrounded by people for whom rugby was the be-all and end-all, and doing it for not a lot of cash.

When I joined the Highlanders, not only did Jamie Joseph quickly realise I wasn't a nuisance (well, maybe I was a little bit), he also realised that I wasn't happy just to get on. I'd grown up watching Super Rugby on Sky, all those great New Zealanders like Jonah Lomu, Ma'a Nonu, Carlos Spencer and Christian Cullen doing incredible stuff, and I wanted to be a part of it. That's why I said, 'You know what, I'll make a bit of money next season. Why would I not go and play in New Zealand, where all they care about is rugby?' In the end, Jamie was saying to me, 'Anyone who's prepared to come to New Zealand and play for peanuts to better themselves is all right in my book.'

Each one of my experiences in club rugby was madder than the last, an even bigger mountain to scale. People said I was mad to leave Wasps and go and play in France, because it would be the end of my international career. But it wasn't. People thought I was mad to go and play in New Zealand and that I wouldn't cut it. But I did. People were wondering why on earth I'd go and play in Japan – why would anyone do that? But I played with so many good guys and learned so much about myself. That's been the template of my life: always hunting new experiences, always wanting a challenge that is more unlikely than the last. Which is why Jamie Joseph called me Gulliver.

PAUL DORAN-JONES:

'James's worst traits? Where do I start? I have to be honest, he can be pretty self-absorbed. When we were playing together at Wasps, he came and lived with me for a bit. I'd just split up with my missus and had a new daughter, so I had house rules. I said to James, "Listen, when my daughter's not here, you can do whatever you want. But when she's here, it's two men and a baby, so you'll need to put a lid on it." James seemed cool with that.

'A few days after James moved in, he came out of his bedroom in the morning and shouted, "Doz, it's your day off, so I've left you a little list of things to get from the shop." I looked at this list – milk, bread, loo roll – and said, "Jim, are you fucking serious?"

"Yeah," he replied, "we're out of loads of stuff."

"Jim, have you bought any milk since you've been here?"

"No."

"Well, that's why we've got no fucking milk. This is not a serviced apartment."

'He also kept dumping his bedclothes next to the washing machine. I'd say to him, "Who do you think is *washing those?" It's fair to say that we had a few teething problems. And that said a lot about James. He was so used to being the most important person in the room, and other people doing things for him, that he just couldn't get his head around the fact he'd have to do things for himself for a change. But here's the thing about James: if you put the flag up and say, "Jim, I'm in a bit of trouble here and need some help," he'll never let you down. He's one of the most loyal people you'll ever meet.'*

OLLIE PHILLIPS:

'Hask fills his life with so many things, never stops moving, that he struggles to be in the now. I think he's scared that if he pauses for even a second, he'll have to reflect on all his insecurities and vulnerabilities.

'I'd consider Hask to be one of my best mates. I love the bloke and I'd die for him. But I haven't seen him for about five years. He'll often say, "Mate, it would be awesome to catch up. Next time you're in London, let's meet for a coffee." But if you expect him to deliver on that, you'll be sorely disappointed. The fact is, he's never going to ring. He's just got too much other stuff going on, is spinning more plates than ten other people put together.

'To be friends with Hask, you have to deal with the fact that he spends most of his time in Hask Land and that you're just one of hundreds of small cogs in his life. When it comes to Hask, you've got to understand the animal you're dealing with. It's nothing personal, that's just how he rolls.

'People might think that if you haven't seen someone for five years, they can't give much of a shit and can't be much of a friend. But if you understand what Hask is all

about, you won't be disappointed, and you'll appreciate and love him for who he is. And when the proverbial hits the fan, Hask will be there. If you really need him, he'll leave Hask Land. At least for an afternoon ...'

Dozzer never stops going on about the time I stayed with him in Clapham. It's one of his favourite stories. I knew he would get it into the public domain somehow. We will often jokingly remind each other that 'This is not a serviced apartment' any time we ask each other to do something. As is often the case, I remember things slightly differently to him. I was training a lot and backwards and forwards with England at the time, and his place was a bit of a tip when I moved in. It looked to me like his cleaner may have gone on holiday some time back and never returned, so I left him a note one day saying, 'It's your day off, here's a list of things we need to get and do' in case he had a spare minute. Anything he didn't have a chance to do, I would then pick up the slack and sort. He also forgets the bit where I paid for some cleaner to come in and nuke the place. And I did once leave my bedclothes in a pile next to his washing machine, but only because it had his three-day-old mouldy rugby kit in it and I didn't have time to sort it. Dozzer's quite emotional in both a good way and a bad way. He can be irrationally angry about things; however, once you understand what he has been put through on a number of fronts and how amazingly he has dealt with it all, you understand. I talked about it in *What a Flanker* 'the podcast' with him. He essentially gave up his rugby career to look after his daughter in the face of some horrific problems.

It does make me smile, as the way he tells that story you'd think I was sitting on his sofa with a little bell, ringing it whenever I wanted something doing, as if he were my butler.

As for Ollie's observation that I never stop and struggle to be in the now, I could say exactly the same thing about him! The man never sits still. He's like water, always moving, impossible to pin down. If he is not sailing the world he is cycling up a mountain or setting up a new business. He is, however, not wrong in ascertaining that I have definitely not stopped as often as I should to reflect on things, or not always taken the time to address issues. I know he is right because it's the same thing Chloe says I need to do. I do spend time with a therapist working on myself, so I have made some progress.

Ollie is the biggest networker I have ever met, and that is saying something. He was always off doing this, that or the other, meeting this person or that person. His wallet was like a breeze block because of all the business cards. When we went to Monaco for the grand prix, we'd have boats picking us up from our hotel and ferrying us to pool parties, we'd drink all day for free, and it would all be down to Ollie's connections. Ollie would turn up to family dinners with a bunch of complete randoms who I'd never met before. I'd be sitting there thinking, 'Where did you find these people? Who are they? What the fuck are they doing here?'

One evening, I was out for dinner with my mum, dad and a couple of old school friends who had been over to watch me play, when Ollie turned up with the designer Karl Lagerfeld, the famous burlesque dancer Dita Von Teese and this wonderfully flamboyant old guy who turned out to be Kate Moss's agent, Robert Ferrell. Shock horror, we all got drunk and I think I kissed Robert (I know, another man) and my mate Kert definitely kissed him. Robert took a real shine to old Kert, who from where I was standing seemed to really love the kiss too. Or so we remind him whenever all the lads get together. I'd like to say this sort of thing was unusual, but it happened all the time. Not the kissing men part; that happened twice, well maybe three times.

With Ollie taking the lead, we went everywhere and met everyone. One day, he bumped into the owner of Ladurée, the famous macaron café. A few days later, we were treated to a free afternoon tea, which normally would have cost about 300 euros. Ollie also made a friend called Olivier, who ended up moving in for a bit. He couldn't afford to pay all his rent, but luckily he owned a wine-tasting business at the time called Ô Chateau and would pay half his rent in the finest reds. As the landlord I'd pop in, have a glass of Petrus or Château Margaux a couple of times a week and that would be his rent paid. It also worked a treat if I was ever entertaining; I could roll in and order the charcuterie board and a couple of the finest wines in Christendom and the deal was done.

There's nothing worse than being analysed by an amateur psychologist. But Ollie's not far off when it comes to my friendships. I don't have millions of friends, and I'm certainly not close to many people. But the way I see things, if I'm mates with someone, I'll always be mates with them. There is not a statute of limitations on friendships, I understand they need servicing to keep them alive, but when you are a doer it's hard to put the brakes on and just socialise. However, since I have retired I have made much more of an effort to see my friends and catch up.

As I have mentioned before, Ollie has the best contacts' book of anyone I've ever met. As I said in my last book, Ollie is probably the best-known rugby player in the world. Everywhere I go, someone will sidle up to me and say, 'I met this rugby player. You might know him.' And I always reply, 'Ollie Phillips, right?' For Ollie, socialising is central to his identity. For me, it's almost an incidental thing. I am much more of an ambivert. When there is a crowd to impress and perform in front of, I am all over it, but I am equally happy on my own. If anything, I am a huge loner at times. I like nothing better than being on my own, eating on my own and doing things that I want to. Chloe finds it hard to understand. I think it comes from being content with myself and not needing anyone for anything. I make my own happiness and entertainment. A lot of people are surprised to hear this. It's like when I signed for the Highlanders and everyone was saying, 'Oh, you'll struggle down there, it's too quiet, you will miss the social side, you will go mad.' To be honest, I loved it. I loved how quiet it was. All the meals on my own, doing what I wanted when I wanted, shooting, boxing, fishing whenever I felt like it and then exploring on my days off.

I adapt to my surroundings very quickly and don't get too bogged down. I always find it funny when you see Welsh and Irish players move over to France, and they only ever last one year of a two-year contract and have to come home for personal reasons. It's because they have expectations that life will be the same as home, they are used to living close to friends and family. They have a certain lifestyle that they are used to and playing abroad is nothing like that.

Maybe Ollie finds it difficult to understand how we had that intense friendship in France for two years and now he doesn't hear from me for months at a time. But it's nothing malevolent on my part, it's just because I'm trying to be the best possible version of myself. If I had more hours in the day, maybe I'd be better at the friend thing. But when you're as focused on work as I am, it doesn't leave much time for anything else. If I have the choice of going to a social event or paid work, I'll choose work every time. And if a social event is likely to affect my performance the following day, I'll maybe show my face for an hour before ducking out. I spent my life dating sober and attending events for 30 minutes, getting some business cards and vaporising. Chloe always used to tell me off, only half-jokingly, for organising parties and leaving early, because I had training the next day. But my rugby, and being the best at it, was always my priority. I'm still like that today. Unless I really want to go to something, or I'm being paid, I won't go. That might sound ruthless, but it's been my recipe for success. I will never attend a dinner unless I am working; I can't stand small talk, or just sitting there doing nothing. I would always rather take part in something or leave.

Having said all that, I've become a far more social animal since I retired from rugby. Now if I'm doing a DJ set, I might invite some friends along and have a bit of a party with them. I'll often text an old mate and meet them for a quick beer or coffee. Before, I never would have done that, because I would have seen it as interfering with my journey. That's one benefit of retiring: I turn up at a place now and think, 'Who lives around here?' or fire a message into a WhatsApp group saying, 'Lads, anyone fancy a feed or a beer?' The only downside of trying to socialise is that when you live in Northampton it's not always easy.

Chloe tells me that people sensed that I was focused on other things and not on friendship, which is why they didn't think they could talk to me about serious stuff. I had team-mates who suffered with mental illness but would never have talked to me about it. That's a shame, because if people had reached out to me with their problems, I would have been there for them, and maybe I'd have understood. Ollie's right, I do live in Hask Land, but if you really need me for anything, I'll gladly leave Hask Land. I'll probably be back in Hask Land in time for tea, but I would never leave a mate hanging.

4

USED-CAR SALESMAN

DYLAN HARTLEY, ENGLAND TEAMMATE:

'James's worst trait is the fact he's a workaholic. He never
stops, and I often tell him that he needs to slow down.
Even when he was still playing, he always had other stuff
going on outside of rugby. But that's why he's a high
achiever, and why I also admire him for it. He can do it, I
can't.

'I'd heard a lot about James before I met him. He had
a reputation for being super-professional – and he was
light years ahead of everyone else in terms of the way he
looked after himself and approached performance. The
other thing people talked about was his personal website,
which is why we used to call him "Dot Com" and joke
about "Brand Haskell". Having your own website just
seemed crazy back then, but he was just ahead of his
time.

'Whatever James decides to do, he really goes for it,
dives in headfirst, and doesn't give a shit what anyone
thinks. He's played professional rugby, he's released quite
a few books, he's produced music, he's got loads of
podcasts, he's had supplement and coffee businesses. He

achieves more in a year than most people achieve in a lifetime.

'In America, that sort of can-do attitude, being entrepreneurial – even if you fail – is celebrated. But in the UK, lots of people perceive trying and failing as a bad thing, something to be embarrassed about. I don't see it like that. It's a good thing to experiment and try different things, even if they don't always come off. Some things James has tried have turned to gold, other things not so much. But that's him just working things out, and at least he gives it a crack, while other people are sitting on their arses and willing him to fail.

'People want James to fail because they're insecure and envious. When James came out and said he wanted to be a DJ, people wanted him to fail. When he said he wanted to be an MMA fighter, people wanted him to fail. The MMA thing didn't work out, because of his injuries and Covid. But at least he gave it a go. However, he has made the DJing work, and is now releasing his own songs, which probably makes his knockers feel like shit. What probably kills them more is the fact he's making money and laughing all the way to the bank.'

It's true that I went to private schools, but while most of my housemates were minted or were the stereotypical fee-paying-school attendees, I never had any money, or I should say the expected level of money you would associate with going to schools like that, and nor did my parents. It's not like I'm looking for sympathy, I'm only talking about my experience and I'm aware that everybody is different. I'm just suggesting that our relative skintness had a profound effect on me, and explains my attitude to money and work to this day.

My parents lived a bit of a hand-to-mouth existence – though you wouldn't have known it from the outside, as appearances are really important to my folks – and they basically ploughed every penny they earned into school fees for me and my brother. Which, when you think of the amounts, was huge. Yes, it was their choice, but it was always touch and go. It put huge amounts of pressure on them to keep working and shelling out. They always gave me and my brother everything we needed but to the detriment of their finances.

One of the things with this was that I never had any pocket money or my own money as a kid. The first money I had was when I signed for Wasps. I did get summer jobs, but I was always playing and touring so it made it very difficult. It was actually quite a good thing playing for England Under-18s and Under-19s because the travel expenses went straight to me. That's how I sort of survived and could get things I wanted.

I'd always be getting in trouble at school for asking other kids for their food and snacks. I'd go on summer camps, run out of cash after a couple of days and be like a broken record for the rest of the week: 'Can I have your banana? Have you got another bag of crisps? Let me have a bit of your Coke …' Teachers would accuse me of bullying the kids.

'I was only asking for a few of their nuts!' I said.

'Well, you're big and intimidating,' they claimed.

'It's not my fault, I only asked if I could have some peanuts!'

'Well, bring your own food, Mr Haskell, otherwise it's bullying.'

We had a teacher that wrote a book about my prep school, and I asked if I could sell it for him. When I was a kid, I could sell ice to the Eskimos, so I was flogging this book to everyone with a pulse. Bear in mind, it wasn't Harry Potter, it was a very dry history of our school. I'm not sure why I offered to sell it,

I think it was that performance thing again. I just thought this looks fun and was a chance to show off. But because I was selling so many, my logic told me that it would be okay to skim a quid off each sale. It never occurred to me that at some point the teacher who wrote the book was going to think, 'Hang on a minute, I've sold 50 books and I've only been paid for 45.' I am of course exaggerating; I only skimmed off the price of one book or maybe five.

When speech day came around, I was going from car to car, giving everyone a big spiel about this book – selling it as some kind of dream, making it sound as exciting as *The Lord of the Rings* – and refusing to take no for an answer. Imagine Del Boy down the market on his best day. Afterwards, this teacher came up to me and said, 'James, have you got all the money?' and I replied, 'Yep, I've definitely got all the money …' Okay, what I did wasn't right, but he only sold as many as he did because of me. I call it business wastage, and to be honest the Mars bar he offered me for hours and hours of hard graft was not going to cut the mustard.

Every Wednesday, my grandma would come and visit me at prep school. I'd sit in the back of her car, drink hot chocolate from a flask, smash down a Toffee Crisp and read the *Beano*. Paradise. On Sundays, we'd have big chapel services, attended by all the kids' parents. Afterwards, the kids would sit in the back of their parents' cars and plough through bags of sweets and bottles of fizzy drinks. All except for me and my brother, because Mum and Dad would always forget to bring anything. I'd look forlornly at my schoolmates, with their faces covered in chocolate, and say to my parents, 'Where's our sweets?' Mum would reply, 'Sorry, we forgot.' And then they'd head straight off because they were always so busy with work. Now again it sounds like me and my brother were like Oliver Twist and the gang. I did not want for anything, I am just relating the fact that we would see my parents and more often than not they had shot out the door late to get to chapel, forgotten to bring any sweets and then went off. Of course, there were times they did remember to bring some sweets. I know there are starving kids out there in the world with nothing, including any clean water. So before you say, 'This guy has lost the plot,' again it's all relative and it's my narrative and no one else's.

Anyway, one Sunday, after they'd gone and we were once again empty-handed, I got hold of a load of hymn sheets, told all the other parents that they were newsletters and sold about a hundred of them for a quid each. I'm not even joking. I'm not sure how I got away with it. I honestly just walked into the chapel, picked up these printed service programmes from that day's service and went from car to car selling them for a pound. I may have said the money was for charity, but don't quote me on that. How no one grabbed me or gave me a clip around the ear for selling that crap, I do not know, but I charmed my way around every parent and they all paid. Needless to say, I took some cash home after that, which kept me in sweets and meant I could buy stuff off the other kids instead of 'pressuring' them into giving me stuff. I didn't try that particular trick again, as it was a one-time deal and was clearly daylight robbery.

I had all sorts of businesses at prep school, anything that could raise a few quid for sweets and comics. I did some decorating, teaming up with Ed Cooper and Leo Mellis and painting the apartment of the teacher who wrote the book about the school. I guess he was an easy target. I remember trying to convince him we'd done 150 quid's worth of work; I had a clipboard, measuring tape out and paint swatches, but sadly he refused to believe we had done that amount of work and he fobbed us off with a fiver and a packet of sweets each. I learned a lesson there: get the quote agreed before you do the work. I had to stop Cooper going back there and trashing the joint until he paid. Coops had a very different business style to the rest of us.

We also had a car-washing business. It was a professional set-up, using a load of gear nicked from my dad's shed. I was always nicking stuff from my dad, and he was always saying, 'What the hell have you done with my gear, you bloody idiots?' He never stopped having to buy himself new kit and tools that we'd lost or broken. No wonder he was forever going on about how much our schooling cost him. One time, my brother dug a pond at school and my dad ended up buying the liner and the fish to go in it. A few days later, some jealous kid who had been phased out of being involved in this new pond decided to break a thermometer and pour the mercury into the pond water, and of course all the fish died. I assume that kid is now behind bars or a yet-to-be-caught serial killer. He was odd enough back then (I remember his name, but who needs him coming around and trying to do me in once this is published?), and killing animals at a young age is a proper sign of being a nut bag and future killer.

My dad went fucking mental as he was probably a grand down on the project to keep my brother happy. So when my brother told him, I recall my dad saying, 'Fucking hell, Edward, that's three hundred quid on fish down the drain. What the fuck are you lot up to? I am not paying any more money. Get some other mug to shell out.' And with that there was no more junior pond as no other parents were stupid enough to put their hands in their pockets. So outside the junior section was just a big muddy hole with an expensive liner in it. Eventually, a teacher nicked the liner and that was it.

Having taken all my dad's buckets, sponges, shammies and cleaning fluids for our car-washing stint, we earned a hell of a lot of sweets. It was a great business and we were on fire before I sub-contracted a job to someone and they somehow damaged one of the teachers' cars. I'm not sure how this happened but when he went to start it, it wouldn't go. He said that the garage told him it was due to water getting into the actual engine, a feat they had never seen before. That put a bit of a spanner in the works, as customer satisfaction is key and with limited faculty cars to wash, one bad review and we were dead in the water, and no amount of my charm could save us. Then a rival gang saw our moment of weakness and started up their own car-washing business, profits took a hit (there were only so many Chewits to go round) and we ended up having to go to the mattresses and scrap it out. It was very much like the prohibition wars in Chicago. We would find their equipment store and trash it so they couldn't work, they would pour dirty water on a freshly cleaned car, making us look bad. We would swap their cleaning fluid with bleach, causing proper damage to their customers. It got messy until it culminated in a big scrap behind the school, like in the film *Anchorman*. Sadly, no one got speared with a trident, but I did put a kid in a wheelie bin. After that battle royale, car washing was banned by the school.

Retelling some of these stories, they sound as if they're from the 1950s, or as if they took place on an inner-city housing estate. And I suppose that shows how much things have changed in such a short space of time, and how much more freedom and autonomy youngsters had back then, especially if you were an entrepreneurial kid at a boarding school.

It's not like I saw myself as a wheeler dealer, the idea just came to me and I had to act on it. It wasn't all about the money, I just loved trying it on and getting an edge. And I also craved attention. Thinking about it, that's exactly like Del Boy. Here's a perfect example. I'd just arrived at Wellington, so must have been 14. During one biology class, we were examining a pig's heart. Like all my classmates, I was establishing my reputation – was I going to be a nutter, a clown, a popular kid or a loser? So when the teacher popped out for a minute and one of my classmates shouted out, 'Oi, Haskell! I bet you wouldn't take a bite out of that pig's heart and swallow it,' I immediately replied, 'Yes, I will, but how much are you going to pay me?'

One kid said he'd give me 100 quid, another said 200. They were throwing these numbers out there and I bit hard. I was like, 'Right, I'm going to do it, but I'm taking names.' I whipped out a notebook and started going round the class, taking individual bets. Surprise, surprise, the big talk about lots of money quickly disappeared and was replaced by two pounds here, a fiver there and the odd 'I'll give you a quid, Haskell.' In no time, I had everyone's name down. Then I marched over to this pig's heart, picked it up and took a big bite out of it, chewed it and swallowed it. When the teacher came back in, the first thing he noticed were the teeth marks and giant hole in the heart. There was a look of pure panic on his face. He said, 'Listen, if any of you have eaten that, you might get ill, because it's not sanitised.' Obviously, everyone was in hysterics, but I didn't own up to it and luckily no one snitched, even though public schools are rife with little turncoats.

Afterwards, all the other kids were taking the piss, calling me a wanker for eating a pig's heart. But I just kept saying, 'No, you've got it all wrong. I've just made 40 quid because you're all gonna pay!' They didn't think I'd bother, but I spent the next couple of days making sure they did. It's not like I fancied myself as an enforcer, I was just absolutely adamant:

'I honoured the bet, now you're gonna pay me.' I had to sharpen a couple of the lads up as they weren't overly eager to hand over the readies, but as always, a little bit of pressure and the money came rolling in. That money kept me in Domino's pizza for a month.

PAUL DORAN-JONES:

'James's parents had some labourers doing some work on their house, and these Eastern European lads had this amazing supply of porn mags that they stashed in the garden shed. Somehow, James got his hands on some of this porn and stored it in a big chest in his room at school. Whenever he opened it, it was like that scene from Pulp Fiction, *when they open the briefcase and it gives off a golden glow. Some people would be lost for words, some would literally gasp, others would be grinning and rubbing their hands together. That porn stash formed the basis of our first joint-business venture. And Hask hasn't stopped coming up with business ideas since – some as mad as our Eastern European porn mag racket, some with a bit more mileage ...'*

Dozzer loves this story. It's one of his favourites. It all started with a guy who did a bit of work for my mum and dad, odd jobs and the like. I'll call him Frank. One day, Frank and some other lads were doing some work on the house. When I paid them a visit in the shed at the bottom of the garden, they were sitting there reading porn mags. I must have only been about 14, but Frank said to me, 'Do you like porn mags?' I obviously replied, 'Of course.' And a couple of days later, Frank turned up with three cardboard boxes full to the brim with every porn title known to man – *Razzle, Escort, Men Only, Shaven Ravers* and my favourite, *Club*. You name it, Frank had it. And if he didn't have it, he'd get it for you.

Having got my grubby teenage hands on this mountain of porn, I decided to turn it into a business. At Wellington, I had a jumbo-sized briefcase (a chest probably sounds better, but I think Dozzer is embellishing), so I jettisoned some of my schoolwork, replaced it with porn mags and started selling them to fellow pupils for two quid a pop, or renting them out for one quid. After a while, pupils were queuing outside my room. I'd be sitting at a table, with the briefcase open, and I'd say to them, 'Right, what do you need?' The younger kids would often be a bit tongue-tied, so I might say to them, 'You know what would be right up your street? A little bit of *Razzle*, perhaps? Or maybe a *Knave*? Nothing too hard, more of a beginner's porn mag. Very accessible.'

If they bought a *Razzle*, we'd sneak into their room, nick it back, remove the front cover and sell it on to someone else, then charge them for losing it. Or if they rented and subsequently soiled said *Razzle* (usually all over the traditional 'pile-up', which you might have to google), me and Dozzer would go from all smiles to aggression. We'd close the door, sit them down on the bed and say, 'Tut, tut, tut, what has happened here? I see the pile-up is no longer visible, because it's stuck to the previous page. That's no good for business, is it? Whatever am I to do with a soiled *Razzle* pile-up? Without the pile-up, this magazine is virtually worthless. I tell you what, buy us a Domino's pizza and we'll call it quits …'

We had a proper little racket going for a couple of months, until things started getting a bit out of hand and we had to fold the business sharpish. I blame Dozzer. Typically, he had vaulting ambitions, was dreaming of global domination. But once my partner took control of the merchandise, I never saw any of it again. I didn't see much of the cash, either. It was like a Mafia takeover. And because word of his hostile takeover was sweeping through the corridors of Wellington like wildfire, he eventually had to cut his losses (which meant stuffing the porn mags in bin bags and chucking them in the woods).

About ten years ago, I was rooting around my parents' shed and found about two thousand porn mags hidden behind lawnmowers, crates of out-of-date lager and all the other old shit you usually find in sheds. Because it would have been too embarrassing to take them down to the tip and there were far too many to dump in the woods ('SHAMELESS HASKELL CAUGHT FLY-TIPPING PORN'), I decided to burn them on a bonfire instead. Which was a great plan, but as anyone who has tried to burn masses of paper will attest to, if you don't rip the paper up and just throw it all on in one go, it doesn't burn properly. You have to keep turning it and revealing more fresh pages to be burnt, which I could not be bothered to do. So what you have are pages and pages of undamaged content still left. Which only rears its ugly head when a few days later a wind picks up. Which then carries fragments of fanny, tits and arse on the wind. These then coat everything in a six-mile radius. As you can imagine, it's a tricky question to answer when your mum asks why all her trees and front lawn have been covered in images of lady gardens and ads for quick telephone relief from Lusty Linda. I decided not to tell her she'd been unwittingly harbouring one of the largest collections of vintage porn in the country for at least two decades, and was complicit in a pretty successful bulk-order porn-mag-flogging business.

ALEX PAYNE:

'Hask is the only rugby player I know who has a PA. That tells you everything you need to know. He's got so much going on in his life, he needs Steph to tell him what time to get up, what time to eat, what time to bath, what time to go to bed. If Hask was Action Man, he'd have every outfit in the range – and be changing them six times a day. And I don't care who you are, you'd do well to keep up with him.'

EDDIE JONES, ENGLAND HEAD COACH:

'James Haskell is a used-car salesman in a rugby player's body.'

Eddie's right, I am a bit like a used-car salesman, and being tackled in rugby is very much like making love to a beautiful woman – you brace yourself, hold on tight, particularly if it's a rear-ender, and pray you make contact with twin airbags as soon as possible. Eddie used to call me a 'wheeler-dealer', and a lot of that came from my dad, who pulled me in lots of different directions after becoming my agent. He wanted me to be breaking moulds, transcending rugby, so that bigger companies and brands would want to work with me. I never lived up to the hype, sadly – my dad thought I was destined to be the next Lawrence Dallaglio – and while we fell some way short we certainly gave it a crack.

Dylan Hartley called me President Business, from *The LEGO Movie*, and he and Chris Ashton would always be taking the piss out of me for my entrepreneurial spirit. Chris called me the 'King of Shbizz', 'shbizz' being short for 'shit businesses'. He'd come up to me and say, 'Hask, mate, what shbizzes you got on at the moment?' I always took it in good humour, used to joke that my dad was like Henry Winkler in that flashback scene from *The Waterboy*, when someone steals his playbook, he loses the plot and ends up making phone calls to his nan on a disconnected phone while wearing high heels. I suggested to Chris that I had walked in on my dad as he was pretending to talk to Apple about a big sponsorship deal for me, only to see that the phone wasn't even connected. He never wore the high heels, thank God, at least not in front of me. Me and Dad have had supplement businesses, a shooting business, a speaking business, health and fitness businesses, training academies. We've tried it all and have sheds full of merchandise and leaflets for businesses that never quite flew. Those sheds are chock-full of broken dreams, and a lot of wasted money.

Often the problem was that we'd try to get big too quickly. Like the time I said to my dad, 'Maybe we should start a training academy,' and suddenly we had a sponsorship deal with Lexus and a load of equipment, like branded tackle bags and water bottles and marquees. A couple of weeks later, a five-day training camp was set up, with other camps planned for all over the country. And because this was in 2008, the arse suddenly fell out of the economy, Lexus lost hundreds of millions overnight and pulled their sponsorship. So we tried to do it ourselves, signed up a few players and the first camp was amazing. The kids said it was the best five days they'd ever had, being coached by professional players, but it never made any money and soon petered out.

Then, because I liked shooting, I said, 'Why don't we do shooting days, where we take corporate groups out, each team shoots with a player and then we all have dinner?' We did a couple of those but the players kept letting us down. The issue with both these businesses was trying to be both promoter and deliverer, especially when one of your sales team was a fully committed professional rugby player. If we could have just turned up and executed it would have been fine, but we had to sell the places, find the players and staff, set the event up and then put it on. The shooting was great but players' days off would change, meaning you sold spots to shoot with England players and none were available. It happened to me a number of times when I couldn't attend my own events or I would arrive very late. Not good. What made it hard was I already had another salary but my dad didn't, so he needed these extra businesses to pay the bills, hence why he pushed so hard.

The supplements brand was called Hades, which was bolted on to a coffee brand called Angry Squirrel (one of my nicknames for Ollie Phillips – more on that later). The coffee van was knocking out 300 cups a day and people loved it, and Hades became *Men's Health* supplement of the year. But because of bad management, and trying to get too big, too quickly (again), it imploded.

There's no getting away from it: these businesses represent a string of financial disasters. But I learned a valuable lesson, which was that if you don't have a passion for what you're trying to sell, and you're only doing it for the money, you're destined to fail. My dad didn't really give a shit about health and fitness and supplements and coaching and coffee. Health and fitness is a central part of my identity, which is why my book *Perfect Fit* sold a shedload of copies. Eating healthily is very important to me, which is why my book *Cooking for Fitness* sold a shedload of copies. Even the supplements business should have been a roaring success, but we got carried away with how much people seemed to love it and failed to cut our cloth accordingly. And, looking back, I wasn't *that* passionate about supplements, although they still could have been a long-term success if we'd done things differently.

Everything I do now, business-wise, I love being involved with. And I stick to what I know best. I like to use the analogy of starting up an Indian restaurant and then a Chinese restaurant opening next door; if your place suddenly falls empty and the Chinese restaurant has queues snaking out of the door, you don't start selling Chinese food; you knuckle down and make your Indian food better – because you know about Indian food, but you don't know anything about Chinese food. Or that other old story about digging for diamonds in your own backyard, rather than aimlessly roaming the earth looking for diamonds elsewhere. Saying that, we kept finding diamonds and throwing them in the bin. And occasionally we'd have our very own diamond mine, blow it up and have to start all over again. But I refer you to that great quote in *One Flew Over the Cuckoo's Nest* when Jack Nicholson tries and fails to lift the sink unit and throw it through the window: 'Well, I tried, didn't I? Goddamn it, at least I did that ...'

5

A VERY NOISY BEHEMOTH

DAN COLE, ENGLAND TEAMMATE:
'The stuff Hask comes out with on his podcast, in his books and in his public speaking is probably 5 per cent of his banter that has worked over the years. I spent the best part of a decade listening to the other 95 per cent. He came out with so much shit in changing rooms and at dinner tables, but most of that has been weeded out. He was basically like a stand-up comedian, using us as a test audience to refine his act. Mind you, we did encourage him. We'd ask him to tell us some stories about Ronnie Regan, because we knew they were among his favourites, and he'd go on for hours.

'Hask probably came across as over-confident and flippant to outsiders, but he took his rugby very seriously and was always prepared. We knew he'd done his homework, we knew he was experienced and understood what it took to win big matches, so when he made a joke before a game it would loosen the room, rather than make people nervous. People assume Hask would be a distraction because of his brashness, but he wasn't at all.

'Especially towards the end, Hask just knew how to be a good teammate. If he was in the starting XV, he knew his role. But if he was on the bench or wasn't in the squad, he was still good to have around. Every game for England is important, but one of the things you learn as you become more experienced is that you can't be on it all the time, otherwise you'll burn out pretty quickly. And Hask was very good at dialling things down, understanding when the mood needed lightening. I remember him being banned for one Six Nations game and Eddie Jones keeping him in the camp for that reason. Eddie even asked him along to training at the 2019 World Cup in Japan, and he wasn't even an official member of the squad.

'As well as training hard, and pushing the players in the starting XV, he brought an energy to the changing room and the dinner table. Some players can't do that, because they can't handle not being in the starting XV. And Eddie didn't like those kinds of blokes. A Six Nations can be tough going, especially if you lose a couple of games, and sometimes you'll sense a flatness in the changing room or at the dinner table. The last thing you need in those situations are mopers and moaners. But Hask was able to spark things, just with a witty one-liner. Thinking about it, he was almost like a team mascot.'

Poor old Coley has been there almost from the beginning of my England career, and he spent most of that time gritting his teeth, with that grim Leicester demeanour, trying not to laugh. Coley's serious, negative but in a fun way, tough, lovely and not a show-off at all. I do remember that whenever he was asked to perform, this secret side of Dan did come out and he would sing and dance. It was amazing to watch. He did it once post-match in the Spirit of Rugby at Twickenham with about a thousand people in the audience and brought the house down. I'm supposed to be the antithesis of everything he's about in every way, but we always got on well.

I remember bonding after a Scotland Six Nations game, which we drew. We had the Monday off and went on an all-dayer in Fulham, and me and Coley were the last men standing at 3 a.m. in some terrible bar called Havana's. And on the 2017 Lions tour, me, Coley, Joe Marler and Justin Tipuric spent an awful lot of time in escape rooms all over New Zealand. We'd be in those rooms together for an hour at a time, supposedly trying to solve puzzles, but actually on our knees pissing ourselves with laughter. Coley is very cerebral and clever, me slightly less so, and Marler is something else completely. You'd think we wouldn't get on because we were all quite different, but we did.

Humour-wise, Coley's a sniper, a master of dry one-liners. In stark contrast, I've always taken the Tommy Gun approach, spraying bullets all over the room and hoping at least one of them will hit the mark. So Coley would have waded through a lot of my shit in changing rooms and at dinner tables all over the world. The same old stories, over and over again.

Looking back, I cringe when I think of some of the times I tried to make people laugh. I was always performing, probably because I knew I wasn't everyone's cup of tea but wanted to be liked. I recently spoke to my good friend Adam Bidwell, who used to live with my old teammate Alex King, and he told me that after my first day at Wasps, Alex King phoned him and said, 'Bidders, you won't believe what turned up today – this fucking 17-year-old kid, an absolute specimen, loud as anything, who's walked through the changing-room door and started taking the piss out of everybody. I've never seen anything like it.'

That made me smile, because it makes total sense now. I wasn't really aware of being different at school – my dad had convinced me that it was everyone else that was different, not us – but now I can see that I'd been a man in a child's body for a while, craving an adult environment. That Wasps changing room should have been an absolutely terrifying place for a teenager, full of legends like Lawrence Dallaglio, Simon Shaw, Phil Greening and Josh Lewsey, but apparently I swanned in like I owned the bloody place.

The first time I did media training with England, they set it up as a proper interview, with a camera, lights and a microphone in my face, before a journalist started firing personal questions at me. And instead of being shy or getting flustered, like some of my teammates, I was fine. I got it straightaway, answered the questions I wanted to answer, rather than the questions they wanted me to answer. I remember people being quite taken aback by that, and I think my apparent comfort in my own skin put people on edge. Even now, I notice how people's body language changes when I walk into a room, because me being comfortable in my own skin makes them feel uncomfortable. When I first met Ellis Genge, he was determined not to laugh at my jokes, and Tom Wood was the same. It's like they're thinking, 'I am not going to be defeated by this big idiot and his loud energy. I refuse to let him amuse me in any way.'

When it came to interacting with the media, I felt that my job was to be engaging. If other players wanted to talk about it being a game of two halves and how much they respected the opposition, that was fine. But I was always aware (although not as much as I am now, as an ex-player looking in) that there needed to be players who gave a bit more than that, for the sake of rugby. But I was also a safe pair of hands, because of my confidence in front of a camera. When a coach needed a player to chat on a slow media day, or deflect from some controversy, they'd often wheel me out.

Eddie Jones knew that I wouldn't rise to the bait or give in to pressure and say something stupid. Like Eddie, I saw it as a game, a performance. That was one of my favourite things about being a rugby player, sitting in the middle of the room, surrounded by 20 journalists with notepads, microphones and dictaphones. When it was over, I'd be disappointed. I wouldn't give the media anything they really wanted, but at least I might make them laugh.

ALEX PAYNE:
'I can't recall the first time I met Hask, but I probably heard him coming before I saw him. I do remember interviewing him when I was a young reporter at Sky and he was playing for England Under-18s. I vividly recall this hulking, blond, very noisy behemoth bounding around, saying hello to all the reporters and comfortably owning the show. From the very beginning of our relationship, he was a cacophony of noise and colour.

'Even as a youngster, Hask was great value, always gave you something. I've conducted God knows how many interviews where it's like getting blood out of a stone, but Hask was always fun, lively and energetic. And he asked questions, which not many do. He was interested in what I did and how things worked at Sky. He wanted info, and he wanted in on things.

'In this world of sanitised sportspeople, where players have media handbooks that are ten inches thick and

every answer is recited, Hask was quite happy to state an opinion, tell journalists what he actually thought. That opened the door to certain journalists getting stuck into him. And once he'd opened Pandora's Box, he couldn't close it. If you're bombastic and state strong opinions, open your arms and say, "I'm here and I'm going to say exactly what I think," people are going to react against that. That's what happens in the UK; we build characters up so we can knock them down. But the biggest compliment I can pay Hask is that we miss him now he's gone.

'What people should remember about Hask is that his teammates and coaches love him. He creates an enormous wake, and people want to tuck in behind him. He brings a massive amount of energy, there's always stuff happening around him. And when he's on his A game, you've got to have your armour on and your sword sharpened, because if you don't, he'll gobble you up and spit you out. But the odd thing is, he gets quite angry that rugby fans all think he's Captain Banter. Having built this caricature of himself, he then turns around and says, "I'm not really the person you think I am."

'It must be exhausting living in Hask's head, because he's non-stop, constantly bouncing from one thing to another. But I don't think there's anyone who gets close to him in modern rugby. I often talk about the Sky Sports News test: when it's on in pubs and bars across the land, it's normally on mute. But Hask is one of the few rugby players who will make people reach for the remote control and turn the volume up. And now he's retired from rugby and beholden to no one, that works perfectly for the podcast.

'*We want* The Good, The Bad & The Rugby *to be a space for people to say what they really think. We like the media handbooks to be left at the door and for individuals to talk about the things that matter to them. And because Hask is a proper team player, has been there and done it, been involved in a fair bit of controversy in his time, they're fiercely loyal to him and trust him.'*

Chloe hit the nail on the head when she said that I'm always performing, a storyteller, because I crave the attention – probably a little bit too much. I enjoyed rugby, but you probably could have replaced it with anything. It was more about executing skills I'd learned and performing at the highest possible level for people's entertainment. Everything I've done since retiring from rugby has been a performance – podcasting, after-dinner speaking, writing books, shooting, my brief MMA career, putting content out on Instagram. It's all about telling stories – even DJing, which is telling stories through music. You are the centre of everyone's night, and people have such an emotional reaction to music that it's about creating that buzz.

Chloe said to me once, 'Do you even like music? Or are you just a geek, more fascinated by the technology?' She had a point, because I was never a massive music person when I was younger, and it was more about the learning and the technical side of things when I started DJing. But it became more and more about the music and the buzz I got from being up behind the decks, making people dance and laugh and wave their arms in the air. It's actually been so good to get that education and to learn about music and the origins of house music. Simon Dunmore from Defected Records really opened my eyes to house, disco, soul and funk. He quickly got me away from my early interest in EDM and showed me the light. I have really enjoyed this late musical adventure I am on. Chloe is a huge music lover and has steered me towards 90s hip hop. I tried to DJ hip hop but sadly it was too hard and a very different style to what I like.

Well before the music career, I learned the importance of fun and laughter to a team environment very early in my time in rugby. On my first pre-season training camp with Wasps, in the middle of nowhere in Poland, I just didn't do what a schoolboy was expected to do. When most players were relaxing in their rooms, I was in the canteen with all the hardcore members of the team – Lawrence Dallaglio, Simon Shaw, Fraser Waters, Alex King – eating biscuits and telling stories. I could see some of the old guard looking at me as if to say, 'This kid really shouldn't be here.' But I just loved it, even if it meant making tea for everyone. I was never difficult when I was asked to do things. I was made to clean a lot of the lads' boots, including Lawrence's (although, to be fair, he also used to give me his cast-offs). Whenever Lawrence called, I'd come running. I probably would have got rid of a body for Lawrence if he'd asked me. He once phoned me at 6.30 a.m. in the morning and told me to meet him at the club. I rightly assumed he'd been out partying and forgotten his kit, so needed some of mine, plus his old boots. So I rolled out of bed, raced down to London and managed to get the kit and boots to him before the team run without anyone seeing.

I would make drinks, get people's food, tidy up, but if it meant I was able to be part of other things I would do it. Some young players now, you ask them to do that and they shout bullying or say no, fuck off. They know you can't do anything about it. If you read *What a Flanker* you will know that I didn't really stand for that and would often have to return to a bit of the old school to get things done. When you are young you don't appreciate why certain things have to happen, but when you are older you understand. Whatever those established pros asked me to do, I'd do it, to the best of my ability.

But just because I was subservient, that didn't mean I didn't have input. And I learned to love those moments most of all, whether it was sitting around drinking tea in a Polish canteen, meal times, 'sappuccino' sessions in someone's room, slagging absolutely everything off, or sitting on the back of the bus trading stories. It was 25 lads with different personalities and different takes on life, all living out their dreams, many of them armed with razor-sharp wit. Some of those sessions would be like duels, rugby's version of rap battles.

When I was playing for the Highlanders in New Zealand, they were sticklers for team tradition and hierarchy, far more so than in English rugby. The first time I got on the team bus I plonked myself down near the back, which was my customary position with Wasps, Stade and England. Nasi Manu, a brilliant player who should have been an All Black, gave me a serious look and said, 'Mate, you're gonna have to move.'

'Why?' I replied, a little bit bemused.

'Because you're a new player and they have to sit at the front.'

'You serious?'

And from the look of his face and demeanour, he was.

I reckon if I had not moved, it would have kicked off. I was a seasoned international, with 40-odd caps to my name, and I was reduced to being a little schoolboy again. I gathered my things, walked sheepishly to the front and took a seat behind

Jamie Joseph, who was chuckling away to himself. I also had to carry bags, clean stuff and fill up the water bottles, so I was basically that 17-year-old kid at Wasps again. But I was quite happy to go along with it, because that was just part of their culture and what I had to do to be part of that team (although it would have been nice if someone had told me beforehand). I like teams with traditions, and I enjoy playing a part in keeping those traditions alive. And because I toed the party line, I had very nearly graduated to the back seats by the end of the season.

At least Nasi had asked me nicely. If people challenge me or threaten me, things can end up quite different. During one Wasps team social, in a pub in the middle of Birmingham, this prop kept going on about wanting to knock people out. I hated all that hard-man bravado, like players slapping each other around the face, trying to get a reaction. So in the end, I said to him, 'Look, just stop saying silly things like that.'

And he replied, 'What the fuck! I'll knock you out as well!'

'No, you wouldn't.'

'Yeah, I would.'

'Come on then, let's go outside.'

To be clear, I was drunk as we were on a team social. I went outside, took my jacket off and suddenly realised we were standing on a street in the city centre at about three o'clock in the afternoon. So I said to this bloke, 'Look, if you just apologise, we can go back inside and forget about it.'

'No, I'm not apologising. I want to knock you out ...'

So we had a scuffle. I whacked him. And when he hit the deck, I thought he was dead. I was standing on the high street with my life flashing before my eyes, thinking what another fine pickle you have got yourself into. I was imagining the newspaper headlines: 'HASKELL KILLS TEAMMATE ON

TEAM SOCIAL', or 'HORRID HASKELL SET FOR LIFE IN PRISON'. I felt awful. Why couldn't I have just left it? I always do these stupid things and then think: What was I doing? Even though it was the other bloke who started it, I was the one who was going to be in trouble. I was looking around for CCTV cameras while trying to rouse him from his slumber. Luckily, he fully recovered (although he had a cut down one side of his face and a big black eye). Then everyone got upset with me because the bloke accused me of sucker-punching him. One of our wingers, who shall remain nameless, actually wanted to fight me too, and I spent the rest of the afternoon explaining that this prop had started on me and that I'd given him every opportunity to back out of it. (I was also on guard the whole time, because this player was quite drunk, and there are few things more dangerous than an irate Islander with a few beers inside him.) The thing that saved me was one of the academy players had come out with us at the time and saw the whole thing, knew it was a fair fight and said that I had given the bloke a chance to back down, which he had not taken. Without this witness, I may have been the one not waking up.

When I was still playing, I was always putting myself under pressure to entertain and worrying if I was going to get a laugh or not. I'd even worry about running out of stories to tell on the coach. Here's just one example. When England were in a training camp in Denver ahead of the 2015 World Cup, we all went whitewater rafting one day. That sounds great on paper, like the perfect bonding session. But because the coaches were obsessed with getting us fitter than the All Blacks and flogging us to within an inch of our lives, all the boys were absolutely fucked. They trained us into the ground, so some lads were in hell. They put us onto a coach straight after the session to give us three days' R&R. That sounded great, but the issue was they were taking us into the Rockies and the river was a four-hour coach ride away. Jonny May cramped up so much he looked like something from *The Exorcist*. He was lying in the aisle, howling and growling, his legs in the air and his hands curled up like claws. Jonny is a pretty weird bloke at times, but I could feel his pain. The lads were in hysterics, as Jonny was clearly in agony. Some of the lads tried to help him but it was an impossible task. He was not right for hours and was just left in the aisle of the bus moaning and wimpering.

There was no air-conditioning on the coach, and no radio. Luckily, the staff were on another coach, so I sparked up my laptop and portable speaker. The lads had put me and Luther Burrell in charge of the music as we were both budding DJs. As you can imagine the pressure was on, as the traffic was getting worse and worse and the lads' patience was non-existent. Being honest, it was the most pressure I have felt as a DJ; one wrong move and I was stuffed. Fortunately, I went through my back catalogue and found some classics to save the day. I basically played non-stop for the entire journey. What could have been a very bleak coach trip was transformed into a darkly comic one, filled with singalongs, moaning, telling funny stories and laughing at Jonny. That had been my role in the England camp for a few years, the bloke tasked with keeping morale up. On every coach journey, the rest of the lads would tell me to go down the front and entertain them. It didn't matter how long the journey, they would all chant 'Haskell! Haskell!' until I got up and basically told a funny story. If you want a tough, judgemental crowd who wanted you to fail then look no further than a rugby team. It was great practice for all the corporate work that I do now. It got to the stage where I was spending more time preparing those stories than I was preparing for training, I really did put myself under that amount of pressure. I did nothing on the field in 2015; all my work came on the coach and during training and meetings.

Having finally arrived at the hotel, me and a few of the lads ate our own bodyweight in fried buffalo wings before getting our heads down for the night. Like I said in the last book, I always felt like I was on thin ice with England coach Stuart Lancaster, so tended to play things as safe as possible. But five other lads disappeared into the night and didn't show up again until the wee small hours.

The following morning, we all got herded onto the coach and it was immediately apparent that there was some scandal in the air. When any of the lads had got up to no good, Jonny May would make a loud tick-tock sound, like the *Countdown* conundrum clock, to put pressure on them to confess their sins. So there was Jonny, standing at the front of the coach, tick-tocking like a weirdo. He was relentless and would not stop until the guilty party got up. After about ten minutes of this, I stood up and said, 'Right, what the fuck happened last night?' And between me haranguing people and Jonny's very annoying tick-tocking, we finally got the lads to admit that they'd been out all night shagging women. Thankfully, that story never made it back to Stuart, and he was able to keep pretending his regime was whiter than white, when all the players knew it was just like all the previous regimes, except people were better at hiding things.

Down at the river, we split into teams of five and given our own large boat and paddles (except for Kieran Brookes, who decided to paddleboard down the river and rapids, which was utter madness – when we'd done police riot training, he hadn't been able to carry a shield for more than five minutes, so we knew he would run out of puff pretty quickly). It wasn't long before all the boats were on the river and we were paddling along. As usual things got out of hand, the boys started to lose the plot and were trying to capsize each other's boats and basically get whoever they could into the rapidly flowing and freezing river. It was a recipe for disaster, because parts of the river were quite shallow, with rocks dotted all over the place. Not only that, but some of the staff got quite fired up. The team doctor and Dave Barton, the media guy, were swinging punches at the lads, as they tried to jump on their boat. They didn't quite get the joke and were really trying to hit the lads. I remember Dave standing there swinging haymakers, frothing at the mouth and shouting at the lads, 'Fucking come on then!' We were all laughing, thinking, 'Calm down, Dave.' Andy Farrell, who I always got on with but who loved getting one over on me, boarded my boat and tried to drag me under. I managed to survive, just about. My boatmates came swooping to my rescue and chucked Andy into the water to much cheering and laughter.

In the end, I was enjoying myself so much that I decided I was going to grab Stuart Lancaster and launch him into the water. I had spotted him in his boat pretty unscathed and thought one in, all in. Attacking the head coach made no sense and was certainly not going to help my slim selection chance, but it felt like something I had to do for the story alone. I remember thinking, 'This is going to be the greatest moment ever, the lads are going to fucking love it.'

I swam up behind the staff boat and everyone went silent. All the lads were sitting there holding their breath and thinking, 'Oh my God, Haskell is going to chuck Stuart Lancaster into the fucking water. Brilliant!' But just as I was about to grab Stuart by his lifejacket, he turned around at the last second and stared straight at me with his disappointed school-teacher's eyes that said, 'Don't you dare.' My hands were inches from his lifejacket, but instead of going through with my plan, I saw my England career flash before me. So I said, 'Sorry, sorry, sorry, I am so sorry,' and sheepishly swam back to my boat. It was like one of those cartoons, where the character is suddenly put into rewind. I was about to grab him and then moonwalked back out of the boat into the water, swam back in reverse and out into my boat as if nothing had happened. The lads were all looking at me disgustedly, calling me a pussy under their breath, and I was sitting there with my head in my hands, muttering, 'Sorry, lads, I couldn't go through with it …' And you want to know the really weird thing? I felt like I'd let them all down. It's my biggest regret from that World Cup.

EDDIE JONES:

'When I was Saracens coach, I met James and his father because I wanted to recruit him. That would have been 2008 and it didn't come off, because he wanted to stay at Wasps. But I always thought he was a good player. Then when James was playing for Ricoh in Japan, I had lunch with him, so I got to know him a bit better. He was open and well spoken, and I liked how off the field he was driven, really wanted to make a name for himself. He seemed like a good guy to have around a team.

'Coaches have to have relationships with their players – that goes for any business, not just rugby – and me and James clicked straightaway. I like having characters in my teams and James was good fun. He always had a bit of banter and wasn't afraid to be self-deprecating. His teammates enjoyed him because he always had good stories and was willing to share them. Laughter is such an important part of life, and James was always making people laugh. At the same time, he put the work in.

'You can't overestimate how much a bloke like James can bring to a team environment. That's why I invited him into the squad at the 2019 World Cup. There were a few new players he hadn't played with and he spent one lunch regaling them with old stories. He's a good old-fashioned entertainer, a raconteur, and blokes like that just makes the place happier.

'James was someone I could take the mickey out of as well. That lunch took place right at the top of a hotel in Tokyo, a beautiful setting. When James walked in, we decided to give him a bit of an introduction. I pressed play on the video, and it was a very short clip of James tackling Australia's David Pocock. Then I said, "That's basically the one highlight of James's career." James being James, he laughed about it and had a fair few things to say.

'James was misunderstood by fans and journalists because he was different and outspoken, which opened him up for criticism and ridicule. But I respected him greatly as a player and for what he brought to the team. Even today we stay in contact, send texts to each other. Were me and James mates? Yes, as far as a coach and a player can be mates. He's a good man.'

When Eddie picked me for England, he instantly recognised how much I loved the 'fun' aspect of the game and that I could fulfil an important role in the team. While in previous regimes I felt I couldn't always be myself, in Eddie's regime I knew exactly what my role was, on and off the field.

I'd been in changing rooms that were really dry and serious, all about the rugby and nothing else, and there's much more to life than that. So I'd spark conversations and try to make things happen. I was never really part of one clique, I'd bounce from group to group, trying to lift the spirits. It's not like I was a court jester at a medieval banquet, annoying the hell out of everyone. But if there was an opportunity to take the piss or tell a few stories, I'd be in there like a shot. When I hadn't played well or wasn't feeling confident about my game, I'd be more withdrawn. But when that happened, players would say to me, 'Listen, we need you to bring some energy. What's happening?'

When Eddie first picked me for England, we were ranked something like eighth in the world. So he walked in to our very first meeting with him and said, 'Are you telling me you lot are the eighth most talented group of players on the planet?' He told us that we could become the best team in the world, but it was going to take sacrifice and hard work to a degree that none of us had experienced. And at the end of the meeting, Eddie said to me, 'Hask, what's your grip strength like?' I replied, 'Erm, it's all right, I think. Why do you ask?' And he shot back with, 'Because you're fucking hanging on for dear life, mate.' Everyone started roaring with laughter and he kept on with that sort of stuff throughout that Six Nations.

I'd play well and he'd say, 'Hask, you're doing all right, but you're hanging on by a couple of fingers now.' Or he'd slam one of those green protein shakes down in front of me, while I was with some other lads, and say, 'Hask, your training was shit yesterday, mate. You were looking really fucking old. Get some vitamins into you.' But because he said it with a mischievous chuckle, rather than a serious face, like some of my previous coaches, I was able to ride with it. The other lads loved it. If he was coming after me then it was a good day.

We'd all been scared when he first turned up, because he had a reputation for being fiery, so nobody dared answer him back. But as time went on, I started to gently take the piss out of him. He'd often leave camp in the evenings to attend speaking engagements or events. I would always check in with him and ask him how he was. He would say, 'Good, Hask, good. Been speaking at a dinner last night.' I would laugh and say, 'Excellent, just getting paid in suitcases of cash these days, are we?' He would give me a wry smile and walk off.

It became our running joke. I would see him leaving in a suit and say to him, 'Off to do some deals, Eddie?' He would reply, 'Just one suitcase tonight, Hask.' I'd send him pictures of people with giant backpacks, suggesting that with the amount of work he was doing he could do with one of these, and he'd text me back, 'Excellent, mate, get me one, the other suitcase is filling up fast.'

Every now and again Eddie would come to line-out sessions and start disrupting proceedings. Steve Borthwick, the forwards coach, would be trying to be all serious and Eddie would pop up and start taking the piss out of my jumping, which would in turn have all the lads laughing. Or we'd be in a meeting, Steve would be talking, Eddie would be bouncing a ball against the wall and he would then throw the ball at someone a few times to see if they could catch it. He'd suddenly say to a player, 'Mate, how's your mum?', 'How's your missus?' or 'Did you see the game at the weekend?' You could see the player thinking, 'Shit. Is Steve going to tell me off for talking to Eddie?' And everyone else would be looking at Eddie and thinking, 'Mate, Steve's trying to talk here.' Paul Gustard, the defence coach, would be running through some videos and

Eddie would start taking the piss out of somebody's haircut – 'Mate, what the fuck is that on your head?' – or be wandering around with a cricket bat, pretending to hit people. I honestly could not love him more as a coach, he always struck the right balance.

With Eddie, I think most of the time it was a test: a test for the players and a test for the coaches. There were a few times that we were supposed to head down to the training centre as a group and meet the coaches early in the morning to do a session. However, they were either really late or didn't turn up. Luckily, we just amused ourselves, went through our moves and took control of the time. Thank God we did because we realised that the coaches were watching us on CCTV to see if we did anything and were being self-sufficient. It could so easily have gone the other way, and we could have employed the rule we used to have at school, that if the teacher was late by more than 15 minutes you could get up and walk out. Eddie would have gone mad if we had all sacked off and gone for a coffee.

You may not think it having read my books or followed me on social media, but I was always the first to get my serious head on during training or on England camps. When I was captain of Wasps, Christian Wade would fall asleep in meetings, while a coach was talking. And I'd have to nudge him awake and say to him, 'Wadey, fucking wake up, you muppet! No wonder we don't get anything right on the field when we've got people like you nodding off in meetings!' Or I'd berate players for not taking notes. I'd say to them, 'How are you supposed to remember everything if you don't write it down? You're not that bright!'

I suppose you'd say I was ruthless either way. When it was joking time, I'd be in the middle of things. But when we had a job to do, I'd be very intense. If players were training like idiots, I'd tell them they were training like idiots. That didn't always go down well. Like the time Danny Cipriani went into a 'tackle' and was supposed to at least put a shoulder on his man, or grab him, but he did his favourite move of a light finger-tip touch, so the player just split the first-team defence and scored. We had a shit defence at Wasps that year and I'd had enough of us taking a casual approach to training. I said to him, 'Danny, for fuck sake what are you doing? Get your fucking shoulder on and stop him, or you can fuck off. No wonder our defence is so bad when you're not even bothering to tackle in training.' He replied, 'Fuck off, Hask.'

That to me was a red rag to a bull. Not only was he not training properly, but he was now coming at me, something I hate when it's unjustified. So I replied while marching towards him, 'Danny, you speak to me like that again, I will kick fuck out of you in front of all your mates in the backs. Make your tackles or go home. If you don't want to be here, we have plenty of people who do.'

But I was right and Danny was wrong. There was a time for levity, even during training. And the laughter of others was like rocket fuel to me. But I had high standards and was deadly serious about my job. Of course, all is forgotten afterwards and these moments are not uncommon in most training sessions. I have been on the receiving end of way worse. It's never personal, and Danny is a great human being and an amazing player.

Come to think of it, I've always been like that, able to get things done despite all the other ridiculousness going on in my life. When I was a kid, just starting out going to pubs and clubs and trying to blag my way into places, I had a mate called Ed Cooper, who was the king of gate-crashing (readers might remember Ed from the first book – we'd drink cans of cheap lager together in supermarket car parks, like a couple of tramps). Ed was that kid who was permanently saying, 'Come on, Haskell, we're going to such and such club, I'll get you in, don't worry about tickets,' not dissimilar to Jay from *The Inbetweeners*.

The only time it ever really came off was when we went to Party in the Park. Me, Ed and a couple of other lads spent hours trying to get into the VIP backstage party, ended up buying wristbands off some leavers and just marching past the bouncers. They tried to stop us, but we just kept walking and looking like we belonged. But that wasn't enough for Ed, who then spent ages trying to blag gold passes, which would give us access to the artists' area. Our persistence eventually paid off, and we were now rubbing shoulders with Robbie Williams, the Sugababes, Hear'Say, and the cream of early noughties British pop.

For a 16-year-old boy, it was like entering Narnia. Free booze, chatting to Lionel Richie and to Mutya from the Sugababes, Rob Thomas my other mate wandering around in Lemar's pinstripe blazer that he had nicked off a rail by the stage. Even being custard pied by Will Young had a certain beauty to it. I remember going up to Will and saying to him, 'Mate, how are you? I was at Wellington College too ...' and he looked at me like I was shit on his shoe and just walked off. Hear'Say's manager ended up giving us passes for the after-party at Café de Paris in Leicester Square. On our way out of Hyde Park, I did my one and only drug deal. This fella came up to us and said, 'Mate, do you want to buy some weed?' and I said to the lads, 'Do we want to buy some weed? Do we even like weed?' and obviously they all nodded and said, 'Oh yeah, we love a bit of weed.' Which was not true as most of them including myself had never tried it, but there is always a first time. So I asked this bloke how much and what did he have. He said it was £20 for an eighth of hash. He might as well have said it's £20 for X+Y×4 = Z, I had no idea, but feeling the lads' gazes on me and trying to make myself out to be cool I said, 'Yep, let's take an eighth of hash,' and I paid this bloke 20 quid for this very tightly wrapped little brown lump, but when I unwrapped it, which took fucking ages as he had put about 30 yards of clingfilm around it, this hash turned out to be nothing more than a small piece of wood from a tree. It still had the bark on it, for Christ's sake. I was like, 'Lads, it's a piece of wood,' they were like, 'No, it can't be,' and I said, 'Yes, it really is a piece of wood.' They could not believe it and were equally amused and disappointed. We went looking for the bloke, but he had turned quicker than milk and vanished down one of the tunnel underpasses next to Hyde Park. Twenty quid for a small piece of wood; no wonder I never bought drugs again.

When we finally made it to the Café de Paris, Chivas Regal were doing free whisky cocktails. And as with the weed, we all said, 'Oh yeah, we love a bit of whisky.' I think Madonna turned up at some point, but we were so steaming it could quite easily have been Madge Bishop from *Neighbours*. As was often the case when I sensed things were getting too much for me, I got on the phone to Mladen, the gardener/handyman/chauffeur/all-round hero who worked for my parents. That was a horrible drive home, all three of us lads with our heads out of the window, heavy breathing and desperately trying not to be sick. And when we finally made it back to my parents' house, I puked in the bin and grabbed about an hour's kip before my mum shook me awake and reminded me I was supposed to be attending a touch-typing course in Wokingham.

That was a weird 24 hours or so, from partying with Hear'Say to learning to touch type in a council-funded session. I have never wanted to be out of a room more than on the day after that party in the park. The hangover was real, and my ability to type out 'The Quick Brown Fox' a million times was totally compromised. I think the teacher thought I had some sort of disability. However, after a very shaky start, I fully committed to it and completed that course. In fact, it's one of the most useful skills I ever learned. I can touch type, drive a digger and I am a qualified barista. That's all the qualifications I have to my name.

Looking back, I was never going to turn out any different to how I have. I've been surrounded by males since I was a small boy. I went to an all-boys boarding school from the age of nine, which can be a pretty brutal environment, survival of the fittest and all that. I became a professional rugby player at 17 and was thrown in with a load of experienced pros, many from the amateur era who had already been around the block a hundred times. No wonder I was always trying to impress people; no wonder I could be so ruthless when it came to the verbals. Spending so much time with males – the most alpha of males, at that – is going to take you down some pretty weird paths and it's only really since I met Chloe that I've softened up and become a little more rounded.

I've often said that my life would be a lot easier if I wasn't the way I was. But there's no point thinking about it too much, I am who I am, whether that's because of nature, nurture or both. And as well as being easier if I didn't have this constant need to perform and addiction to adulation, life would be far less exciting. I'm pretty certain there is nothing after we die, so I don't think this is a dress rehearsal. Life is pretty short for everyone, and pretty difficult for lots of people. So if you're lucky enough to have lots of crazy opportunities involving lots of fun, you've got to say yes to as many of them as possible.

It's like that line from Jeremy in *Peep Show* when Mark gets caught hiding in a cupboard and accused of wanking over someone's wife: 'Cheer up, Mark, at least now you've got a funny story to tell people.' Why wouldn't you want to be the person sitting around a table with lots of stories to tell? My favourite thing about being a rugby player was sitting on the back of a bus, in the changing room or in a coffee shop, telling stories and making people laugh. Mostly, it was an unconscious thing. When me and Ollie drugged a neighbour's dog in Paris, we supposedly did it because it was barking too much, but we really did it for the story. When I egged that woman's car, I supposedly did it because she nicked my parking space, but I really did it for the story. Those moments justified everything I did. They were like the cherry on top of a magnificent cake. And I still have that attitude now. If I get things wrong and self-sabotage sometimes – like arguing with anonymous idiots on social media – so be it. As long as it doesn't lead to me being cancelled …

6

CAN I HAVE A WORD?

SUSIE HASKELL:

'As a child, James was full of fun, mischievous and always at the centre of anything that was going on. But he was also misunderstood, which made me very defensive of him. Because he was the biggest and the gobbiest, he got the blame for everything. He'd be painting in class, sweeping his arms, knocking paint off tables and sending kids flying. And the following day, someone from the school would tell us he'd been knocking the other kids about. Another time, my husband and I were called in by the headmaster because a boy's mother had accused James of soaking her son with water. The truth soon came out. In fact, it had been a hot day, James had rescued his friend from hordes of kids crowded around a water fountain, his friend had wet his pants and, because he didn't want to tell his mother, blamed James.

'Then there was the time James came home with bandages all over his head. He also had trainer marks all over his neck. Apparently, two of the older boys had given James some Smarties and told him they were drugs. They then pinned him to the playground floor, with a

trainer on his neck. We had to take James to A&E, to have bits of tarmac removed from his head. Most of the time, once we'd investigated things ourselves, it transpired that James was trying to help someone or was just too big and getting in the way.

'When the video thing happened at Wellington [when James was accused of secretly filming Dozzer in bed with a female pupil], I didn't cope with it terribly well. We had at least 20 cars of press outside our house, cameras with zoom lenses pointed at our windows. James and his brother Edward were locked in our office and my husband was constantly on the phone to a lawyer. It hurt me terribly, but when James told me what had actually happened, I knew he was telling the truth, because he's never been able to tell me a lie.

'James was blamed for something he did not do. He made the camera work and walked away. He wasn't actually hiding in the cupboard, like the press suggested. I taught James to respect girls and be kind to them. But when there are lots of boys together, all goading each other – which there were in this case, it wasn't just James and Dozzer – things like that happen.

'James never meant to hurt anybody, but I got terribly shunned by other parents and vilified as the mother of a peeping Tom and a pervert. His brother suffered terribly. There were so many people who were just so vile. The Mirror *doctored a photograph of James, darkened the skin under his eyes and made his cheeks all sunken, so that he looked really evil, nothing like James at all. Piers Morgan was the editor at the time, and I've always said that if I ever meet him he'll get the rough side of my tongue.*

'*But what goes around comes around. When bad things happened to those people later in life, I wondered if they reflected on how badly they treated me and my family. And the more famous James became, they suddenly wanted to be friends with us again, so that they could meet him. A few years earlier he was nothing but a pervert. But that's human nature.*'

What readers have to remember about my mum is that while she's a lovely, lovely woman and very dear to me, some of her recollections of my childhood are – how does a son put this delicately? – somewhat romanticised. You know how mums are: they want to portray their offspring in the best light possible, so they're prone to view things through rose-tinted glasses, gild the lily, use a whole load of artistic licence. It's great that she's so proud of me and my achievements, but it means you sometimes have to read between the lines, like with a coded letter. And sometimes her pride can make me wince.

Let me give you an example. A few years ago I was round my mum and dad's, and they were having some work done on the house. I was in the kitchen eating breakfast when this builder walked in, said hello and started explaining something about the bathroom upgrade to my mum. He had no idea who I was, had probably never watched a game of rugby in his life. But it just so happened that there was a copy of *Gay Times* on the worktop, with me on the cover wearing not a lot. And I could see my mum looking from me to the builder to the magazine, thinking, 'How can I shoehorn the magazine into the conversation?' And the most cringe conversation followed, which went something like this:

MUM: 'Tell you about that, did he?'

BAFFLED BUILDER: 'About what?'

MUM: 'The magazine. I thought you mentioned the magazine?'

BAFFLED BUILDER: 'Sorry?'

MUM: 'Yeah, that's my son on the cover of the magazine.'

I was looking at my mum, shaking my head, when this builder turned to me and said, 'Oh, is that what you do, then? Model for gay mags?' I smiled and replied, 'Yeah, that's what I do, mate, model for gay mags.' This builder smiled back, turned on his heels and walked out of the kitchen, while my mum was shouting after him, 'No! No! No! He's actually an England rugby player!' Once the builder was out of sight, my mum pretended to throw the magazine away, by gently placing it on top of the bin. Of course, she was going to pick it out later. It was textbook David Brent and could have been a scene straight out of *The Office*.

I reckon I could have burnt the school down and mum would have told the story as, 'James had put on an artistic firework display for all the underprivileged kids to enjoy and a freak wind blew one of the fireworks onto the roof of the science block, which had not been properly maintained, and before you knew it a horrific blaze had started, which James then risked his life to put out.' And it wouldn't have mattered how many times I told her that it was my fault, she'd have stuck with her version of events. So while Mum remembers me begging my teachers to go to the ballet as a kid and demanding they do it for our cultural development, and doing a big, stir-ring thank you speech afterwards to a huge throng of people and students, I have vague recollections of Mum persuading me to go and me causing havoc and talking a load of shit on the back of the bus whether the other kids wanted to listen or not. I'm sure I was told to 'Sit down, Mr Haskell!' a number of times.

But Mum's right about the video incident – and I was always getting blamed for things I didn't do. If I was playing with a kid and he fell over and started crying, the teacher would assume I'd pushed him over. If a kid threw a wooden brick at me and it hit me in the head, which meant I'd throw a wooden brick back at him which hit some part of him, I would end up being hauled in front of the teacher as I was too big for these sorts of games, and just because so-and-so threw one didn't mean I had to throw one back. Their favourite thing to say to me was, 'Mr Haskell, you say so-and-so told you to do it?' Well, if he told you to jump off a cliff, would you do it? They never ask that of adults, do they, as an adult would say, 'No, I'm not a fucking idiot. One leads to someone getting water bombed and the other leads to my death. Not quite the same thing.'

I did once say something similar to a teacher, and he pulled out his trump card and just said, 'Well, now you are being cheeky,' which is code for, 'You have done me over but I am going to utilise the authority card to get me out of this embarrassing situation.'

I want to be clear that I was not like Nelson from *The Simpsons*, a big lumbering idiot who took great delight in the misfortune of others. It's not as if I was turning people upside down for their lunch money. A lot of the time, it was simply a case of me being bigger and more boisterous than all the other kids. Or the banter would be flying, one of the kids would take it to heart and tell their parents I'd been bullying him. I'd be thinking, 'Hang on, one minute you're in on the joke, the next minute it's got a bit too much for you, you've got upset and told on me. How's that fair?'

I was always the first to stand up and thank people, and always desperate to help. During one school event, which I had been asked to help with, I decided to put on a wig and serve people drinks. I was even putting on a funny accent and people thought I was part of the entertainment. No one asked me to do this part, I was just meant to clear tables. I have no idea why I did it and it makes me cringe just thinking about it. It was a strange mix of performance and genuinely wanting to give people a hand. I loved being helpful, was always asking the mums, 'Can I do this, Mrs Smith? Can I do that, Mrs Jones?' It must have been a praise thing that I wanted. It was an odd blend of always being in trouble but being the most helpful and nice kid in school, with some parents raving about me while others wanted to string me up. I can't imagine it was much fun for my parents.

My school days weren't easy at times. In fact, some of my experiences make it sound like I was at boarding school in the Victorian era. When I started at Wellington, I had a head of house who ran the place like a warlord. And like any Hitler, he had his Himmler. We'd be dragged out of our rooms at four in the morning, while still in our boxer shorts, stood up against the wall and shouted at for no apparent reason. I was made to clean up sick with a fork and had a bucket of water thrown all over me while I was sleeping.

Most of the dirty work was done by the boys who ran the house, like the time eight lads wearing balaclavas burst into my room and hammered me with bars of soap in socks. It was like a posh version of *Scum* – 'I'm the papa, now!' – and properly shook me up. There was also the time a couple of kids threw beer all over me and locked me in a trunk for three hours. I would love to meet the two main ringleaders from all those years ago, the head of house and his henchman. I know society says you're supposed to forget what happens at school, put it down to youthful ignorance and exuberance, but if I met one of those two guys in a social situation and they said, 'Do you remember me?', I'd reply, 'Oh yes,' then perhaps test their mettle like they tested mine. Anyone can attack a kid, but a fully grown meathead with a chip on his shoulder is another matter.

When I went to Wellington, and was bigger than most of the other kids, I wouldn't take shit from anybody. On one of my first days at Wellington, some guy pushed me into a cupboard and threatened me, and I headbutted him. When the housemaster saw what I'd done – this kid wasn't in a great way – he was open-mouthed, just couldn't comprehend that one of his new intake of 13-year-old boys had stuck the nut on a classmate. I wouldn't describe myself as aggressive or violent, but I don't like anyone trying to embarrass or threaten me. If I feel cornered, I will lash out.

Another time, this kid from the year above knocked my books out of my hands as we passed in the corridor; I picked them up, not saying a word, and let it slide. However, it happened for the following three days in a row, every time I entered the corridor. He smelt blood and I had seen him doing it to all my other dormitory mates. So the next time he did it to me I went to pick the books up while he cheered. I then picked him up and dump tackled him on his head into his room and gave him a little bit of a working over. Then I caught the same kid stealing food from my mates, and when I confronted him and he decided to hit me with a tennis racquet on the head, I battered him again until he was on the floor. On the way down he ended up biting my thigh, like Mike Tyson with

Lennox Lewis's leg. And while he was hanging off me like a shark and I was punching him in the head, the housemaster finally turned up. On both occasions no one else stepped in, they just left me to get dealt with by older boys. I had blood pouring from my thigh, but the other bloke was in a far worse state, which meant the housemaster took his side. He screamed at me, 'Haskell! What have you done?' and I screamed back, 'I didn't do anything!' Lucky the witnesses who didn't come to my help with action later turned up with witness statements, and the other kid got detention and was eventually suspended as our housemaster hated him more than anyone, including me.

Of course, when you get a reputation for fighting at school, older kids start taking an interest. One day, this guy said to me, 'Listen, Haskell, I know you think you're hard. But if you ever try that shit with us, we'll burst into your room with eight lads and hockey sticks and smash the shit out of you.' I pointed out that you could batter Mike Tyson with eight people and hockey sticks so it hardly makes you tough, which didn't go down well. It never happened, but there was always that edge about the place. It was a stereotypical, old-fashioned, dog-eat-dog public school environment. And because I was sharp-witted and constantly trying to make people laugh, housemasters were always dragging me into their office and accusing me of bullying. I wasn't a bully, I just liked being in the thick of it when banter started flying. And there always seemed to be one kid who'd end up taking it personally and grassing me up.

I've talked about my mum defending me to the hilt. Well, she wouldn't take any prisoners either. Mind you, having said that … when my parents' franking machine at home kept going wrong, they called an engineer in. This bloke tried and failed twice to fix it, and the third time he came my mum decided to lock him in the downstairs office until he'd completed the job. She claims that when she finally unlocked the door there was an awful smell; the poor man had fixed the franking machine, but it's possible he'd also shat himself. She might have added a bit of polish to that story, but the basic facts were certainly true.

When my mum goes off, she terrifies people. And I've seen her go off plenty of times, because she has a very keen sense of injustice and is fiercely loyal. My mum deserves a medal, because she's spent her life having to defend me and my dad, usually after we've said or done things to upset people. When the video incident happened at school, there were plenty of other kids involved who never got implicated. And my mum just couldn't understand why they didn't put their hands up, so that maybe the blame would be shared around a bit more, and why she was getting judged by other kids' parents. They were all shaking their heads and tutting at her for having a deviant son, when their own children had seen the video and laughed about it. I know she rowed with quite a few friends over it, because she couldn't let that kind of hypocrisy go.

Once you get a reputation for starting trouble, it's difficult to get rid of it. It even stuck with me throughout my rugby career. In one England training session, Geoff Parling punched me in the face because he thought I was taking the piss (I've spoken to Dan Cole about this, and his recollection is that I was winding Geoff up and Geoff was having a few off-field issues). I was in the bin juice for this particular game. We were going through a team run practice, which means the bin juice players just provide light opposition. So when we went into a line-out and they set up a drive, I was in the middle of it and lightly had a go at Geoff. I kept saying, 'Maul, maul,' then said, 'I bet they didn't teach you that in the CIA' (I had watched *Meet the Parents* the night before) as we stopped the drive and laughed. Geoff said, 'You taking the piss?' and hit me, then 'You fucking taking the piss?' and hit me again, his voice quivering with emotion. I didn't move or flinch, not because I'm hard like Bruce Lee, more the fact I couldn't believe this was happening, and somehow I knew I was going to get into trouble. We watched it back post-training and it was the oddest thing; I got hit twice and just stood there looking at him. I was obviously in shock as this was a non-contact fun session and Geoff had gone 0–60 in 0.2 seconds.

Graham Rowntree, the forwards coach, came running over and screamed, 'Haskell! What the fuck have you done now? You're always causing trouble!' before checking to see if Geoff was okay.

Before I could reply, Geoff did a complete U-turn from anger to shame and said, 'Sorry, Hask, sorry, Hask,' before Graham walked him off to one side. I think he'd got some bad news pre-session so was a bit on edge. The session carried on but the lads were all laughing and taking the piss that even when it wasn't me, it was my fault. They kept saying, 'Haskell, what the fuck have you done now?' That was the good thing about my time with England: if the other boys noticed that I was being treated differently or harshly that made it okay, it made me feel like I wasn't doing anything wrong or going mad. We nicknamed Geoff 'Feather Mitts', as he gave me two of his best shots and didn't even bruise me.

That was my time with the England squad in a nutshell before Eddie came in, always in trouble over something and not always understanding why.

* * *

I was permanently in detention at school, for things I had and hadn't done. I was in there pretty much every week, one of the serious and serial offenders. One of the teachers at my school created these special detention sheets that he actually rolled out into lots of other schools. They would buy them and then get their students to use them. They were meant to educate as well as punish. I think I was his guinea pig as he was always changing them and refining them. He would ask me how I found that day's papers, what did I learn, or what I thought of this and that, all the while making notes on a clipboard. I should have charged him commission, but he was the same teacher who had written that book which I sold and whose apartment we had painted.

There was always this section at the end of the paper you had to fill in which showed a picture of some stereotypical parents with a big speech bubble next to them. The question was: 'What would your parents say about what you did and your behaviour?' I'd have to write an explanation of my misdemeanour, say how disappointed they were in me, how much I had let them down, how I was bringing shame upon the family … but once you have done this over a million times and you know they are never going to read it, by the end I was writing stuff from my parents like, 'This is victimisation of our son! Your mother and I know you shouldn't be in there! Stay strong, we both love you, these people will get their comeuppance.'

I've always had a thing about injustice. I have never been able to accept being blamed for things I didn't do or people not standing up for me, even when they know I've done nothing wrong. Like the time, just before what should have been my first school dance at Papplewick with actual real girls. I was messing around an hour or so before the bus left with

135

some schoolmates in a dorm and some kid got hurt and the school chaplain banned me from attending, which was devastating. I had been waiting months for this, I was doused in Lynx Africa and had my best Paul Smith shirt on. While everyone else went off and kissed the night away, I had to write out a thousand times 'Why we don't play on bunk beds'. Does anyone else find that 'religious' practitioners are often the most unforgiving and aggressive people? Certainly in my experience they are, and I've had a lot of interactions with them at school and outside. I could be wrong and maybe I got a few bad apples. This particular chaplain was not my biggest fan, after a kid came running out of his house with a big smile on his face shouting at the top of his voice, 'Chaplain gave me a bumhug! Chaplain gave me bumhug!'

I thought, 'I bet he did,' and reported it to a teacher. It turns out the kid was foreign and he had meant to say, 'Chaplain gave me a HUMBUG.' Word obviously got back to him that I was the party concerned and from that moment on my card was marked.

There was another interaction with the cloth that didn't go my way after I got a little bit carried away with my prefect responsibilities and was once again accused of bullying. I'll come back to that prefect story in a bit, but I first have to provide some context. When I was at prep school, even the kid who regularly put his finger in the light socket and ate glue was made a prefect, but not me. So when I was made a prefect at Wellington, I probably let it go to my head. I wouldn't describe myself as officious, but I did perhaps enjoy my power a little too much and ran a tight ship.

Anyway, this one kid's room was an absolute shambles, crap everywhere, Pot Noodles growing God knows what out of them, dirty underwear, unwashed plates, papers, wall to wall shit everywhere. He never cleaned or tidied it, nor did he clean himself; both the room and him stank to high heaven. There is nothing worse than an adolescent who doesn't wash; it's rank and needs to be dealt with in the harshest way. I had told him many, many times to go shower and sort his room out. Even the housemaster had been on to me to get him to sort it. So I said to him one day, 'Listen, you and your room are in a right state. Go shower now and then give it a clean from top to bottom.' He grunted at me and tried to pretend I wasn't there, both things I hate, so I marched past him, grabbed all his stuff, chucked it in the corridor piece by piece and said, 'Now put it back nicely one item at a time.' As I went to leave, he shoved me. So I gave him a backhander, a bit like Archy gives Johnny Quid in *RocknRolla*. The famous Archy slap, or the famous Haskell Slap to be more precise, pushed him back into his room and told him never to do that again. He showered and made his room look superb. Everyone was happy, or so I thought. Lo and behold, this kid went home that weekend and told his parents I'd attacked him.

The following day, I got called into the deputy headmaster's office. I said to him, 'The guy pushed me. What was I supposed to do?' and the deputy headmaster replied, 'Turn the other cheek.' I was going to have to do some detention as a punishment and needed to see my housemaster next as he wanted to speak to me as well. As you can imagine, I was not best pleased. So straight afterwards, I phoned my dad and asked his advice, which was, 'You need to tell your housemaster that if he's not going to support you in your role, he needs to find someone else to do the job.'

Whatever my dad said, I did at that time. So I went to see my housemaster and said, 'The boy's room was a mess. You asked me to get him to tidy it, so I asked him to clean it, he pushed me and I gave him a backhander. What's the problem? If you're not going to support me, how am I supposed to do the job you asked me to do?' My housemaster replied, 'How dare you talk to me like that. I did not ask you to use violence, you silly boy. We'll find someone else …'

Dad's plan had worked, but not exactly as he'd imagined. When I phoned him back around two minutes later, he said, 'That was a quick meeting. What happened?' and I replied, 'I'm not in charge of anything anymore, I'm back with the div kids and exchange students.' My time in charge of anything other than the school library at my first school had come to an end within three months.

The thing about my dad is, it's his way and that's the end of it. It goes back to that idea of 'the Haskells against the world'. My mum likes to toe the line, but my dad is a non-conformist. He went to Wellington as well, and some of my teachers taught him. He must have been a bit of a nightmare, because they'd say to me, 'I remember your father. I hope you're better behaved than him.' Dad always tried to bend the rules to fit him, rather than the other way round. He had told me at the time that he was head of house, head of the school and a top sportsman. When I did follow in his footsteps at Wellington and went looking for any evidence of his achievements on the great swathe of wooden boards, I couldn't find them. I asked him about this, but he said all records had been lost in a great fire. Oddly, no records of a fire were found either. Which he said was down to a big flood.

My dad is a very proud man, and pride gets you into trouble sometimes. That's why as I've got older I've learned to be less proud. I'll fight my corner if I think I've been hard done by, but I'm less likely to dig my heels in, and more likely to put my hand up and say, 'You know what? You're probably right.'

Years after I left school, I was asked to open a new building at Papplewick. When I was a pupil there, I was labelled as a bit of a troublemaker. But now my name was on a plaque on a wall (a removable plaque, mind you – they're not completely mad). My mum loved that more than anything else in the world. When the new headmaster Tom Bunbury, who I have always got on really well with, invited me to the opening, I said to him, 'I will of course do this, what an honour, but on the one small condition that you give me a prefect's tie.' He said, 'What do you mean?' and I replied, 'I never got made a prefect or in fact anything while I was there. So if you want me to open this building, I want a tie.' He said, 'Leave it with me,' unsure of whether I was taking the piss or not. However, on the day in front of the 300 people who had turned out to watch this new building being opened, he made a lovely speech about me and called me up on stage to make me an honorary prefect of the school. I was chuffed, I felt like I'd finally earned it, and that tie has pride of place in my collection. I was really touched that they had asked me to do this unveiling, and to this day it remains a big highlight for me.

Before the talk and ribbon cutting, I did a tour around the school and went into the science laboratory, where they have a room full of spiders, lizards, rats and all manner of creepy-crawlies. I got shown into this lesson where all the young boys went mad and covered me in every creature you can imagine. At various points I had a tarantula on my face, a giant python around my neck and a scorpion on my arm. I didn't flinch, to the boys' delight, so I got awarded the herbology colours. I went from having no ties and no honours to two ties and two school honours. Not a bad trip.

PAUL DORAN-JONES:

'I think it's fair to say that James and I were a bad influence on each other, although it's always made out that I was the one who led him to the dark side. Whenever James recounts stories, it always seems to be, "Dozzer came up with this idea, Dozzer made me do that ..." That was especially the case when his parents found out about any nonsense we'd been involved in. He'd point the finger and I'd be thinking, "I'm pretty sure it was Jim's idea ..."

'We got into a lot of scrapes at school, there's no doubt about that. Some of what went on could have been lifted straight from The Inbetweeners. A few of us would often skulk over to The Wellington, the pub on the edge of the school grounds. We were sitting there one night, having a few beers, when the deputy headmaster walked in with one of his mates. Everyone got busted, apart from James, who was in the toilet at the time. He heard the commotion, tried to clamber through the toilet window and got stuck. No wonder, because he was the size of a house at 17. We thought he'd escaped, but apparently he was stuck in that window for about two hours.

'Each house at school had a pool table, and if you got seven-balled, you'd have to do a naked run. That was the long-standing tradition. One week, four of us got seven-balled. That was a huge event, especially because one of us was a girl. The rules said you had to exit the swimming pool and run the length of the first XV pitch, the so-called Big Side. There was me, Jim, the future Scotland international Thom Evans and this girl, plus about 700 kids spectating. But as soon as we appeared, the deputy head came out of nowhere and started *chasing us. Thom and Hask were faster than lightning, so left him for dust. And because chasing a naked girl around a field wasn't a great look for a teacher, he decided to concentrate his efforts on me instead.*

'*He must have been chasing me for about half an hour, like a Benny Hill sketch. I was a bit of a dumpy chap, so just couldn't get rid of him. In the end, he grabbed me as I was just about to run back into the school. He had me by the ear, because I had nothing on apart from a pair of trainers.*

'*It was lucky we were both quite academic because that tended to get us out of jail. But our luck ran out when the video incident happened, with the blame falling mainly on me. One of the lads in the house was part of the audio-visual club, which had just bought a load of new kit. Suddenly, it was a case of, "Right, I know what we'll do: whoever brings one of the girls back to their room next, we'll film it." I still maintain that it was Jim's idea, he still maintains that it was mine. As far as I was concerned, I just happened to be dating one of the girls at the time. Although I use the term "dating" loosely. And it was only ever going to be me, because Jim couldn't pull in a whorehouse at that time.*

'*I'm aware that the excuse that it was nothing more than boys being boys doesn't wash its face now, but it wasn't malicious. It was just a really ill-considered, stupid idea. I got expelled and Jim got suspended, which led me to believe he'd struck some kind of deal with the headmaster. I wouldn't put that past him, but I think that's even a stretch for him. Then again, I did have a bit of previous, because I'd already been kicked out and let back in after being caught climbing out of the girls' boarding house and it was Jim's parents who wrote to the headmaster to let me back in. But because I wasn't allowed to board, I ended up living with one of the lads' mums on the edge of the campus. That was a bizarre set-up. I was like her live-in companion for six months, while her son was boarding. I'd ride my bike into school every morning and see him in classes.*

'That video incident certainly tested mine and Jim's relationship. It was the end of our time at school together, so we didn't speak for a while. But we didn't let it ruin our lives. Because I hadn't signed professional forms yet, my deal with Wasps fell through. But instead, I buggered off to study at Trinity College in Dublin and got a Masters in Medicinal Chemistry. In hindsight, that was the best thing that ever happened to me. And things didn't turn out too bad for Jim, either.'

Because Dozzer is supposedly from 'the wrong side of the tracks' in High Wycombe, when asked about his childhood he will go on about the mean streets of his home town and all the scrapes he used to get into. He likes this 'boy done good' narrative and became convinced that was why he got the blame for everything. But while I was always happy to egg him on, when perhaps I should have told him it was a terrible idea, he has to take some responsibility for his own actions as I do for mine. I mean, if we are being fair, I was marginally a worse influence on him than he was on me, because I probably agitated more than he did. But when he got suspended for climbing in and out of the girls' house at Wellington, after getting caught with his big arse hanging out of a window, that was on him.

Dozzer didn't come from a particularly privileged background, so he was quite shocked to suddenly be surrounded by a load of big posh idiots pretending they were tough. I remember his dismay when some bloke in his twenties, with his shirt off and covered in tattoos, walked onto the school grounds and started kicking off with one of the pupils. Within minutes, there were about 150 kids gathered around this bloke, many of them saying horrible things, like 'My dad could buy you,' or 'Do you live in a shed?' But whenever he challenged anyone and lunged at them, they shat themselves and ran back.

I vividly recall Dozzer giving me a withering look, as if to say, 'You bunch of absolutely fannies.' And it dawned on me what a bunch of privileged, deluded idiots we all were. It was awkward and embarrassing how people were acting. They got all giddy but not one person had the balls to face up to this bloke, let alone throw a punch. All they had to do was rush him and he wouldn't have been able to do anything about it. Eventually, one of the kids said to Dozzer, 'Why don't you do something?', and Dozzer confronted this bloke and told him to fuck off and leave it. Dozzer actually had a bit of a fiery streak when challenged and was certainly not a pushover like the rest of these fops and dandies. We spoke about this incident a lot afterwards and Doz flagged just how embarrassing it was, how wrong it all was the things that people were saying to this guy and what a bunch of weak people we were. That always stuck with me. I hate fake tough guys, people who talk a huge game and under-deliver. I was a bit like that as a kid. Trying to be hard, but soft in the head.

Back to the England rugby team. One of the weird things about the 2011 World Cup debacle was that we'd been in a really good place the previous year. The summer tour to Australia in 2010 was brilliant. Having told all the former

Leicester coaches – Martin Johnson, John Wells, Graham Rowntree and Brian Smith – that they were too negative and needed to cheer the fuck up, the lads enjoyed themselves, the coaches then seemed to relax and there was a great buzz around the place.

There were a lot of laughs on that tour. One evening, some of the lads were walking past Dozzer's and my room and heard banging house music, which only just masked a loud creaking sound. Obviously, they wondered what the hell was going on, so stopped to listen. It was then they noticed the door was creaking off its hinges and bowing at the top. So they knocked on the door to find out what was going on. I opened the door in my pants, sweating like a lunatic. Dozzer was also in his pants, and also sweating like a lunatic. They all came wandering in and asked us what we were up to; we said we weren't doing anything, and we thought we'd got away with it. But just as they were leaving, they noticed a TRX door attachment. We'd been doing extra fat-burning sessions in preparation for a post-tour trip to Las Vegas. The lads were aghast: 'All you two are thinking about is Vegas! You'll burn yourselves out – you're not even eating properly!' They had a point. Both of us thought we weren't going to be involved in the Test team, so we hadn't eaten any carbs in about a month and were doing extra beach weights in the official lifting sessions and full-body circuits in our room every night. We were training our arses off in the rugby sessions to burn off as many calories as possible. The rest of our down time was spent topping off our tan on the roof of the hotel.

Most evenings we banged on some house music and spent an hour sculpting the rigs. We assumed no one would notice, but when you have 120 kg hanging off a wooden door doing chest presses and front squats, someone is bound to smell a rat, which they did. We both got fined for this. We said we would stop, but we didn't.

I ended up being on the bench for the first Test in Perth, in which Lewis Moody missed eight tackles off the back of the line-out, mainly on their fly-half Quade Cooper. Afterwards, I assumed that I was going to get the start for the next game, but when I was called into my one-on-one with forwards coach John Wells he said, 'Listen, Hask, I know Lewis has missed a few tackles but he has got credit in the bank so we will give him another chance as we know he can deliver.' I was a bit shocked, as if I'd missed that number of tackles you would never have seen me again. So I asked what I had to do to get that much credit. Wellsy laughed and said, 'I'm not sure it's possible. Make sure you train hard this week,' and that was the end of the meeting.

When I say the former England coaches were on better form on that tour, these things are all relative where Wellsy is concerned. He was pretty much the same as always: an amazing technical coach, a nice guy, but a dour, no-nonsense type of man in every other regard. The only time you saw him smile or be positive was in contact sessions. Most coaches try to run on 'Lombardi Time', named after the great Green Bay Packers coach Vince Lombardi, who expected his players to be 15 minutes early for meetings and training. If they weren't, he'd consider them late. One day, I turned up five minutes before a meeting was supposed to start, and casually walked down the middle of all the players to the front. This was where the coaches made me sit. I used to try and sit at the back, but they would always drag me forward. Graham Rowntree loved this. 'Where is Haskell? Get to the front, kid.'

As I walked past, all the other lads were tutting, whistling and 'oohing'. I replied with a 'Fucking chill out, keenos,' but no sooner had these words left my mouth and were still hanging in the air than Wellsy leapt out of his chair and roared with the rage of a thousand gods, 'Haskell, sit down, boy. We'll have none of your fucking arrogance here!' It was like being told off by Gandalf. I sat down like a good boy and didn't say a peep. The rest of the lads some 15 years later still talk about it.

Anyway, because I thought I wouldn't be involved in the second Test, when an Old Wellingtonian asked if a few of the lads wanted to meet up for lunch, I said yes. This guy was an investment banker and renting Hugh Jackman's apartment in the heart of Sydney, so I knew it would be a case of no expenses spared.

The following day, which was a day off, eight of the lads met up with this guy and some of his investment banker mates on Sydney Harbour. The plan was to have some lunch, jump on a boat and have a few drinks, while they took us on a tour of Sydney before we hooked up with rest of the lads to go out for the team meal later in the evening. So I was sitting in this restaurant, drinking ludicrously expensive white wine in the sun, life was good and the stories were flowing. It was about halfway through the meal when I noticed a woman sitting on the adjacent table. It's not like I could have missed her, because her breasts (and when I say breasts, think of two Swiss balls bolted to her chest) were desperately trying to escape a bright red military jacket, like the guards at Buckingham Palace wear. She was flanked by a couple of shady-looking blokes, who kept staring at us, but we just ignored them and hoped they'd go away.

After a couple of hours, the Old Wellingtonian said, 'Right, the boat's ready to depart. And we've got a couple of surprises.' We got up to leave and the woman in the red jacket sidled up to us and said, 'Can we have a photo with you?' (Normally, I was wary about that sort of stuff, and with good reason: I'd heard a story about Phil Greening being stitched up at Twickenham, when a couple of girls asked to have a photo taken with him and lifted their T-shirts to reveal their tits. The photo appeared in the *Sun* and Clive Woodward went mad.) But because I'd already had a bottle of Cloudy Bay, I readily agreed. I made sure that I was standing right on the edge of the photo, in case she unleashed her fun bags, at which point I could dive out of the way of the shot. I didn't alert the other lads to my concerns as I didn't want them all getting the same idea. However, when one of her companions started unpacking his professional camera and attaching lenses, I started thinking, 'Shit, something is not right about all this.' He took his snaps, with the woman in the middle of all the players. She kept her jacket on so we thought nothing more about it.

When we got on the boat, we were greeted by four or five women serving champagne in their lingerie. So I said to the Old Wellingtonian, 'Listen, who are these girls?'

'They're PR girls,' he replied.

'They're not hookers?'

'God, no …'

The rest of the lads didn't seem that bothered, so I relaxed a little. I got myself settled down in the back of the boat with a bottle of Corona, a few of the lads went up top to talk to these girls, and everything seemed to be going swimmingly. Admittedly, it was all a bit odd, what with the waitresses wandering around with almost nothing on, but I certainly wasn't complaining. However, just as the boat was embarking, I looked over my right shoulder and saw the photographer from earlier swivel around in his chair with the most professional-looking telephoto lens I had ever seen. It looked like he was wielding a telescope, so I shouted to the lads up top, 'Get the fuck down!' It was like we were about to be torpedoed, and it's quite possible our careers would have been, had I not seen the photographer first, hit the deck and squeezed myself under the gunwale. Some lads saw what I was looking at and ducked down, others were too busy talking to women to be bothered about anything else. The boat left harbour with me lying down the side and my feet the only things on show.

Thankfully, that's as dramatic as the trip got. We had a few drinks, sailed under the Sydney Harbour Bridge and everyone was on their best behaviour. The waitresses weren't prostitutes, they really were PR girls. And if they wanted to serve drinks in their lingerie, that was their prerogative.

As it turned out, I was on the bench for the second Test, but I was the only player who didn't get on. That was the only time it had happened to me, and I was livid. And things went downhill from there. While the lads were celebrating their win, the first time we'd beaten the Aussies down under since the 2003 World Cup final, Dozzer came up to me and said, 'Hask, something's gone wrong, we are in the shit.' Just as I was trying to work out what he was going on about, England head coach Martin Johnson appeared over Dozzer's shoulder and said, 'Can I have a word?' This was the story of my life, constantly getting called into corners for a chat. It was never a good thing, no one has ever pulled me aside to give me good news, and it's always the start of some drama that finds its way into the papers. If I had a pound for every time I'd heard the phrase, 'Can I have a word?', I'd be a very rich man. I first heard it at prep school, I didn't stop hearing it at Wellington and I heard it far too many times as a rugby player. At Wasps, Dai Young was constantly saying to me, 'Can I have word?', and I'd feel like a naughty schoolboy again. I'd usually say to him, 'Whatever happened, it wasn't me.' And Dai would reply, 'Yes, it fucking was!' Sometimes it was, sometimes it wasn't, but it always required a little chat in an office or a tucked-away corner somewhere. It was pretty tiring at times.

Johnno pulled me and Dozzer into a room and said, 'Right, have you lads been sleeping with prostitutes?' Now, it's not great being accused of sleeping with prostitutes by anyone, but being accused of sleeping with prostitutes by Martin Johnson is on a whole different level. Me and Dozzer were going red, pulling on our collars and stuttering. It was like that scene from *Star Wars* where Darth Vader chokes one of his Death Star officers just by raising a finger. When we denied we'd been sleeping with prostitutes, Johnno replied, 'Are you sure? We've been told you filled a boat with prostitutes and had sex with them all over Sydney Harbour.'

We denied it again and again, but Johnno just refused to believe us (I should have told him I found his lack of faith disturbing, but he probably would have killed me). And then he hit us with, 'Well, the *News of the World* have got hold of the story and they're running with it.'

When we got back to the hotel we were called into a room for a crisis meeting. The media man informed us that the woman in the red military jacket was the madame of Sydney's biggest whorehouse and that she'd told the *News of the World* that we'd ordered the lingerie girls from her and that we had gone on a sex trip with them. I'm not sure why I was always the one who got the talking to, as there were eight other lads involved, but I supposed once a ring leader always a ring leader. Upon hearing this potentially career-ending story and with a seething Johnno looking on, I promised him this was not what had happened and that I would get onto the organiser and find out. So straight after this meeting I got on the phone to the Old Wellingtonian and screamed, 'What were you thinking, putting eight England rugby players on a boat with a load of whores?! You're a fucking idiot!' This guy insisted he'd hired the girls through an agency and that they weren't prostitutes at all. I relayed this to the media guy; he had a word with the paper, and while they conceded that the women were only PR girls, and that this madame was making it up and just trying to get into the papers, they still ran the story with the headline: 'BOATS AND HOES'.

They printed the story with the picture that had been taken as we were leaving the port. I was nowhere to be seen, thank God, but if you looked closely you could see my feet sticking out as I had dived for cover. As always, though, the bastards still bloody mentioned me in the copy. 'The organiser of the trip James Haskell, etc.'

They had zoomed in on the picture and enlarged a section that showed the faces of the lads sitting in between the women. Doz was clearly visible on the front of the boat, Corona in hand, shirt off, taking a photo in between a couple of the girls. One of the lads who was on the boat and clear as day in the photo was shitting himself, because he was getting married after the tour. If his missus had seen a picture of him in the paper, chatting to some random girl wearing just her bra and knickers, the wedding might have gone up in smoke. As for me, I'd already been caught up in an England sex scandal, so knew how damaging they could be. Fortunately, because we'd beaten Australia for the first time in ages, the story barely made a splash and we all lived to fight another day.

On the 2008 tour of New Zealand, when four England players were accused of rape (they were cleared after an RFU inquiry), the story ended a couple of players' England careers, and in classic RFU style they weren't really given any support.

On this same trip, David Strettle was the victim of a kiss-and-tell story, also published by the *News of the World*. The waitress involved said she and David had made passionate love, he was like 'the Duracell Bunny' in bed, but also claimed I'd tried it on with her earlier that evening and she'd blown me out ('out', not 'off') as she only had eyes for Strets. I'd never even spoken to her, but it's just another classic example of my name getting thrown into the ring when I had done fuck all. Now, before you say there is no smoke without fire, I have been fingered for a whole host of stuff I never did. However, my missus at the time wasn't convinced and said to me, 'Why would she mention you if you weren't trying it on?' I was like, 'Babe, I don't know, I wasn't even there,' but she wasn't buying it.

What that story shows is how easy it is for sportsmen to get caught out. Most people out there are great, but there are plenty of others who are desperate to trip you up. Things you'd get away with if you were a plumber or some bloke who worked in the City – whether it's hanging out with some scantily clad women or shagging a waitress after a night on the beers – can sink you if you're a famous sportsman. That's why I'd be terrified to be a young rugby player now, because society has got even more puritanical and the people looking to entrap you have so many more tools at their disposal, what with smartphones and social media.

Towards the end of my rugby career I was usually the guy trying to keep everything from spiralling out of control. Because I'd been burned quite a few times, I could smell the danger. I cared about being an England player or a British & Irish Lion, and I knew that players being anti-social could turn a successful tour sour and reflect badly on the coaching and backroom staff. So I saw it as my responsibility to manage situations and save people from themselves.

My behaviour didn't really change much when I got drunk, apart from getting even louder than usual. But that wasn't the case with some of my England teammates. When they got hammered, there was almost nothing anyone could do to control them. On the flight home from Australia in 2016, one player was crawling down the aisle, because he'd been celebrating so hard. Other players were throwing peanuts at him and hitting innocent onlookers instead. Then this player started wrestling with a teammate, which must have been quite alarming for everyone else in business class – two 18-stone blokes rolling around on the floor is not what you expect when you've paid a couple of grand for a flight. One player was standing on his seat, swearing his head off. Another player had thrown up on his blanket. I was saying to them, 'Lads, we've just had the best tour ever, beaten Australia 3–0, and you're fucking it all up. Go to bed!' Most listened, except one player, who no matter how hard you reasoned with him would never stop. I took him back to his seat about ten times, while all the other lads slept on. He kept sneaking up and peering around the curtain, trying to get to his mate at the other end of the cabin. He tried crawling under the seats to reach him. It was not good and the air staff were getting upset. I wasn't captain – Dylan wasn't on the flight – and it wasn't my job, but I saw where this was going and managed to nip it in the bud.

Eddie Jones got wind of all this some time after and wasn't very happy, and had to address this particular problem player. Despite a few members of the public filming the idiocy on their phones, we got away with it.

I didn't think it was possible, but things got even worse when we landed in Dubai and the Wales team joined our plane. They were returning from New Zealand, so had been drinking for even longer than us. We were at one end and they were at the other, and a few of their lads spent the whole journey shouting at various players and playing drinking games. They would shout, 'Haskell! Haskell! Give us a wave!' Which I did. Then they would go, 'Care! Care! Sing us a song!' Which he did. They then tried, 'Haskell! Haskell! Show us your six pack!' When I refused as I didn't think it was quite on, and I didn't really know them, they all started booing and jeering. One of them lost a bet and had to have a selfie with Chris Robshaw, which was very funny, especially as they woke Chris up to take it and they had never met each other. Things carried on like this for a while, but when the captain came out and said he would make an emergency landing if the Welsh lads didn't behave, they all returned to their seats. They didn't stop drinking but at least they sat down.

Another flight that could have gone horribly wrong was the return flight from NZ with the Lions in 2017. One player who was known to be a nightmare on the piss was living up to his reputation. He got so drunk that he was just climbing over seats and walking through all the lads' business-class pods without a care in the world. He then thought it would be a good idea to practise his dive passing with rolled-up inflight magazines. He was getting progressively more drunk – hitting people with passes, rowing with people, singing his head off – and I eventually said to a couple of his teammates, 'Lads, you've got to stop this. This is just crazy.' They looked at me as if I was mad, before replying, 'Mate, we can't stop him. And I wouldn't try if I were you, unless you want to get punched in the face.'

Things went from bad to worse and no one was doing a thing about it. I could see that this was going to end in a fight. So I decided to take drastic steps. We'd each been given a sleeping pill, so I got three of them, crushed them up and stirred them in with a vodka cocktail. I called him over and said, 'Mate, well played this tour, it's time to do a shot together.' I gave him the spiked drink and he took it down in one. He then stumbled off down the aisle, knocking someone's drinks off their table. It was like watching a toy run out of batteries. He got slower and slower, and quieter and quieter, until he started yawning, went back to his seat for what he thought was a moment and even though I could see him trying to fight the enveloping darkness, he eventually conked out and started snoring, with his mouth gaping and saliva running down his chin. To this day, he doesn't know I drugged him. He just woke up in the UK with little memory of what happened. We didn't have much choice, and it's quite possible we saved him from some horrible newspaper headlines. Not many of the lads know that I did this, but my conscience is clear. Beware if you are a loud dog or a misbehaving scrum-half around me, as you will get drugged for some peace.

For a time during my England career, the squad would frequent an Italian restaurant called Pazzia, near Ascot. We'd tried lots of different restaurants, but the owner of Pazzia absolutely nailed the brief: we'd walk through the door, the starters would already be laid out and we'd descend on them like a swarm of giant locusts, before steaming through 30 pizzas and bowl after bowl of fudge cake and ice cream. We'd be in and out of there in an hour and a half, no messing about. We tried other places in the area but no one did it like Pazzia. Before my time, Jason Leonard had worked out that the bill was always around a certain amount of money and that if it was under that week he would order the finest wines on the menu, tell them to keep the corks in and take them home with him. I heard about this and so started replacing the cheap wine some of us were drinking with some mega vintage gear, a bottle of Barolo or Bordeaux for example. All the lads would dip in for a glass. It was only when the Stuart Lancaster regime took over, and the lads became too scared to drink because the officious team manager would go through the bill item by item and snitch on us, that we sacked it off and stuck with water and soft drinks.

You will remember the story in *What a Flanker* about the South Africa wine debacle when the same team manager grassed us up once again and it became a bit of an issue. But this was during the Martin Johnson era, when things were a bit looser. In those days we'd drive ourselves in car pools to the restaurant instead of all bundling onto the team bus, as long as we weren't drinking. And during one trip down there, things got a bit out of hand.

I was going through one of my idiot pretend-soldier phases, and me and Dozzer had recently paid a visit to a BB gun shop in North London. I basically discovered that I could buy what I wanted, when I wanted, and I always wanted a mad electric BB gun. My parents would never let me have one or afford such an expense when I was much younger. So one day, while driving past one of those Airsoft shops with Doz, I stopped the car and to his surprise said, 'Right, I'm getting a BB gun.'

He was like, 'What, Hask?'

'A big, fuck-off BB gun, mate.'

I know, reader. I am a huge child.

When we were in there, the bloke behind the counter kept losing his shit because I was handling the weaponry. But before he could chuck us out, I'd bought an M16 with a sight and fake silencer. Oh, and a couple of pro-level smoke and paint grenades. Dozzer, who's not into this kind of stuff, thought I was a total loser. So while I shopped, Doz struck up a conversation with an eager young shopper. He had seen this kid with a huge wad of cash and asked him what he was buying with that. This spotty kid said in the most IT consultant voice, 'I'm going to buy a light support weapon, or an FN Minimi to be precise.'

'What you going to do with that?' said Doz.

'Well, what I would do is kick the door in and lay down covering fire,' he replied nonchalantly.

'If I saw you come through the door with that and start spraying people, I'd chin you and take it off you.'

Doz was joking, but this kid was having none of it. He started twitching and convulsing, just like that hitchhiker from the movie *There's Something About Mary*, the one who Ben Stiller picks up in his car who has the corpse in the sleeping bag.

He replied to Doz, 'No! No! No! You can't do that. Airsoft is non-contact! Nobody's coming up and doing that. You won't, you won't do that.'

Sensing he could have some fun, Doz said, 'I promise you, I'd have that off you in two seconds. That gun's mine.'

The kid was now hitting the side of his head, and kept saying, 'No! No! You won't take my gun, you won't take my gun.'

The shopkeeper had had enough and threw us out.

Military-style weaponry could get you into so much bother. Once I was driving down to Pazzia with a bunch of teammates when one of the lads in the back of the car suddenly said, 'Fucking hell, Hask, what's this?' I glanced in my mirror and said, 'Oh, that's a smoke grenade.' And this lad replied, 'You're kidding me?', before pulling the pin out. I should probably say that I had gone full professional with these grenades; they were proper army quality and not the crap you get at paintball places. I immediately started panicking, because I knew how much damage those grenades could do if they went off in a car. (I'd previously rolled one under Dozzer's car, which was actually his mum's Vauxhall Astra, at Richmond Rugby Club, thinking it would just give off a bit of smoke. But Dozzer ended up falling out of the driver's seat onto the ground and coughing his guts up on his hands and knees. Within a few seconds the whole car park was blanketed with bright green smoke, which also started fanning out across the A316 and stopping traffic.)

Anyway, back on the road to Pazzia, I told my teammate to give me the active grenade before lobbing it out of the window, only for it to roll under someone else's car at a junction. I was going berserk, bashing the steering wheel and calling my teammate an idiot. The other lads were watching in fascination to see what had happened to the grenade. It had rolled under a car and due to busy traffic the car sat there while the smoke grenade did its thing and belched white smoke. The driver shot out of his vehicle like a rat up a drainpipe once he noticed the smoke. Other people were out of their cars, watching on in horror. Meanwhile, a thick wall of white smoke had spread across the road, bringing traffic to a halt and causing mayhem. We somehow managed to extricate ourselves from the situation without getting fingered and had a good laugh about it over dinner. But when I got back to my hotel room, I couldn't help thinking what the headlines might have looked like: 'ENGLAND PLAYERS BLOW UP CAR'/'ENGLAND PLAYERS IN SMOKE BOMB NIGHTMARE'.

You might be thinking, 'Well, if you're driving around with smoke grenades and a bunch of idiots in the back of your car, you deserve everything you get.' And you might be right. But the point I'm trying to make is that while it's often me who's holding the grenades, it's often someone else who pulls the pins, both literally and figuratively. Like another time we were eating out at Pazzia and a gang of girls intercepted me as I was on my way out. As I was chatting, one of the lads walked past and said, 'Hello ladies, are you popping back to the hotel?' He only meant it as a joke, but they followed us all the way back to Pennyhill Park. I tried to lose them, took all sorts of funky routes, drove like a movie getaway driver, the other lads in the car giggling but also slightly concerned as Lancaster had a 'no girls back to the hotel' policy and would have hit the roof. At one point we thought we had escaped, only for this carload of chicks to appear behind us on the long, winding hotel drive. I raced up to the car park and hid my Range Rover among a load of others, switched the lights off and climbed out silently. The other lads legged it with me, as we hid behind cars and tried to stifle our laughs. The girls pulled up and got out. They were not giving up. I was 29 at the time and found myself with another teammate of similar age crawling into the bushes, thinking what the fuck were we doing. That's how sketchy things had got with England and that management team; we hadn't done anything wrong but didn't want the drama. I could ill afford any problems because I was on ice thinner than Alun Wyn Jones's hair. That's how paranoid I was. Although, to be fair, if anyone had asked the lads why they were in that predicament, they would have mentioned me. No doubt about it. That was the story of my life: a small, seemingly innocent incident that had suddenly snowballed into a potential disaster. Eventually, one of the single lads took the heat for us and fended them off. He got one of their numbers and sent them on their way. By that stage I had made it back to my room and denied any knowledge.

* * *

I don't think I told you the stories of my Paris stalkers. Correct, there was more than one. When I moved to France, Twitter was still in its infancy. But me and Ollie latched onto its potential earlier than most sportspeople and started recording and posting mini four- or five-minute podcasts, all about our Parisian adventures. So, for example, after Ollie had informed me that you can eat the produce while doing your supermarket shopping (as long as you paid for it), we recorded ourselves having a six-course meal in our local Carrefour. It was just ridiculous stuff like that, but fun to do. And after a few of these podcasts, we started getting direct messages from people on Twitter.

One day, I received a message from an Australian girl. Her photos made her look super-attractive, and she was very flirty, so I immediately got sucked in. The age of the catfish was not yet upon us and it never occurred to me that people weren't who they said they were. We were soon chatting so often that I was even asking her for fashion advice, as she had told me she was a high-end Sydney fashion stylist. I remember I was in Louis Vuitton one afternoon, looking to buy a holdall bag, and I called her up to ask her opinion on it. I wanted to go for the traditional LV pattern, and she told me not to and instead go for the black one, which was more expensive. That bag cost me about 800 euros, 300 more than the other one I wanted. But she knew fashion, or so she said, and who was I to argue?

She said she was coming over to Europe for the summer for work and we should meet up. But every time we arranged to meet, she never ended up coming. Eventually, she messaged to say she was coming to Paris. But as the day of her arrival got closer, I started to get cold feet. It suddenly dawned on me that I had no idea if this woman was who she said she was. So, fearing more scandal, I said to Ollie, 'She's staying at the Mercure near the Eiffel Tower. You need to go in, I can't be in a hotel room with her on my own. If she says anything, no one will believe I didn't do it. You are harmless so I'll wait outside in the car while you go and check her out. If you're not back in ten minutes, I'll come up and kick the door in, because she'll probably be trying to murder you. Just tell her that I am waiting downstairs and that we will take her to lunch, in case she asks why you are there and not me.'

As it turned out, she didn't try to murder Ollie. But my hunch had been correct, because she was considerably larger in person than she was in her photos, and when I say larger I'm being kind. In fact, she wasn't the same person. Now it turns out that Ollie had been chatting to her at the same time, so not only was I done over, so was he. I couldn't understand why he agreed to go in and see her so eagerly, but the truth came out that he had also been working some angles, or I should say she had been working on him. She'd clearly earmarked Ollie as the weaker of the two of us, and thought he'd be more forgiving of her lies than I was. She must have sensed that I was beginning to question her bullshit the more we spoke. And she was right, because I'm not sure how I would have reacted if I'd been sent into the hotel instead of him. I certainly wouldn't have given her a kiss like Ollie did.

You might have to strap yourself in for my second stalker story, because it's quite long. And terrifying. One day, a random punter messaged me and Ollie, telling us she had a friend who lived in Paris and would love to meet us. We both ignored her, but this person kept messaging us incessantly, almost every day. And because me and Ollie were single at the time, and this person had implied her friend was quite pretty and feeling lonely in a strange city, we eventually agreed to meet her.

We didn't tell her where we lived, but instead arranged to meet in a restaurant nearby. Ollie bottled it, the experience with the white whale of Sydney having put him off, but I remember walking into this restaurant, clocking this girl and thinking, 'She's not quite how her mate described her, but she's nice enough.' But within a few seconds of striking up a conversation, alarm bells started going off in my head. She was very pale and clearly wearing a wig. And she had bandages and a hospital tag on her wrist. I was thinking, 'Jesus, what have we got ourselves into here?' But then I started thinking, 'Don't worry, it's all about the story …'

Meeting people for a drink has always been a very expensive pastime for me, because I can never just have a drink, I always have to eat as well. It doesn't matter how dull the other person is or how much I don't want to be spending time with them, I always get ravenously hungry and start ordering food. So I ordered some pasta and started stuffing my face, while she was picking at her bandages and not really saying much. Eventually, she warmed up a bit and started telling me her story. She said she was recovering from cancer and had also recently had a stillborn baby. This seemed like a lot of tragedy for one so young, so I was obviously very sympathetic. However, she insisted she was through the worst of it and was now working as a PA in Paris, although she couldn't tell me who for. I kept digging, but she claimed she'd signed a confidentiality agreement and would only tell me he worked in the media.

When Ollie asked me how it had gone, I said she seemed a bit odd but nice enough. A couple of days later she messaged me to say that her boss was supposed to be having dinner at the Moulin Rouge, couldn't make it and would we like to go with her instead. We had never been and thought why not. It might be nice to have a female friend to water down some of the high levels of testosterone flying around. So me and Ollie rocked up to the Moulin Rouge, watched a show, and steamed through a three-course meal and a bottle of champagne each. The three of us had a nice time and a few laughs. We offered to pay but she said that her boss had taken care of it all. We were very thankful and said please pass on our kindest regards. Everything seemed fine, and because the girl's hotel was on the other side of Paris we invited her to stay at our place instead in the guest room, which she did.

But when I got up the following morning early for a rare physio appointment, I caught our guest trying to sneak out without saying goodbye. I asked her what was wrong, and she said she wasn't feeling well and something about losing her passport. And as soon as she'd left, I got on the phone to Ollie while I headed into training and said, 'There's something not quite right about this girl, she gives me the creeps.' I was concerned that she could say anything, and no one would believe our side of the story.

Stupidly, I didn't follow my instincts and ended up meeting her for a coffee a few days later. This time, she told me she'd started writing for the French version of *Cosmopolitan* magazine and showed me an article she'd written. It was all about the British expat scene in Paris and she'd referred to Ollie as the 'angry squirrel', which was something I'd called him in a previous conversation between the two of us. She told me the editor loved it and wanted to detail more of our adventures. The article all looked legit so it put my fears on the back burner. Then she told me she was staying in her boss's apartment for a couple of days, so I started grilling her as to his identity again. She still refused to tell me, but eventually I said, 'I know it's something to do with fashion as you have mentioned that a couple of times.' I then started listing different designers to see her reaction. When I mentioned Tom Ford, she smiled. So I said, 'Is it Tom Ford?' and she replied, 'Oh, I couldn't possibly say,' before giving me a wink. I couldn't believe it – I loved Tom Ford, he'd been the head designer at Gucci, and here I was having a coffee with his PA. I was thinking free shirts, free suits, free shoes. And then she said, 'Listen, we're going to Monaco for the grand prix, would you and Ollie like to come? He's having a party on his yacht.' Suddenly, this girl was no longer giving me the creeps. Ollie and I had already been planning to go, due to his contacts within Red Bull. So I said we would both love to be there, but are you sure it's going to be okay?

That evening she called me, said it was all arranged and that Tom was so happy that we were coming. She had told him all about us and he was a big fan of mine. It wasn't beyond the realms of possibility: Tom Ford is gay, I have done lots and lots of things for the gay community, appeared on loads of front covers, so he might have had an idea who I was. It was a stretch, but not impossible.

She then said that he was such a big fan of us both that he'd love to put us in one of his suits for the day. So she sent over this tailor's form, me and Ollie measured each other up, filled it in and scanned it back. The following day, she messaged saying, 'The tailors have asked if you've written the measurements down right, because they're a bit unusual.' That just made me think it was all legit, because rugby players do have weird measurements, owing to the fact we've all got massive necks, wide shoulders, small waists and thighs like giant hams. We even had a laugh about it, and I was massively excited at the prospect of rocking up to the Monaco Grand Prix in a Tom Ford suit I got for free and partying on his yacht with loads of celebs. I mean, who wouldn't be?

The last message we had from her was that she was sorting out a hotel stay at Hotel du Cap, that the suits were being made and all was good. We heard nothing from her for a week after that, which was most unusual. Then a week before the grand prix, I said to Ollie, 'Look, this is a bit weird, because she said she was going to book flights and accommodation.' Eventually, she sent me the flight and hotel details (business class and five star respectively), but when I phoned the airline and the hotel a few days before we were due to travel, they said they didn't have any bookings in our names. I texted her to find out what was going on, and shortly afterwards I received a text from another number, saying, 'This is Tom Palmer-Smith, so-and-so's assistant [we are calling her 'so-and-so' because this person is still alive and will most definitely appear again if I say her name]. Unfortunately, so-and-so has had a stroke after being in hospital for a routine procedure. It's touch and go whether she's going to pull through or not.'

Now I have mentioned that she claimed to have had cancer and various other issues, so her going into hospital was not unusual. Upon hearing the news, we were shocked to start with, but that was quickly replaced by a very eerie and uneasy feeling. For a start, there were no flights, no hotel, no sign of any suits, and Tom Palmer was a teammate of ours at Stade Français, so what were the chances of her having an assistant with the same name, just with Smith stuck on the end? So I said to Ollie, 'This has got all the hallmarks of a serial killer. I'm going to pretend we're not going to the grand prix and tell this Tom Palmer-Smith, who is obviously the girl on another number, that we'll be waiting by the phone for any news. But get in touch with your lady friend who works for Red Bull and say to her we will take those places for the F1. Then you book yourself, me and Dozzer flights and a hotel in Monaco.'

Two days later, we were getting steaming drunk on free vodka Red Bulls next to Michael Fassbender on the Red Bull energy station in the heart of the Monaco grand prix, when we got another message from 'Tom Palmer-Smith', informing us that the girl was likely to pass away in the next couple of hours and asking if we had any final messages for her. We'd had a few drinks and were very tempted to call an end to this charade of bullshit, but thought that like the ending of any good crime novel it was better to drag this out to a final dénouement. There was also the tiniest chance that she could actually be dying. We really had no idea. I texted back mildly antagonistically: 'Oh my God, that is awful. Ollie and I had both thought she looked very unwell for a long time. She had a very pale and haggard appearance. I do hope she doesn't die. Send our love. We will be waiting in Paris for any news.' Now I knew, or was about 90 per cent sure, it was this girl pretending to be someone else messaging us, so I was having a slight dig at her appearance because I knew it was her reading it. I was hoping she would slip up and then we could call her out.

The next day as we were preparing to leave, somewhat hungover, we got another message from this 'assistant' claiming that against all the odds the girl had made it through the night and things were looking much more positive. The doctors had changed their prognosis and felt she was on the mend. The assistant wanted us to know he had not left her bedside the whole time and while she had been at her lowest ebb she had been muttering our names in her sleep. Apparently she had woken up and we were the first people she had asked about. The assistant said he had shown her our get well messages, but that she was very upset that we had said she 'looked unwell and haggard' and it had made her cry.

I decided to up the ante a bit. It could have been the hangover or just my boredom with this whole affair, but I sent him a text saying, 'You must be the most incompetent personal assistant I have ever known. Why would you show her those messages on her waking from a near-death experience? If you were my assistant, I would have fired you. The word prat springs to mind.'

The assistant claimed to be outraged by my insolence, and had never been spoken to like that in all his years working. I think I told him to get fucked and left it there.

On returning home from the grand prix, the girl then sent a message claiming she'd just been released from hospital and that everything 'Tom Palmer-Smith' had told us was true. I decided to play it cool, told her not to worry about it and focus on getting well. However, she kept messaging me and Ollie incessantly, apologising for ruining our weekend.

If she had left it there then it might have been fine, but because she started pushing her bullshit stories more and more, Ollie and I both decided that it was time to look into this girl and gather some actual evidence. We already had a fair bit, but we needed more to complete the picture. Aside from all the crap about Tom Ford, *Cosmo*, cancer, and being a high-level PA, she had told us that she had an older brother in Norfolk where her family was from. We got on Google Search. We found out where she lived, her Facebook page and lots of other weird things. Ollie called the number for the family home and a man answered, confirmed he was the girl's dad, and when we asked how she was he said she'd been with them the whole weekend and was most definitely not ill. He said she didn't have an older brother, she had a younger one. The father started to get a bit agitated with the questions and hung up.

We then hatched a plan to confront her once and for all. I had to go back to the UK for some England training, while Ollie was over doing some sevens stuff. So instead of telling the girl we'd rumbled her, we sent her a message suggesting we meet in Richmond, if she happened to be in the UK. She agreed, and me, Ollie and Dozzer headed over to Starbucks in Richmond, because we wanted it to be as public as possible. Not only did we want to confront her with all our evidence, but we also didn't know what she might do when we did so. We were clearly not dealing with a woman of sound mind. We arrived early and took three chairs facing a fourth chair right in the corner, and none of us ordered hot drinks, because we were afraid she might dash them in our faces.

She turned up and it all started out quite friendly, until I said, 'Listen, we need to tell you something. We know that everything you've told us is utter nonsense. We know you don't work for Tom Ford. We know you don't write for *Cosmo*. We know you don't have an older brother. We know you weren't in hospital in Paris. We know all the stuff about cancer is bollocks as well. You made it all up and you must be mentally unwell.' She was wearing a low-buttoned shirt, and as I was talking her chest was getting redder and redder. I was worried she was going to explode, start tipping tables over and throwing chairs. Instead, she kept muttering, 'I don't know what to say, I don't know what to say …'

I replied, 'Listen, we should be as embarrassed as you are for falling for your lies. We were both greedy and wanted to use you as much as you wanted to use us for the sick fantasy life you wanted to lead. You don't have to say anything else, just never contact us again. If you do, we will contact the police and seek a restraining order.' Ollie had his say, and Dozzer just nodded in agreement. (I'm not even sure why Dozzer was there, presumably for moral support. He is never one to miss any drama. That being said, she had said she would get him a ticket as well for Monaco so he had been mildly stitched up, before Red Bull came to the rescue.) After soaking it all up while saying nothing, the girl said she needed to go to the bathroom. Half an hour later, she was still in there. So now we were thinking that maybe she'd climbed out of a window or tried to kill herself. If you know Starbucks toilets there is normally only one, and it's unisex and disabled in one. As I watched this mounting queue develop, I was getting the fear. I could see the headlines now: 'HASKELL AND CO. IN STARBUCKS DEATH'/'WOMAN TAKES HER OWN LIFE WHILE ENGLAND PLAYERS LOOK ON'. But just as we were about to inform a member of staff, the girl reappeared and said, 'Look, I need to tell you something. My family and myself were held hostage a while ago and the kidnappers made me do this, they were trying to extort money. I can show you the evidence.' By this point we were almost laughing. I say 'almost' because it was actually quite sinister. Now I know you, the reader, might be thinking what the fuck is going on. I very much had the same thought that this was getting beyond madness now. Feeling still very concerned, we said, 'Listen, just leave us alone,' and with that we walked back into the real world hoping never to hear from her again.

No such luck. Two weeks later, I received an email with a load of attachments, including police documents and scans of hospital reports. None of these attachments had this girl's name on them and they were all obviously faked. She also sent a padded envelope full of the same printouts to my family home. Which was not good; she now had my UK address as well as my Paris one. Once again, I ignored it. But this was one problem that just would not go away.

For the next six years this girl would send me cryptic messages from random phones, all pretending to be girls that I had chatted up. She'd even contact girlfriends. One girlfriend even started replying to her, revealing relationship secrets, which the crazy girl would then relay back to me, trying to use them as leverage against me or just to drag out a conversation. She was obsessed with me for some reason. I couldn't understand what was going on, until I spoke to my partner and asked who she was talking to about us. She then revealed the bombshell that it was this nutbag. My then partner didn't know the full story, and when I told her she was as sketched out as me. The stalker had told my ex that we were having an affair and provided enough detail for her to believe it. My ex then decided to share stuff about me with her. Which of course fuelled the stalker's fire. I told her I had never had an affair and that this girl was making it up. I was then able to prove this. As you can imagine, my relationship did not last much longer after that.

One birthday, this stalker sent a leather iPad cover and a card to my parents' home address, with the message, 'My Darling James, here's a little something for you. The iPad will arrive separately.' That iPad would have been a silver lining, but it never arrived. How unhinged do you have to be to send someone an iPad cover for an imaginary iPad? But believe it or not, things got even crazier.

Because I was genuinely worried that this girl might appear from nowhere and stick a pickaxe in my head, I'd occasionally google her name and my name together, just to see what came up. One day, I discovered that she was apparently climbing Kilimanjaro for a stillbirth charity and had set up a fundraising page. And on the page was a fake donation from me, with the message, 'Good luck, little one, I know you can do it. Love James Haskell.' Then someone from Twickenham called me, wanting to confirm my attendance at an upcoming event. This girl had claimed to be my friend and booked two tables on my behalf. I had to tell this bemused woman from Twickenham that the girl was insane, that I didn't know her and that I definitely wasn't coming to the event.

One day after England training, I was updating Dozzer on the latest news of my stalker and Ben Youngs overheard me. Ben is from Norfolk, where this girl was from, and he immediately twigged that this must be the same girl that dated one of his mates. Apparently, she pretended to be pregnant with his child, which was quite traumatic for the poor bloke. I don't think her family were too pleased either, but they brushed her obvious insanity under the carpet. So she had previous and I was not the only victim.

Fast forward eight years and I received a call from a random number. This bloke said, 'Is this James Haskell? Listen, I've been dating this nutcase. I think you might know her …' I couldn't believe my ears. I said to this bloke, 'Fucking hell, mate, you need to run,' and he replied, 'Too late. We went on a couple of dates, I slept with her once and she told me she was pregnant. She said she was going to keep the baby. Now I can't get hold of her. She's trying to ruin my life.' This guy was in tatters, absolutely broken. He had spoken to her family as well, but they refused to believe any of it. We had got the same vibe from a friend of a friend, who had heard his story, remembered me saying something similar about a girl and thought it might be the same one. So he had given him my number, although I'm not sure what he expected me to do about it. This went on for some months, as she was sending baby scans to him that were all dated wrong, and then she said she would get rid of the baby, but had she? This bloke was in hell. She would contact members of his family to say he beat her. It was a nightmare. Thank God I never shagged her, otherwise can you imagine the drama? I'm not actually sure what happened with this guy and her. I assume that she was faking the pregnancy, she lived out her fantasy and then it ended. You can only lie for so long.

I feel sorry for her, but it does not excuse the levels of madness she went to. Even today, I wake up some mornings and wonder if she's going to pop up again. Maybe she's concentrating on other people now, trying to ruin their lives instead. Or maybe the police finally caught up with her. Even writing this all down for you lot is terrifying. Just imagine the lies you would have to tell to keep this charade up. The sad thing is there are thousands of people out there doing this, and it's even easier in the digital age. I now don't trust anyone as far as I can throw them. There is a clear moral to this story. Never meet up with random strangers who contact you on social media. Unless you're my wife, of course, who did exactly that when I contacted her on Twitter …

7

SOME SAD CLOWN

DAN COLE:

'There are two sides to Hask: the brash, funny man and the softer, more self-conscious Hask. You know what sums him up? His banter. When he's sounding off, he looks like he doesn't give a shit, but then he'll go into a panic because he thinks he's upset people. You'll hear him saying, "Shit, did I go over the top?"'

SUSIE HASKELL:

'Not everything came easy to James. We didn't know it at the time, but he was dyslexic. He'd memorise books I read to him, so when he spoke the words back to me he wasn't actually reading. One day, when he was about six, I collected him from school and he was sitting on the steps, reading a book with a dinner lady. I said, "Is there a problem with James?", and she replied, "No, I'm just teaching him to read." When I asked the headmaster about it, he said, "This boy will never be able to read and write."

'That didn't make sense because I knew he was bright. I could tell by the things he talked about and words he

173

used. We were in the supermarket once and I parked him up away from the shelf, like I usually did (otherwise he'd take food from the shelf and start eating it, because he had a voracious appetite). Suddenly, this woman touched me on the shoulder and asked if James was my son. When I said yes, and asked what he'd done, she asked how old he was. I told her he was three, and she replied, "Don't be ridiculous, he's just been telling me all about the crystal chandeliers at Versailles. How would a three-year-old know about that?" I had to explain that my husband and I had just been there and showed James a video on our return.

'A lord and lady came to visit his first school one day, because they were thinking of putting their son in there. James was chosen to show the lord and lady around, as he always was when the headmaster wanted a pupil to join the school tour and add some colour, and after he'd told them all about the sports their son could do, they asked about the other subjects. James replied, "Oh, I can read now. Nick helps me when we're in bed." Nick was a little boy in James's dormitory, who had great patience and taught James to read in a few weeks. The lord and lady were a bit taken aback, not only by the fact that James had been taught to read by another pupil, but also by the fact they were in bed together. For the record they weren't in bed together, they were just in a dorm together with side-by-side beds, but James had not told the story properly. As you can imagine, there was some explaining to do from the slightly embarrassed headmaster.

'They say your childhood shapes you, and James's childhood certainly shaped him. He was ridiculed for all *sorts of reasons, including for having great big feet. But that's where his stubbornness and single-mindedness comes from, because he was determined to prove people wrong.'*

Honestly, sometimes I listen back to what my mum says and wonder if she is getting me confused with another child she had. There is no way I was talking about chandeliers from Versailles. Yes, I was definitely beyond my years and spoke much more like an adult than a child, hence why I was always asked to show parents around because I could talk the hind legs off a donkey and was a good representation of the school. I'm sure I spouted some beyond-my-years chat to this woman in the supermarket, but take it with a pinch of salt. She was probably asking my mum what I was saying as a polite way of telling her can you shut this little fucker up and let me shop in peace.

I don't remember any teachers writing me off to my face, like Mum seems to. She likes to tell the story about me making a picture out of pasta at my first school, and the teacher telling me it was shit, crumpling it up and throwing it in the bin, thus destroying my confidence and denting me emotionally for ever. I don't quite remember it being as brutal as that, but Mum seems to think it scarred me for life, had a profound effect on me, and meant I was destined to spend the rest of my life desperately trying to prove people wrong. But I do remember my parents constantly being at my prep school, speaking to teachers who just didn't get me. When my first book *Rugby Fit* was published, Mum was so proud. She said to me, 'There was a teacher who said you'd never be able to read and write properly.' She is right about that; some teachers labelled me a complete lost cause and most likely to end up as a menial low-level worker.

I still have a chip on my shoulder now, which is probably why I'm always bouncing from one thing to the next, because I'm obsessed with confounding people. I imagine that when most people are invited to appear on *Celebrity Mastermind*, they treat it as a bit of a giggle. Not me. My specialist subject was the Harry Potter movies (when I was younger I actually auditioned to appear in one of them, but that is another story for another day), so on the plane over to Belfast I had my head in this Harry Potter crib book and was frantically scribbling notes. People must have been looking at me and thinking, 'God, what a massive geek.' Then when I got to my hotel I spent most of my time revising in my room. We were in lockdown because of Covid-19, but I would have done the same if we weren't.

When I was introduced to Omid Djalili, who was also on the show, the first thing I said to him was, 'Man, I loved you in *The Mummy*.' I got that right, but the next thing I said to him was, 'I also loved you in *The Young Ones*.' Quick as a flash he replied, 'Yeah, you've got me confused with Alexei Sayle.' He then turned and checked himself in, leaving me standing there like a lemon, wishing the floor would open up and swallow me. The woman who was chaperoning us had to walk off, because she couldn't cope with the awkwardness. I went straight back to my hotel room, saying, 'Fuck, what an idiot!' to myself a million times before I called Chloe and said, 'I just called Omid Djalili Alexei Sayle. I knew he was in *The Mummy*, but I thought he was also in *The Young Ones*. How bad is that?' Chloe told me not to worry about it, but I was absolutely mortified. The fact that it apparently happens to Omid all the time didn't make me feel any better. If he had put me at ease that might have helped, but it definitely irked him.

The following day, we had a pre-show briefing. I don't know if you've ever done a speed awareness course, but there's always one bloke who starts talking back and causing arguments, when everyone else is just trying to get through it as quickly as possible. On mine, the instructor showed a speed limit sign and asked what we should do when we saw it, and this bloke replied, 'Speed up.' He started going on about speed limits being 'a money-making scheme for the government' and calling traffic police every name under the sun. I had to confront him as it was becoming unbearable and I said, 'Listen mate, these people don't have the power to change anything, you are wasting our time and no one wants to be here. So shut up and just give the answers they want.' I got a round of applause before sitting down. Looking big and angry has its benefits … Anyway, on *Celebrity Mastermind*, because Omid had been on the show a few years earlier, he was similar to that bloke on my speed awareness course, and he kept saying stuff like, 'Is that really how we're doing it? It's just that when I did it before, it was a bit different …' And while he was going off on one, and dragging the meeting out for 30 minutes longer than necessary, everyone else was puffing out their cheeks and rolling their eyes. It was textbook alpha male behaviour. I found it funny, as he is a lovely bloke but was just obviously excited to be on again and was simply making it about him and his past experiences, which we are all guilty of doing from time to time.

Omid's specialist subject was *Curb Your Enthusiasm*, which seemed quite manageable. But Zoe Williams, the TV doctor from *This Morning*, had plumped for Nelson Mandela, which sounded pretty tricky, and Charlotte Crosby from *Geordie Shore* had plumped for whales and dolphins. I couldn't get my head around that. When I asked her why, she replied, 'Because

I love whales and dolphins.' And I said, 'Yeah, but there's loads of them.' I could tell people thought I'd taken the easy option with Harry Potter – there were a few pitying looks – but I was sitting there thinking, 'Why the hell would you choose Nelson Mandela or whales and dolphins? I don't care how much Charlotte has revised, there's no way she knows the Latin for the humpback whale or Bolivian river dolphin. Who does?'

When it came to the actual filming, I sat down in the famous chair and John Humphrys started grilling me about concussion and whether rugby was too dangerous for kids. I said to him, 'John, I think you've forgotten where you are. You're not on Radio 4 anymore, this is supposed to be a light-hearted celebrity quiz show.' He laughed and said, 'Yes, sorry, let's keep it light.' I killed the Harry Potter round, only got one question wrong, which left me level with Omid. And after he finished his general knowledge round, Omid turned to me and mouthed, 'Beat that.' I was sitting there thinking, 'Oh, right. I wasn't really bothered about winning, all I really care about is not completely fucking up, because I'll never hear the end of it.' But after Omid laid down the challenge, the old competitive spirit reared up and I was eager to win.

As it turned out, I aced the general knowledge round and beat Omid by four points. People were surprised that I had done so well, and me winning I don't think was part of the script. I'm not sure in our group who the favourite was. I would have said Zoe, being a doctor, or Omid as he is clearly very bright, as most comedians are. I'm not sure Charlotte was a front runner because she was a reality TV star known for being a bit dippy, and once I discovered her expert subject I knew things were not going to go well. She scored two points on whales and dolphins, which is two more than I would have scored. It was horrifically hard. However, as always she was mega value and had John, the crew and us laughing out loud. She is such a character and you can see why she has the following and success she does. When John asked me how winning *Mastermind* compared to my rugby achievements, I told him it was right up there, 'because I look like I shouldn't be able to tie my own shoelaces'. What John and the viewers didn't know is that when I was growing up, even I thought I'd never be able to tie my own shoelaces. As a final word on this, I should add that Omid actually turned out to be brilliant company, and my fear of him being an alpha male and my concern he thought I was a plonker were both misplaced. After filming, we enjoyed a couple of glasses of wine, exchanged a few yarns and he didn't seem to mind when I single-handedly demolished a charcuterie board we had ordered to share.

While we are on the subject of TV shows, I appeared on *A League of Their Own* years ago as a guest. I was stitched up and asked if I had any special skills, so I said to my agent that I could juggle, if not that well. I was offered good money to appear on the show, so I went on and juggled. Little did I know they had got actual celebs with talent to come on as well and sing, dance and do whatever. I made my small cameo appearance and then got feedback from the panel. Amanda Holden took a shine to me as I was wearing a wife beater and was in good shape at the time. I had a laugh with her and told her I was single. This was filmed in the first month of Chloe and me going out and I was only joking to get extra points through being flirty. However, when it was aired eight months later Chloe hit the roof, saying I had embarrassed her. I tried to explain it was all for TV and it was filmed ages ago but, anyway, I digress. The next judge was Freddie Flintoff, who said, 'To be honest, I expected more,' and as quick as a flash I came back with, 'After watching you box, I think it would be fair to say we expected more as well,' and everyone cheered. I had buried him, the scene ended and I walked off happy with how I had done. Now Freddie was a hero of mine, an amazing British sporting legend, a guy I looked up to and always wanted to meet. At the end of the show, I went up to him and introduced myself and said, 'I'm really sorry about earlier, it just came out. You are a hero of mine and it's an honour to meet you.' He looked a little rattled but was polite enough.

Fast forward to the next season and *ALOTO* got me on again as a guest, this time to sit on Jamie Redknapp's team. However, they wanted to go with the narrative that Freddie and I had a beef to settle. I was like okay, no problem, it's all fun and games. What they wanted to do in a segment was to have me and Freddie go head to head on a beam using pillows to batter each other. Seemed fair, Freddie is a big bloke, I'm a big bloke, all good.

This is where it gets dark. Before the filming started, Freddie came up to me and said, 'Listen, why don't I push you off, you square up to me, we have a push around and make it look like a scrap?'

I was like okay, sounds great, I am all over that. We didn't tell anyone and the filming started. Things went exactly as planned. Freddie pushed me off and we squared up. However, Freddie went a bit over the top, pushed me five times and looked proper angry. Now I thought we were still joking, so putting my best acting into practice I took the hits and looked serious and equally angry. Jack Whitehall came running in and broke it up. The director said cut, all the producers came out and the studio audience had gone quiet. As soon as it was over I was all smiles, but I got this feeling that everyone thought the square off was for real. James Corden came up to me and said, 'Was that real?' and I was like, 'No, no, of course not.' Now I would never get angry on a TV show whatever happened, as we are paid to be there. I would also never let Freddie Flintoff keep pushing me over in real life and not react. I have seen him box, and I'm pretty sure I could serve him up. In fact, it would be light work.

We went back to filming but everyone was concerned there was beef between us. Even my agent was worried. I told him it was Freddie's idea and just a game. I left, thinking nothing more about it. However, when the show aired it went mental. People were saying things like I was a cunt, that I'd got filled in by Freddie, and I was a wanker. It went on and on for months. I had messaged Freddie after the show to say thank you again and for him to keep smashing it. I also asked him, if I sent him a cricket bat to sign for this ill little boy would he do it, as Freddie was his hero. He just ignored me and that was it. I thought fuck it, just move on.

Then when the next series started, Freddie was shown highlights of our head-to-head and said, 'Yeah, that Haskell was a bit of a dick,' and he made it all out to be serious and a real thing. So again it blew up, and I was getting abused once more. So much so I had to do a video saying it was fake and that I respected Freddie. Jamie Redknapp and Jack Whitehall both tweeted it was a joke to calm the building fervour. I'm not sure why Freddie lied on TV and went with it being real. I can't help but feel I got done and it was part of his plan. You live and learn. I still have to hear about it today, with trolls saying, 'You're a cunt,' and 'You got beaten up by Flintoff,' when the reality is, I'm not, I didn't and I wouldn't.

OLLIE PHILLIPS:

'Hask is a far more complex man than his public image, to an unbelievable degree. Sometimes I wonder how much is Brand Hask, how much is real Hask and how confused he's become about who he actually is. One day you'll hear him say, "I don't give a shit what anyone thinks of me," the next day you'll hear him say, "Why don't the pundits and fans like me?"

'The bloke who bowls into a room and holds court for an hour isn't the whole story. That's why he never became unbearable to live with. If someone was around, the show would come out. But as soon as that person left, and there was no one to impress, he'd go off and play Call of Duty for nine hours, with his headset on. He really would flip that quickly.

'Maybe it's that he thinks the world wants to see the risqué, brash, slightly calamitous Hask who's going to break some eggs and piss people off. Maybe that is what the world wants to see, and they're not interested in his softer side. But the fact is, he's intelligent and articulate and has lots of insecurities and vulnerabilities. He's just a total contradiction, in so many different ways.'

CHLOE MADELEY:

'James is a little boy whose sole purpose in life is to please his mum and dad. As his mum has already described, he developed this fight mentality very early on in life, from when he was at prep school. And his dad's motto, that "the Haskell way is the right way", was drummed into him from an early age, which is why he's always been desperate to prove people wrong.

'That's why it's so hard to get James to see things from other people's perspective. If you say to James, "Have you noticed that you always have to be right?" he'll reply, "That's because everyone else is wrong." It's hard to communicate with someone who genuinely never thinks they're wrong. I'll try to get him to a place where he can see that he might be wrong – or at least where he can see why I think he might be wrong – and he'll accuse me of repeating myself. That's always going to be a work-on in our relationship.'

I've been labelled arrogant many times by many people. I don't know what qualifies someone to be arrogant, but Chloe always tells me I've got too much to say about all the wrong things. According to her, the things I could make a lot of noise about – e.g. my rugby career – I don't, and the things I maybe shouldn't make a lot of noise about – e.g. politics or religion – I do.

I don't think I'm boastful about anything, but I do like to have an opinion. It's just that some people seem to think I'm not allowed to have an opinion about anything other than what I'm most known for. They'll say, 'Stick to what you know.' In other words, 'Just tell funny stories about rugby.' I can understand it when people say you should leave medical chat to doctors, but are they saying that the only people who can comment on politics or religion are politicians and clerics? That frustrates me. It stems from being labelled, as a kid, a bit thick, a troublemaker. I'm constantly railing against those labels, trying to confound expectations. It's like I'm on a mission, to try as many things as possible and be successful at them, just to make people look stupid.

There's always been this narrative surrounding me, that I'm 'misunderstood'. Every newspaper article would include the word 'misunderstood' somewhere. I get where people are coming from, but it's a bit more complicated than that. The fact is, I wasn't misunderstood in rugby circles, I just worked really hard, played really hard, and was really loud and a massive attention seeker off the pitch. That was it, there wasn't much more to understand. Journalists always expected me to fall out with coaches, but it never happened. Not once. They thought Martin Johnson would hate me, but we got on fine. I also got on fine with Stuart Lancaster. They said Dai Young wouldn't accept me at Wasps, but he did. They said I wouldn't fit in at the Highlanders under Jamie Joseph, but he loved having me around. It was the journalists who misunderstood me, not my coaches or teammates. And because fans believe what journalists write, they misunderstood me as well.

CHLOE MADELEY:

'I don't get James's full attention. I don't think anyone does. The only things that get his attention are tasks, whether it's shooting, DJing or making music. And then he'll get bored and pick up a new hobby.

'He's very easy to live with, because he'll just sit in his office and work for hours on end. Meanwhile, I'll be pottering around the house doing whatever I want. But that's not the same as being easy to be married to. In truth, he's a bit of a loner. In fact, he's probably better suited to the life of a bachelor. I don't mean that as an insult, it's just the truth. And because he doesn't get too close to people, and doesn't like letting people in, I do feel incredibly special that I'm without a doubt the closest person to him in his life. And I'm very flattered and touched that he chose to give up the bachelor's life to

spend the rest of his life with me. I think it surprised even him.'

However much I don't like to admit it, Chloe is never too far off the mark. She's right, I am a loner. A lot of people don't get that about me. Someone once said to me, 'I see you in Soho House a lot, but you're never with anyone. You just sit at the bar with your headphones on, staring at your laptop, typing away and nodding your head.' They obviously thought that was slightly weird behaviour, not least because Soho House is where creative sorts have meetings, eat, drink and make merry. But as much as I love performing to a crowd, I'm also perfectly happy in my own space. I don't need to be with anyone. I don't get lonely or depressed when I'm on my own, like some sad clown.

I was in the West End recently for work and had a bit of time to kill beforehand. I texted a few people to see if they fancied lunch, and when they all replied in the negative I went and had lunch on my own. I ended up having a whole lobster and a bottle of Sancerre just by myself. Oh, and a prawn cocktail to start. There I was, getting stuck into this massive lobster, with my iPhone propped up against the pepper grinder, headphones on and watching some shit movie, when a mate walked past. He did a double-take, before saying, 'Hask? What are you doing? Are you seriously eating a whole lobster on your own?' I replied, 'Mate, I do this all the time.' He couldn't get his head around it, clearly thought it looked a bit tragic. As far as he was concerned, eating a lobster on your own was something Alan Partridge might do during a breakdown, like driving to Dundee in bare feet. But to me, it was perfectly normal.

I'll walk into a Michelin-starred restaurant on my own and order a five-course lunch. Most people need to share those moments with other people for them to be special, but not me. I don't depend on other people for my happiness, which I think is a good way to be. But the downside of being so self-sufficient, at least for Chloe and probably other people, is that I'm often difficult to reach. When I'm with someone, I'll give them my full attention. But I don't fret or feel bad when I haven't seen or spoken to someone for ages. I have a small and tight social circle, consisting of Dozzer, my other mates Jamie and Robbie, plus Chloe. I'll speak to them every week, but I don't need anyone else.

For some people, it's really important to be surrounded by and in contact with people all the time. They associate the word 'loner' with sad, middle-aged men in anoraks eating broken biscuits from a plastic bag on a park bench, who all share the unfortunate smell of stale urine. But I wouldn't mind sitting on a park bench on my own, eating broken biscuits. I would leave the piss smell, though. Sometimes, I take myself off for car picnics. The other day, I was driving back from London, stopped off for scampi and chips and ate it in my car, while watching a combination of the world go by and some rubbish on Netflix. I'll go on very long walks with the dog, smoke a cigar, listen to audiobooks and not think about anything else. That, to me, is heaven.

But there's a difference between being a loner and being lonely. You can be a loner and still have good people around you, who support you, make you better and keep you honest. Being lonely means you don't have any of that. It means stewing in your own thoughts, not having anyone to turn to. That's why I'm so lucky to have Chloe, because she understands me so well.

Having said that, I don't look to Chloe or anyone else for my happiness, because the only person you can 100 per cent rely on is yourself. That's why I'm constantly booking things in, and Chloe's constantly asking where I'm off to. People think it's weird that I went and got a 360 excavator licence at JCB for a week. They all ask – including Chloe – why would you do that, what's the point? I reply, because I can and it's what makes me happy. I'll go off shooting, live the life of a shooter for a few hours, and then go off and be doing something different. Maybe speaking at Airbus on leadership, DJing for five thousand people at an event or making a new house music track. Every day is different and fun. That's how I find contentment. My life is never dull, that's for sure.

8

I HAVE TO SAY
SOMETHING

DAN COLE:

'My first proper memory of Hask is on the England tour of Australia in 2010. After the Australian leg, most of the players who appeared in the two Tests were sent home. But all the rest had to go to Napier, to play against the New Zealand Maori. Not what anyone really wanted.

'We landed in Napier on a dark, foggy evening and when the bus pulled up outside our hotel the team manager stood up to say a few words. And just as he did so, Haskell jumped out of his chair and roared, "Sit down, Gav! No one wants to fucking be here, we know it and you know it! We want to go home!" We were all in pieces, and we could see all the coaches down the front, trying not to laugh, their shoulders rolling. Only Haskell could get away with that.

'Hask also led two bus sit-ins. The first was before a leaving dinner, prior to the 2011 World Cup. On the journey there, we discovered it had been sold off to corporates and we had been told that it wasn't a commercial dinner and that we didn't need to get paid. However, our then EPS contract said otherwise. Hask *was up in arms. He kept saying, "Hang on, are we getting paid for this?" All the coaches got off, the captain Lewis Moody got off, but Haskell ordered the rest of us to stay put. It was so awkward. The protest only lasted about three minutes, but it felt like an hour. Haskell called Lewis "The Puppet" after that, because he did whatever the RFU told him.*

'Hask's second industrial action took place on the 2017 Lions tour. On the morning of the first Test, the guys who weren't involved found out that we had to be at the stadium a few hours before kick-off to meet corporate guests. It was written in the schedule, but in tiny letters at the bottom of the page, like Willy Wonka's prize contract in Charlie and the Chocolate Factory.

'Once again, Hask led the revolt from the back of the bus. He said to the rest of us, "Right, when all the staff get off, we'll hide under our coats." There must have been about ten of us hiding under our coats, like a bunch of five-year-olds on a school trip. It was so childish. But that was the thing about Haskell: if he thought things hadn't been done properly, he'd speak up. And while the rest of us mumbled and grumbled under our breath, he took action.'

That trip to Napier didn't go down too well with the bin juice, especially as the Test squad were flying home. Me and Dozzer thought we'd be flying straight to Vegas from Australia. All of the non-Test starters spent most of the flight to New Zealand taking the piss out of each other and grumbling about Ugo Monye, who'd sustained a suspicious last-minute back injury and got out of the trip. He had said he was dead keen to play but suddenly couldn't, which meant one of the other lads who was going home now couldn't. It didn't help that someone had described Napier to me as 'the retirement village of New Zealand'. I thought, 'Pretty much all of New Zealand seems like a retirement village, so Napier must be like a cemetery.' Let's just say the mood was quite low when we arrived at the hotel.

So when Gav the team manager stood up at the front of the bus and started giving us a lecture about the fact we were still representing England and how we needed to conduct ourselves in New Zealand, I lost it, as described by Coley. I did it in my usual comedic way and saw an opportunity to make a point and take the piss. Gav was the best team manager we ever had and he loved the chat. The boys loved it, as I said what we were all thinking.

I was a bit of a physical wreck at the time, which didn't help my mood. I was rocking a mohawk and had asked Dozzer to trim it up for me before leaving Australia, but none of us had noticed that the grade 2 clipper blade had a couple of teeth missing off it, so when Doz was cutting my hair in one stroke he was giving a skull cut and a grade 2. My head resembled a chewed tennis ball and I looked like I was a mild sufferer of alopecia. Which as you can imagine made me the centre of every joke going. Then, because I was bored in Napier, I decided that I would do some extra training on my own, as there was honestly nothing else to do, so at the start of the week I did a bodyweight leg circuit. Sadly, this gave me the worst case of DOMS (delayed-onset muscle soreness) I had ever had. Then, to top it all, I had gone from not getting on the field when we beat Australia, to the boats and hoes drama that I could still see the coaches did not quite believe, to being demoted to the bench for our midweek game against the Maori. Things were not going well. I kept waking up thinking that my legs would feel better, but after four days I was still in hell. On the day of the game I kept having to move, as if I sat down or rested then my legs would seize up. I didn't have the heart to tell the coaches. They mistook my constant warming up as a sign of keenness. Which was not a bad thing, as I spent the whole game wandering around like John Wayne. Napier might have been like a cemetery, but the ground that night was like a zombie apocalypse. It was a proper gnarly place, with a really intimidating crowd right on top of the pitch. And the Maori were out for English blood, as usual. In case anyone cares, they beat us 38–25.

Afterwards, we went out for a few drinks. I was standing at the bar, minding my own business, when this Maori bloke stormed up to me, steaming drunk, and started accusing me of throwing ice at him. This place was a bit spit and sawdust, a bit naughty, with a real *Once Were Warriors* vibe. But I wasn't having someone accuse me of doing something I didn't do. I hadn't thrown any ice. I think some of the lads near me had, but I hadn't. However, as I stepped towards him to say, 'Listen, you have got the wrong man,' his missus flew in from nowhere, stepped between us and started shouting, 'Leave it! Leave it!', like a local in the Queen Vic. She was flapping away in my face and when I put my hand on her shoulder, to gently manoeuvre her out of the way, she slipped over on the wet floor. The place went so quiet, you could have heard a pin drop.

When all these Maori boys started getting up from different tables and walking towards me, I almost shat myself. They kept appearing from every corner, and when I looked around the lads I had been with had shrunk into the background. The only person left next to me was Doz. I offered to help the woman up but she knocked away my hand. This was going to get a lot worse before it got better. Luckily, just before I got a hiding of a lifetime and another scandal while on England duty, another group of fans who had been watching the whole episode explained what had actually happened: that someone else had been chucking ice around and that the woman was drunk and had slipped on some water. Thank God, because if they hadn't been paying attention, I'm not sure anyone with an English accent would have made it out of there alive.

I should probably tell you about what happened when me and Dozzer finally made it to Vegas. We took the investment banker along for the ride, the one who arranged the boats and hoes trip. He didn't last long. The poor bloke had completely misjudged things, thought we were there for shopping and 'nice' dinners, kept telling us not to go mad. However, as soon as we checked into the Hard Rock hotel, me and Doz, a bit like a scene out of *Stars in Their Eyes*, walked straight into our room and came back out 30 seconds later in swimming shorts, ready to party. We took the banker to a pool party called Rehab, which used to be this mega Sunday event. We had the time of our lives but somewhere along the line lost him in between vodka cranberries, fake boobs and blaring EDM music. When we got back to the suite on the first night, or should I say early morning on the Monday, we found him in bed with sick all over him. At least it was his sick.

Minus the banker, we spent the next four days partying non-stop. The problem was a load more lads were turning up the following week. So on day five, me and Doz had a serious chat and decided that if we didn't escape Vegas for a few days, we'd run out of money and die. So we hired a car and drove to LA (hitting a kerb and breaking a wheel along the way), before spending 4 July in San Diego. And the following morning, I woke up to find that Doz had legged it. His leaving note said, 'Sorry, Jim, I can't do this anymore, going home.' In the middle of the night, he had called up the lady from the England travel company and got her to change his flight, and while I was indisposed with some female company he had smoke bombed into the night, leaving me on my tod.

I later discovered that he'd got home and then taken out a girl he'd only just met on a romantic four-day holiday to Sardinia, because he thought he was in love. I knew exactly what it was and it wasn't love. I said to him, 'Mate, you've done too much drinking and partying and that's made you all melancholy and romantic, you are just riddled with demons. A couple of days off the piss and you will be fine.' Towards the end of the holiday, Doz discovered this girl had a boyfriend in the UK and it was not quite the love he thought it was. To be fair to him, he does have previous doing this sort of thing. He once got drunk in Hong Kong and sent flowers to a girl back in the UK who he had been on a date with twice. He then drunkenly told her he loved her and that they should move in together and get a dog. He had a bit of a tricky time when he got off the trip extricating himself out of that particular bit of bullshit. The girl had started looking at houses, handed her notice in on her flat and got the dog. To this day he says to me, 'I should never have left Las Vegas early. What was I thinking?' I have never forgiven him for breaching the man code and leaving a good mate behind.

My unforgiving nature often extended to the clubs I played for. I hated it when clubs treated players badly, as happened in my final season at Wasps and which I described in detail in my last book. If players, including me, weren't getting paid what they were due or were being fobbed off with poor training facilities,

I'd stick my head above the parapet and tell the bosses that it wasn't on. That meant I got a reputation as a whistleblower or a rabble-rousing shop steward. And that's why I had to finish my career at Northampton instead.

If I thought I was being bullshitted, I had to say something. Like the time we started wearing GPS vests at Wasps, which tracked how much work we'd got through in a game or training session. The coaches were meant to use that data to tailor an individual player's training, so something like, 'Haskell needs to take it a bit easier on Tuesday and Wednesday, which means he should peak again before the game on Saturday.' But they didn't use the data like that. Instead, they only ever used it to tell us that we weren't working hard enough. It should have been a piece of hi-tech kit to refine player training, but it was just another stick to beat us with.

At one team meeting, Dai Young said, 'Listen, lads, people are complaining about training for too long, but we're only actually training for 50 minutes per day. That means we're not working hard enough.' So I put my hand up and said, 'That's just not true, Dai. I ran my Apple watch the other day and we were out there training for over two hours. I don't think your data included the warm-up, the extra scrums and line-outs.' The head conditioner confirmed that I was right, it did only include the actual rugby sessions and nothing else. Dai obviously hated that. Then he unveiled a graph that apparently showed the second team hadn't been working hard enough either and weren't getting enough metres in per week. And I put my hand up and said, 'The second team don't wear GPS vests when they're training or doing extra fitness.' There was a stunned silence, as again the conditioner had to concede this was true. Then I pointed out there were data points on the graph that could not have come from anywhere other than just being drawn in, as no players wearing vests meant no data. The meeting ended quickly after that, with the lads sniggering and Dai almost bright red with anger.

Dai was pissed as I had basically dismantled his point, but after a while I saw him call the analysis guy into his office. Half an hour later, this guy reappeared with a solitary tear running down his face, because Dai had given him the mother of all bollockings for misrepresenting the data and making him look silly in front of the lads. To be fair to Dai, he was unaware that what he was saying wasn't accurate. Look, I wasn't trying to be difficult or cause trouble, but you can't tell us one thing when we all know it's bullshit.

Whenever I took on the role of shop steward, it was never just about the fact that, for example, the facilities weren't good enough. I didn't really give a shit about the state of the training fields or the fact that people were breaking into teammates' cars or that tramps were wandering in and eating supplements with their hands. Actually, I did give a shit – it was awful – but I could have lived with it if the bosses weren't telling us that everything was fine and we should just get on with it. And when I started speaking up and they ignored me, that just made me even angrier. I found it particularly galling because people had been picking me up on my mistakes for years, rightly or wrongly. But when I pointed out other people's mistakes, I was called a troublemaker.

I don't like being told that everything's fine when it clearly isn't, or that something has to be done a certain way and can't be changed, even when it's obvious that doing it differently would be better for everyone. On the 2017 Lions tour to New Zealand, an ex-player and former teammate of mine who was a boyfriend of one of the sponsorship girls tagged along for the last two weeks. After the final Test, some of the lads went to a vineyard for the day. At some point, one of the players had gone up to ask one of the tour managers if he could buy a round of shots and some more drinks for the boys. And this spare part piped up with, 'Only if you lads buy us a nice bottle of wine.' Nobody said anything, but everyone was looking at each other and raising their eyebrows, as if to say, 'Who the fuck is this bloke telling us what to do? He wasn't even invited and he is not even a Lion or a former Lion.'

Later that night, a few of the lads sent him some voice messages, taking the piss out of him for demanding drinks when he wasn't even an official part of the tour. They had called his room and made themselves a nuisance, told him he wasn't welcome and should shut up. It was probably a bit harsh, but par for the course and nothing that he didn't deserve. At least no one filled him in, which after two days of drinking could have been a real possibility. The following morning I came down for breakfast and found out that a few of the lads had been taken into a room for a dressing down. When I say a few I mean ten lads, and the dressing down had been some long-winded inquiry with people taking notes and lads having to give written statements as to what happened. It was utter crap. I heard from the shamed players that the female partner had been too upset to be in the room, but her boyfriend, the troublemaker, was in there casting aspersions and looking down his nose at the lads. One of the couple's close friends was also on the senior management team and he somehow got himself involved, and had tears in his eyes and a wobble to his voice, saying that in all the years of knowing this lady he had never seen her so low, and that she'd never been made to feel so small and would never go on another Lions tour.

Imagine being in a room hungover and having to listen to this crap? It was pathetic on every level. All the lads were then made to apologise to this bloke. He said, 'While I accept your apology, I feel that you have let the shirt down with your behaviour and being a Lion means you should act in a different way.' He said that they should all 'take a lesson from this unpleasantness'. On hearing this, I firstly had to check that no one had died, no one had been physically attacked and all this fuss was over a couple of texts and some late calls on a hotel phone. Once that was confirmed, I stormed off half-cut to find the team manager.

'This is utter bullshit and embarrassing!' I said to him. As far as I was concerned, if the guy couldn't take a bit of ribbing, that was his problem. He certainly shouldn't have been demanding players buy him drinks and crying when they gave him stick for it. Plus, if he had a beef, he should have come to us, instead of grassing us up. On top of all that, the manager shouldn't have dressed players down as if he was a headmaster and they were a bunch of schoolboys. The tour was over, nothing had happened and they were treating all the boys like criminals.

I hate shit like that, people being pious and officious for no good reason. I told him he could have just said to the girl, 'Listen, the lads were just taking the piss out of your boyfriend, no need to be dramatic.' That to be fair to the lads he shouldn't have even been on a social with them, he wasn't a Lion and was acting like a bit of a dickhead. The manager, who was a good guy, told me that the players' behaviour was unacceptable, and I lost it all over again. I just couldn't get my head around the fact that we'd just drawn an epic series against the All Blacks and they were being upbraided for taking the piss out of some bloke who wasn't even meant to be there.

Remember, I hadn't even been involved in sending the bloke messages, and now I was in the thick of it. I just couldn't stay out of it, because I was so annoyed that my teammates were being hauled over the coals when they should have been enjoying a remarkable achievement. Half the players who got bollocked were not even involved. Imagine spending your last morning on tour writing out affidavits when you should be having a laugh. I sought out the member of management who had been so emotional and told him to pull himself together and stop being so fucking weak. He didn't like that, so we had a row. I knew I was never going to be a Lion again, so honestly I didn't give a fuck. I just told him how it was and walked off, while he tried to justify the unjustifiable. It was important I stood up for the boys and did what was right. A lot of them were young players who ended up going again on tour to South Africa in 2021 and I didn't want them being earmarked as troublemakers. Once the lads heard I had gone in to bat for them, they all thanked me. Which is all that matters.

During England camps at Pennyhill Park, the players would use the spa facilities, which often meant rubbing shoulders with members of the public. Literally. We'd be in the hot tub and an absolutely smoking woman (often in a very small bikini) would slide in and start chatting to us, while drinking a glass of champagne. But whenever that happened, I'd jump straight out and run away. The way I saw it, I wasn't good-looking enough for some random stunner to start chatting me up and assumed it must have been a honey trap. The juice was never worth the squeeze on those occasions. The usual clientele were more often than not slightly overweight, married or divorced women, or couples away for the weekend, not absolute worldies.

Anyway, one day this woman with huge fake boobs slid in beside one of my teammates (who I'll refer to as Norman, to be on the safe side) and said, 'Hello, I'm Cecilia. How do you do?' They had a perfectly normal conversation and Norman thought nothing more of it until a couple of days later, when a hotel worker placed a black envelope in front of him while he was having breakfast. It had beautiful writing on the front in smart gold pen. Norman opened it with some trepidation and the card inside read, 'Dear Norman, it was lovely to meet you in the hot tub the other day. If you're ever interested in some no-strings fun, here's my number.' As you can imagine, the other lads were loving it. But Norman was engaged to be married, and wasn't the cheating type, so dropped the card straight in the bin.

Norman wasn't involved in that weekend's game, and having been in camp the following Monday and Tuesday, was sent home early, having not been picked again. So he was at home with his fiancée when he got a call from Stuart Lancaster, who said, 'Listen, Norman, we've had a man come into Pennyhill Park, shouting and screaming to whoever will listen that you've been fucking his wife, that he wants to kill you and that he's going to tell the *Sun*. We have tried to get him to leave but he won't go until you address it.' Norman was sitting next to his fiancée at the time and frantically denied it. But when Stuart said he'd also been accused of texting this femme fatale saucy messages, Norman's fiancée quite naturally thought there was no smoke without fire. Before hanging up, Stuart landed the killer punch, telling Norman that he'd have to apologise.

Norman was now in a very sticky situation. He hadn't done what he was accused of doing, but it didn't matter how many times he denied it, because the husband claimed they had the saucy texts to prove it and the RFU seemed to believe them. This was like my situation at the 2011 World Cup all over again, with the England management just wanting to make the situation disappear, even if it meant throwing one of their players under a bus. What made it worse was that it happened under the whiter than white regime of Stuart Lancaster, who was always trying to avoid this very thing.

The RFU kept insisting that Norman write this bloke an apology letter, and Norman kept telling them he'd done nothing wrong. In the end, they said they were going to write it themselves and get Norman to sign it.

When the RFU called back some time later, Norman was in the car with his missus, so the whole conversation was now on speaker phone. The person from the RFU read the letter out aloud and it went something like this: 'Dear John, I'm desperately sorry for sending inappropriate messages to your wife, it was completely unacceptable, etc.' By now, Norman's fiancée was pulling her hair out, because she just couldn't comprehend how Norman hadn't done anything when the RFU were forcing him to apologise. But instead of signing this letter, Norman phoned me, told me what was going on and asked for some advice. I told him, whatever you do, do not sign that or agree to it. If you did nothing wrong, then never apologise. I then put him in touch with the lawyers who'd cost me a fortune when the whole New Zealand debacle was happening to me.

Norman's lawyers exchanged letters with the RFU's lawyers, who were still only interested in making this so-called scandal disappear rather than clearing Norman's name. Remember, Stuart Lancaster's regime was supposed to be a clean break from the previous regime, which the media had portrayed as resembling the last days of Rome. As long as everything seemed perfect and holier than thou, that was all that mattered to them. Meanwhile, Norman's lawyer fees were mounting up and his relationship was on the verge of collapse. Then, one of our teammates admitted that it was him and another player who'd been sending this woman saucy texts, having fished her card out of the bin. However, they were too scared to come forward and beg Norman to take the heat.

By now, Norman's lawyer fees had hit something like 12 grand (for the drafting and sending of two or three letters), so he got on the phone to the two teammates who'd stitched him up and asked them to help out. The player who'd owned up agreed to contribute, but the other one refused. So when Norman got a tip-off that this refusenik was on his way to the airport, he jumped in his car, with the intention of filling him in before he got on the plane. Norman was texting this player's fellow teammates, telling them to hold him there until he dealt with him.

If the England management had just believed Norman and told this woman's husband to piss off, this whole fiasco would never have happened. That was what made the situation so ironic – in their desperation to portray Stuart Lancaster's regime as squeaky clean, they'd ended up creating an absolute clusterfuck, just as they'd done with the rogue maid situation in New Zealand. Norman had lawyers chasing him for money he didn't have (although he didn't end up paying anything, because he never signed the letter of intent), he'd fallen out with one of his teammates (he didn't reach the airport before the plane took off, mercifully) and his fiancée had come very close to dumping him. That was the RFU all over back then, likely to fly into a blind panic at the first sign of controversy. If someone had accused an England player of assassinating JFK, they would have got him to sign a letter admitting his guilt.

*   *   *

When Stuart Lancaster took over as head coach, he was desperate to reconnect with the fans and grassroots rugby. There was a lot of talk about heritage and culture and pride in the shirt, and Stuart became very involved in all the little details. Stuart was a keen student of military history and requested shirts with little Victoria Crosses on them. He also dreamt up the 'Arthur Harrison Award' for defensive excellence, which was presented to a player after each match and named after the only England rugby international to receive the Victoria Cross. Arthur's family came in and did a presentation, described how he'd been shot in the head during an engagement with the Germany navy and carried on fighting, before being gunned down on his ship's gangway. There was also a lot of talk about putting the team before money – doing it for the pride, rather than the perks – which sounded a bit rich when Stuart's entire family joined us on a pre-World Cup training camp in Denver for a family jolly. The immortal quote 'All animals are equal but some animals are more equal than others' springs to mind. No one would have given a toss if he hadn't gone on about 'team first' all the time. The lads were pretty fed up by that stage and there was plenty of talking in corners about how he used security to ferry him and his family around like personal chauffeurs. Rest assured, if I ever got into power you would know I was in power. It would be much more of a dictatorship than some socialist sham, but at least I wouldn't hide it.

One of Stuart's gimmicks was this old bell he'd got from the Navy, which he set up at the training centre in Pennyhill. The management didn't really know what to do with it, but finally decided that someone would ring it to signify the end of a game review, on the Monday after a Test match. It sounded quite cute after a win, but after we lost to Wales at the 2015

World Cup the bell rang and someone shouted, 'Iceberg ahead!' (when I say someone, of course I mean me). The coaches were trying to be serious while the lads were pissing themselves, and Stuart was furious, looking around for the gagster. As it turned out, I was spot on – we lost our next game against Australia and sank like the *Titanic*, failing to progress from the group.

Don't get me wrong, I think it's important for the England team to be connected to the fans, grassroots rugby and the history of the sport. Without the fans, grassroots teams and the England players that came before us, we wouldn't exist. But the truth is, all the off-field things that went wrong at the 2011 World Cup had nothing to do with any of that stuff. It was just a bad team environment, our standards weren't good enough and we kept getting stitched up. And while I understood what Stuart was trying to do, some of it was overkill and ended up being a bit annoying. It's nice to get a message from an old coach or a family member every now and again, but it was happening all the time under Stuart. And it didn't always have the desired effect. When they asked my dad to record a video, he looked straight at the camera and said, 'Your mother and I are very proud of you but try not to lose this weekend, James.'

Before the 2015 World Cup, Stuart went big on getting us to learn from people from other fields, to teach us about team-work and leadership. There was the day out at the Metropolitan Police public order training centre in Kent, which I described in my last book and which only succeeded in giving the lads blisters and aching backs and necks. He also got a bloke in from the Special Forces, to talk about working in small teams. Then there was a guy from the Red Arrows, who spoke about the importance of executing the minute aspects of your role to absolute perfection. Some of these talks were brilliant, really inspiring. And when we were told a policeman was coming in to talk about his experience combating terrorist attacks, we thought it would be more of the same. Alas, it didn't really turn out like that.

When this guy was introduced as a hero of the 2013 Nairobi shopping mall attack, all the lads were psyched. Everyone was suddenly leaning forward in their chairs, expecting the yarn of the century, something to rival the famous SAS Iranian Embassy siege. I thought Tom Wood was going to explode with excitement, because anything to do with guns is right up his alley.

So when this guy kicked off his PowerPoint presentation with a photo of his mum, my heart was in my mouth. I was thinking, 'Jesus, this bloke's mum died in the attack. Or maybe he dragged her out of the mall under a hail of bullets.' But then the guy said, 'I was planning a family excursion on the day of the attack, which is why my mother was over.' So his mum hadn't been involved in the siege at all, she just happened to be round his house at the time. It's not like I wanted her to die, but I did kind of hope she'd been in some kind of danger.

I think it's fair to say his story never really recovered. He explained how he'd been sitting at home, planning this family excursion, when his colleague Colin phoned and said, 'John, I'm in the mall and I've just seen four gunmen walk in with AK-47s. I think it's a terrorist attack and you need to get down here.' At that point, we were all thinking, 'Yes! Here we go! John's gonna grab his weapons and stun grenades, get his arse down to the mall and smoke some bad guys.' And when John started explaining that he almost left his 'most important bit of equipment' behind, we thought he meant his M16 rifle or his anti-tank rocket launcher. Instead, he'd had to go back for his miniature forensic kit. We were all like, 'Miniature what?!' He surely must have meant gun, not forensic kit. We were all looking around at each other thinking, 'Oh God, where is this going?'

Every time I thought some danger was about to kick in and I was shifting towards the edge of my seat, John quickly doused the excitement. There followed a rambling sub-plot about him not being able to find a parking spot for his van and blocking people in, before a detailed description of how he'd set up a perimeter, 500 metres from the attack, got some bloke to make a list of everyone in the area and put out boxes in which to store evidence. He said he could feel bullets flying past his head, but that seemed unlikely, given how far away he was and the fact there were only four terrorists, who were engaged in a close-quarters firefight with half of Kenya's armed police force. Instead, it had become abundantly clear that while his mate Colin was armed to the teeth and at the heart of the battle, John was essentially in charge of admin.

John went on to describe how he received a phone call from Colin, telling him he was coming out of the rear fire exit with ten civilians. Weirdly, John put the phone down on him. We were all thinking, 'Why did he do that? He's supposed to be teaching us to think clearly under pressure and he's just told us how he left his mate, who had bullets flying past his ears, hanging on the phone, not knowing if John was going to be there if and when he got out.' His point was that you need to stay calm under pressure and take a moment before sharing information, hence why he had put the phone down on Colin to take the sting out the heightened adrenaline his mate must have been experiencing.

John did phone him back and arranged to meet Colin at the rear of the mall to save these civilians. John then hot-footed it to a rear door. But when Colin and the civilians came flying out of the exit, John shouted at him, 'Have you checked the civilians for bombs?' Colin's just saved ten people from a terrorist attack and the first thing he hears when he escapes is some bloke trying to admin him to death. Colin of course replied, 'Have I fuck, I just wanted to get them out!' So John got his mate to check them all over – while he had, in his own words, a 'hot debrief' with Colin! By now, the lads were exchanging bemused looks and struggling to stifle laughter. This hot debrief was about getting info quickly and concisely when under pressure. Colin explained what was going on, and said he was going to go back in and save more people. John then shouted, 'Don't forget hydration!', before thrusting a bottle of water into Colin's hand. Colin then ran back in under fire while John marshalled the gathered crowd, took names and labelled things in boxes.

Apparently, Colin ended up saving about a hundred people that day, while John was dealing with admin. I think John's lesson was that everyone has their own job to do in a high-pressure situation, and whether you're the hero saving hostages or the man setting up a perimeter, putting out boxes and making sure people drink enough water, it's important that you all pay attention to details and execute your role properly, as one could not happen without the other. But the lads were just a bit underwhelmed. It was like hearing about the Iranian embassy siege from the point of view of a cop who was standing half a mile away, directing traffic. If you have ever seen the movie *The Other Guys* with Mark Wahlberg and Will Ferrell, John was definitely one of the other guys. He was the guy doing the paperwork while the hero cops saved lives. All of which is very important to the running of a team, but I'm not sure you can make a talk out of it.

When John had finished his talk, he asked if anyone had any questions. Tom Wood put his hand up and said, 'Did you have a gun? And did you want to go in there?' John said he didn't have a gun, and that he wouldn't have gone in there anyway, even if he had one. Woody, gun lover that he is, couldn't get his head around that. Then I put my hand up and said to the team manager, 'Could you not have got Colin to come in and tell his story?' The lads had a meltdown after that, laughing their arses off. I couldn't see Stuart Lancaster's evil stare, but I could feel it burning a hole in my head.

I know it probably sounds like we were being a bit mean. But the talk would have been fine if it hadn't been sold to us as a hair-raising tale of derring-do. However, instead of the shooting and death we wanted, we got the story of a man who parked his car badly, got the crowd to move back using the 'power of his commanding voice' and put out some boxes, before putting the phone down on his imperilled mate, shouting 'Hot debrief!' in his face and telling him to drink some water.

When I told that story on *The Good, The Bad & The Rugby*, Stuart Lancaster phoned Alex Payne and said, 'What was Haskell on about? That wasn't true. All the lads absolutely loved that talk. They were inspired.' We weren't inspired, Stuart, you just thought we were. Truth was, we spent the next few weeks shouting 'Hot debrief!' at each other. And whenever someone started to reply, we'd tell them to 'shut up and hydrate'. Once I get something like that in my head, I can't let it go. And, as I've previously said, one of the peculiarities of Stuart's regime was that the management didn't know what the players thought about stuff, because they didn't feel like they could be frank.

DYLAN HARTLEY:

'James was pretty brash and direct and not everyone's cup of tea, but I think some of that was down to other people's insecurities. I had a lot of time for his humour. He was well rehearsed in changing-room banter; if anyone fired shots his way, he fired back pretty quick. A lot of his humour was quite inappropriate, but most things that are funny are inappropriate. And as the world gets more PC, it's good to have people like James who cut straight through the bullshit.

'I never felt like he let himself down. We came through the ranks together, rubbed off on each other, goaded each other. And to have a friend like James who would load bullets and get other people to fire them made life a lot of fun. Life as an England rugby player can be quite boring, because you spend a lot of time travelling and in hotel rooms. So you need people like James to bring energy. Some of what happened, like the maid incident at the 2011 World Cup, was pretty shit at the time. But once we were out the other side, it gave us something to talk and laugh about over a pint. And he's now telling all these stories on podcasts and in books. People don't just want to hear about what happened on the pitch, and I'd hate to have nothing to talk about in my retirement, because I was too vanilla, with no flavour.'

When I first got into the England team, the coaching staff had a strange fascination with motivational videos. And they didn't always make a lot of sense. On the 2008 tour of New Zealand, the media team put together a highlights reel for us to watch. They put a Europop remix of the *Gladiator* theme over the top, which was nice. Unfortunately, it didn't mask the fact that the best player in the video was Jamie Noon, who hadn't been picked for the first Test. Other players in the video hadn't even made the touring party, so I walked out of the room thinking, 'Do they want us to think they brought the wrong players?' (Maybe they did, because the All Blacks hammered us in both games.)

I thought it couldn't get any worse than that, but when we played the All Blacks again at Twickenham a few months later the coaching team went full self-sabotage. Two days before the game, the squad was ushered into a room and one of the coaches said, 'We've got something for you.' He dimmed the lights, pressed play on his laptop and we were treated to a highlights reel of the two Tests we'd only recently lost in New Zealand, mashed up with audio from the Gerard Butler swords and sandals film *300*. This video mainly consisted of Ma'a Nonu repeatedly carving us up and making us look stupid, and cut away to Gerard Butler screaming, 'Hold, hold!' And as soon as the coaches left the room, the boys all dissolved into hysterics. We were literally howling with laughter, with tears running down our cheeks. If I remember rightly, Joe Worsley was laughing so much he fell off his chair.

I have no idea what the coaches were hoping to achieve, but the main lesson I took from that video was that Ma'a Nonu was absolutely incredible. Afterwards, we gave the video editor some serious stick. While he was trying to eat his dinner, players kept shouting at him, 'What the fuck were you thinking? Now I'm shitting myself!' And not only was it bad for player morale, but it caused tension between us and the coaching staff, because they all heard us howling with laughter and spent the rest of the day giving us the evils.

Remarkably, they kept plugging away with these videos. The day before the game at Twickenham, as we were getting ready for the team run, Martin Johnson, who'd just taken over as head coach, said, 'Right, this is massive. You don't really have to think about it, you know how intense it's going to be, but we do have something for you ...' Johnno pressed play on the DVD and it was that scene from *Goodfellas*, where Ray Liotta pistol whips some bloke to within an inch of his life, because he's been hassling his wife. There was no audio at all this time, it was just Ray pulling up in his car, strolling over to the bloke and repeatedly whacking him on the head with his gun. The screen went black, before the words 'England versus New Zealand – Bring the Violence' appeared. Then Johnno said, 'Right, everyone out for the warm-up.' I could sense that the video had not gone as planned as the computer guy was getting a bollocking as we all trundled out into the Friday sunshine.

On the way out, I had a word with Graham Rowntree.

'Graham, I'm confused. Do I have to bring a gun to the game tomorrow?'

Cue all the lads laughing, or stifling laughs, to be more accurate.

'Shut the fuck up, Haskell,' he snapped back.

'But seriously, do I? Because I don't have one at the moment and I'm not sure where to get one from before tomorrow's game. Oi, Borthers, have you got your gun ready?'

'You're an idiot, Hask. Get on with your warm-up and keep shtum,' replied Graham, while Steve Borthwick ran off so no one could see his smile as he was meant to be captain and knew the video was a shit choice.

It transpired that the video guy had fucked up again and forgotten to put the sound on. I'm not sure it would have made any difference. After the team run was over, I shouted, 'Right, lads, don't forget to pack your shooters tomorrow. Apparently that's the only way we're going to stop Ma'a Nonu ...'

You won't believe it, but after all the piss-taking and jokes they played the same video once again in our final team meeting before we left Pennyhill to play the game, this time with sound. It made no sense with sound either, and we got pumped by NZ at Twickenham. I brought the violence and got yellow carded, so all in all it was a terrible day in the office.

People assume that everything about the England set-up is going to be the absolute height of professionalism, but that wasn't the case, at least not until Eddie Jones took over as head coach. Instead of assembling the best of the best, the RFU mainly hired whoever would take the least money to do a job and wouldn't speak out of turn. Don't get me wrong, they were all good guys with the best intentions, but they'd constantly be doing things that would make me think, 'Are you serious?'

Take the team doctor. Simon Shaw had a massive lump on his chin, which was getting bigger and bigger. All the boys were calling him Gungan, out of *Star Wars*. Ronnie Regan gave him hell, turning into half-pirate, half-parrot. Every time Shawsy was within earshot, Ronnie would say, 'Errr, Gungan, Shawsy, Gungan …' Shawsy was getting very down about it, so he went to the doctor and said, 'Listen, I've got this lump on my chin. I really need to know what's going on with it.' The doctor gave him the once-over and prescribed him some pills, but they didn't work. And a couple of days later, Shawsy was back saying that it was no good and he needed outside help. The doc assured him he would sort it and promised he'd consult an expert. Shawsy pretended to leave the doctor's office but instead waited a couple of seconds and then crept back in up behind him while he was crouched over his laptop, and saw that the guy was googling 'How to fix a swollen chin'. After that, everyone started calling him Dr Google, Ronnie Regan more than most.

Anyway, back to the motivational videos. Not only were these an amateurish joke, but they made me think the coaches didn't understand us. Why did they think a violent scene from *Goodfellas* was going to motivate us to play better? Did they seriously all sit around and say, 'If anything's going to get them up for the game, it's that clip of Ray Liotta bashing someone's brains in'?

We hadn't beaten New Zealand for five years, and most of the players involved in England's most recent victory over them had retired, so they had no business making a highlights video. And unlike most of my teammates, I wasn't able to shut up about it. I just couldn't resist. For the record, the All Blacks stuffed us 32–6, while Nonu ran in a brilliant try from the halfway line and was named man of the match.

On the subject of pre-match motivation, Jamie Joseph gave some brilliant pre-match team talks when I was at the Highlanders. Before one big game, he turned up with a cross on a small plinth, which he put on the table and said, 'Right, lads, whenever you build something, you don't start at the top, you start with the foundations and then you start laying the bricks one by one. During pre-season, when you were going to some very dark places, you were laying the foundations. And every training session, gym session and game since, that was you laying another brick. You will always have setbacks and issues like we have had this season, but if you stick to the plan and put the work in then things go well and you are able to finish the project. And once every brick has been laid, only then do you get to put the steeple on the top as the finishing piece.' At that point, he picked up the cross, slammed it upright on the table and said, 'Tonight is your chance to go one step closer to putting that steeple on the top of all your hard work. Three more games between now and the final. Don't waste all the effort, let's build one more layer on what are some incredibly strong foundations.' It really made sense and resonated with all the players. I am sure I haven't done it justice in the recounting of it, but it was one of the best pre-match talks I have heard. We won that game but sadly fell short in the next.

Before another game, against the Crusaders, Jamie put a jug of water and two pint glasses on a table. Then he started comparing the teams. Every time he named one of their players against one of our players, he'd pour some water into one of the glasses of the team he felt had the upper hand in that position. He was honest and brutal about it. He talked about all of a player's qualities, not just his on-field ability but what he was like as a person. Remember from *What a Flanker* Jamie focused very heavily on his players being GCs (good cunts). The only time he really poured more water in for one of their players was when he got to Dan Carter, and I felt a bit sorry for our number 10. But by the end our pint glass was overflowing and their pint glass wasn't quite full. That was Jamie saying to his inexperienced team, 'Look, I know you think they're unbeatable, but when you compare yourselves to them as individuals, one on one, we add up to more than them.' If I am recounting the story right, as I was not there, Clive Woodward did something similar and basically said before an England game against NZ that he would not swap one of his players for one of theirs. It was then that Will Greenwood stood up and said I think we can all agree that we would 100 per cent swap Jonah Lomu for Austin Healey. Of course, everyone pissed themselves.

Those kinds of team talks, with lots of symbolism, can be a bit naff and clichéd, and you can't be rolling them out all season. But if you pull one out every once in a while, they can be very inspiring. Certainly more inspiring than Dai Young's team talk before a Wasps game against Leinster. For about half an hour, he showed us slide after slide of all the negative things the media had written about us. I understood what he was trying to do, but it didn't work on that occasion. By the end of it, I was thinking, 'Jesus, Dai, this is depressing. By laying it on so thick, all you've done is convince us the media might be right.' It's hard being a coach as sometimes you gamble and it comes off and other times you get it wrong. For me, if your whole game and mental state rested on what the coach said pre-game, you had already lost. I didn't really listen as it didn't matter what they said, I was as prepared as I ever was going to be before I played. I had my routine and I didn't need a Churchillian speech to rouse me.

During the most recent 2021 Lions tour, they played Ian McGeechan's famous speech from the 1997 Lions tour over and over again. It was brilliant, one of the best you will hear. However, that was not always the norm with the coaches or Geech. When Geech coached Wasps, half the lads had no idea what he was talking about during most pre-match meetings, so much so that Shaun Edwards would be hopping from foot to foot to interrupt him so he could fire us back up again. The media hype up this part of a coach and captain's role, but if you need words that late in the day to get you up for a game, you are doomed. We are all professional, and while it may sound nice and may give you 30 seconds of surface motivation, it's not going to make much of a difference. I would say that it's 50/50 whether the coach motivates or demotivates with their final words.

The only thing I had to avoid pre-match was a coach trying to motivate me by telling me I was crap, or this was my last chance to prove myself or else I would be dropped. Yes, that happened more than once. It was the demotivation that was my enemy on game day. Coaches often played amateur psychologist without realising they were doing more harm than good.

As with a lot of my personality traits, I get my hatred of jobsworths from my dad. Like me, my dad doesn't put up with anyone misusing their power, and it doesn't matter what uniform they're wearing or what badge is attached to it.

One afternoon, we were having a meeting with my agent in the Gaucho restaurant in Chelsea. The drinks were flowing and everything was going very nicely, until I noticed a traffic warden writing out a penalty fine for my dad's car, which was parked right outside the restaurant. I ran out and tried to explain that my dad had bought a parking ticket, but this traffic warden was having none of it. He had written the penalty ticket and was going to put it on come what may. I ran back into the restaurant, got my dad's keys and showed him that his ticket had fallen off the dashboard but was valid. He still wasn't listening. So in the end I said to my dad, 'I haven't drunk anything, so I'll move your car around the corner before he can slap the fine on. It doesn't count if they don't put it on your car and photograph it.' I had seen that he hadn't done that; if you watch wardens now they put the empty sticker on first, then photograph it and fill the ticket out after. It means you can't drive off like people were doing to stop them making the whole process valid.

I had to move my car first because that ticket had expired. And when I returned, my dad was standing there waving a valid parking ticket in this traffic warden's face, stopping him getting to his car. Whenever he moved my dad moved in front of him. All the while, my dad was trying to explain what had happened, but it didn't matter how many times we told the bloke to cancel the fine, he refused to listen. He wouldn't even look at us, he just kept saying, 'I can't, I can't, I've written it now …' With my dad being old and having sunk a few beers, the traffic warden managed to jink past him and slap the fine on my dad's windscreen, and that was the beginning of the end.

As soon as the traffic warden got his camera out to take a photo, my dad, for some reason only known to him, snatched the camera out of his hand. He then shouted to me to move the car. I was gobsmacked but moved it anyway. I lobbed the penalty ticket into the bin on the way back to the restaurant. When I came back, I saw that my dad was now trying to give the warden his camera back, but every time he was offered it he turned away. This went on for about five minutes until I got so fucked off I took the camera and tried to put it in his hands. He just let it drop to the floor. Finally, when he turned round I dropped it down his shirt and said, 'There you are, mate. Stop being a dickhead.' He then shook it out onto the floor again and left it there. By this stage, it was abundantly clear that all this bloke wanted to do was get us into trouble. The warden was on his radio calling for what I assumed was backup. He was the stereotypical traffic warden, unwilling to listen or compromise.

My dad was getting more and more agitated trying to calmly reason with this unresponsive nightmare of a human being, so eventually I said to him, 'Look, let's go back inside and leave him to it.' But having resumed our meeting back inside the restaurant, we were laughing about the ridiculousness of the situation when the backup started arriving. After about ten minutes, there were three more traffic wardens outside, astride mopeds. And when four police cars and a riot van pulled up, I suddenly stopped laughing, looked at the other two and said, 'Fuck. This could end really badly.' The other person at the table was my agent Duncan Sandlant from Esportif, who was also a lawyer. Even he was looking slightly concerned.

The police entered the restaurant and chatted to the maître d', who then wandered over to my dad.

'Sorry, sir, the police would like to speak to you.'

'Send them in!' my dad replied in a sort of lord of the manor way.

'No, sir, they'd like to speak to you outside.'

As I was exiting the restaurant, one of the coppers said, 'What's your name, sir?' and before I could reply he'd written 'James Haskell' on his pad. Because the traffic warden had told them he was being intimidated by two burly men, some of these cops were armed. The police station was only a few doors down, but it must have been a seriously slow day on the murder and crime front. What did they think we were going to do? Start a shootout over a parking fine? I was used to this kind of thing so started denying everything and saying no comment. However, my dad quickly owned up to taking the traffic warden's camera but fought his corner ferociously. He certainly wasn't taking the rap for dropping the camera. And when the police saw the valid parking ticket, you could tell they were having to make every effort not to sigh and roll their eyes.

Having established that the Gunfight at the Gaucho was highly unlikely to break out, most of the cops drifted off, before we were persuaded to apologise to the traffic warden. It was like being told off by a headmaster for fighting. The police made the traffic warden shake our hands and we had to shake his, all pretending we were sorry. It was quite weird seeing my dad saying sorry. He made it seem sincere, but I could tell he was saying it through gritted teeth.

That's just one example of how quickly a Haskell family situation can spiral out of control. There we were, having a quiet lunch, when suddenly there were four police cars and a riot van screaming down the street and we were being accused of harassment and criminal damage. It wasn't the proudest moment in Haskell history, but … WE DIDN'T START IT – THE OTHER BLOKE DID! If we ever build a Haskell family mausoleum, these words will be chiselled on the front in perpetuity.

Here's another weird thing that happened at the 2011 World Cup, undoubtedly the most shambolic tour in history. We were based in Dunedin, at the Southern Cross Hotel, which wasn't really set up for a professional rugby squad. It was small and claustrophobic and had a casino, which was dangerous for a load of lads who were bored out of their minds (although I should remind you that some of them had already lost most of their tour fee at a casino in Auckland). That's why Dylan Hartley bought an old banger, so that me and him could drive around the city and let our hair down a bit.

So when the media manager asked if we wanted to spend one of our days off driving Land Rovers on a beach, riding a helicopter, doing water sports, playing cricket and football and getting stuck into a barbecue, we almost tore the bloke's arm off.

On the day, I was put in a Land Rover with former England lock Martin Bayfield, who was working for ITV, his camera-man and a Land Rover off-road guru. There were five Land Rovers in total, all packed with players and driving instruct-ors, and the atmosphere on the way to the beach was buoyant. It was a bit like that scene in *One Flew Over the Cuckoo's Nest* when Jack Nicholson busts the inmates out of the asylum for a fishing trip. But we sensed it was going to be a bad day when we came to a halt on this super-flat beach that doubled as a road. Call me a mad dreamer, but I was expecting quick-sand and dunes that were 20 feet high. It didn't help the mood that a couple of the Land Rovers took a wrong turn, got lost and finally arrived an hour late.

After a bit of beach cricket, the instructors told us to jump in our vehicles. But instead of getting us to do doughnuts and wheelspins, the only instruction they gave us was not to drive too fast. So there we all were, driving in convoy at about 30 mph, when a helicopter with cameras attached to the bottom came swooping over. At first, I thought, 'Wow, that's cool.' But after a while I realised that the day had been mis-sold – this wasn't a fun day out for the lads, we were actually being used as props for a Land Rover advert.

Inevitably, the lads soon got bored of pootling around like *Driving Miss Daisy* – we may as well have been on the M25 during rush hour – and started acting up. When I pulled out of the line and raced off down the beach, one of the instructors started screaming at me to stop, but the others soon followed suit. I don't think Manu Tuilagi even had a licence, but he must have been travelling at 70 mph, while Ben Foden was hanging halfway out of the window with Chris Ashton holding his feet.

After a few minutes of chaos, the instructors managed to persuade us to fall back into line. But we'd soon go rogue again. Eventually, the instructors went from vehicle to vehicle, ordering us to behave, but by that stage we were getting a bit mutinous. Some of the lads were calling the instructors 'the fun police', while others wanted to know what had happened to the water sports and the barbecue. What made matters worse was that we each had a CB radio that was connected to every-one else. The lads all got on these and started taking the piss. Every time the lead guy would shout, 'Slow down!' or 'Get off the radio!' you would get a thousand responses of 'Err, fun police!', 'Calm down, Nigel Thornberry!' or 'You are not in charge, we are!' The main bloke was going mental and yet no one was paying any attention. He would say slow down, the lads would speed up and go racing near the waves or do sharp manoeuvres on the sand.

The lads didn't take kindly to being told off like kids on a school trip. What did the instructors think was going to happen when a load of lads in their twenties found out that the fun day they'd been promised was actually an ad shoot that was going to take up their entire day off? They could have been doing other things with their time instead, so they weren't placated by a cold wrap and a bottle of lukewarm water. The barbecue, like the rest of the day, was a myth. And when they told me and a few other lads that we weren't allowed a ride in the helicopter, which had been part of the deal, I was really quite pissed off, as were the others.

Now I was actually sponsored by Land Rover at the time, and when I was taken to one side during a break in the carnage and had the reality of the day explained to me, I decided to sharpen up. This was not a fun day out but a very expensive ad shoot, and the Land Rover top brass were going mad that it was not happening as they wanted. There was no barbecue and no beach games. Land Rover had paid for the helicopter cameraman who had filmed on *The Lord of the Rings* to come and shoot this day at great expense.

I got the lads together and said, 'Look, let's just get this driving stuff done. We have to stop fucking about, they're going mad. Let's let them get their footage and then we can get the hell out of here.' The other senior lads agreed and we spent the next hour or so driving along the beach like pensioners in golf carts on a Californian retirement estate, with the players grumbling into their walkie-talkies.

When we were done, everyone parked up one more time for some photos. It was then that Martin Bayfield asked for an interview for the ITV World Cup coverage. I should add that his cameraman had been rolling all day and had captured most of the madness. So we parked up, found somewhere quiet and chatted for ten minutes on camera. But when we wandered back around the corner, everyone else had pissed off and left us behind. Because they all had the hump, no one had noticed we were missing or bothered to check, and no one from Land Rover or the RFU did a head count. The lads must have seen an empty Range, got into it and just raced back off to the hotel. I thought it was a joke for a minute, but as I looked around and there was no sign of any cars or any people, nothing, the stark reality of being left behind in the arse end of nowhere on a beach miles from our hotel slowly sank in.

Me and Martin were in back of the beyond somewhere in New Zealand with no car, no mobile phone signal and no water. Luckily, there was also a cameraman with us, so I had someone to play up to. While Martin was looking worried and holding his phone up to the sky in a desperate attempt to get a signal, I was going on about me and Martin having to live together in the wilderness for the rest of our lives, our only food the cows in a nearby field.

Half an hour went by, followed by another half an hour. Still no sign of anyone. Bear in mind that my name was already mud, because of Maidgate, and now I'd upset all these Land Rover people. On top of that, my missus was arriving later that day. Me rolling in six hours after 'enjoying' a fun day out driving Land Rovers on the beach would have gone down like a shit sandwich. And then I'd have to tell her about the maid allegations. There was no telling how she might react, and she didn't trust me at the best of times.

After an hour and a half we decided to yomp up a hill to see if we could get a signal. It took us an hour to get up. And just as we were nearing the top, this 4x4 came screaming into view, crammed with redneck Kiwis. It was like a scene from *Deliverance*, and we briefly feared we might be tortured and spit-roasted (food- and sex-wise). They were actually lovely and gave us a lift to the top of this hill, where we managed to get a couple of bars of signal. I phoned one of the RFU ladies and said, 'Have you forgotten something?' She said, 'I don't think so,' and I shouted back, 'Yes you fucking have! You left me, Bayfield and the cameraman behind!'

This woman couldn't believe it. They'd already been home for two hours. She said they'd send a car and we spent the next hour or so on this freezing hilltop, throwing stones at a glass bottle. She kept calling us back to make sure we weren't taking the piss. The glass bottle game was a great distraction until we hit it and it broke, ending any entertainment. In the end, we just sat on the grass, leaning up against a fence and staring into space. That must have been a melancholy sight.

When we finally got back to the hotel, I was confronted by my missus, who didn't believe I'd been left behind. And after she'd calmed down, I had to tell her about the maid. As I'd suspected, the news was not well received.

After the RFU carried out its World Cup review and it all got leaked to the press, the icing on the cake was that Land Rover then cancelled their very lucrative sponsorship of the England team, citing the day out as the reason. They said it had been a nightmare and that the boys had behaved abominably. This all got leaked to the papers as well. Land Rover blamed the team manager for mis-selling it to us, while the manager pointed the finger at them. Land Rover claimed it was made clear all along that this was a mandatory appearance and was a serious shoot, while the RFU said it had been told something very different.

Some of the lads who had got up to the most mischief had their personal sponsorships taken away from them, something I managed to avoid. All in all, it was a fuck-up on both sides and will go down as a day to forget. What happened to the footage that Martin and his cameraman got? Good question and something I asked about for some time after. Apparently, it was seized and will never see the light of day, which is a shame as it would make interesting viewing.

As my career progressed, and especially after camera phones and social media appeared on the scene, the need for rock-solid security became more and more apparent. On the 2008 'rape' tour of New Zealand, and at the 2011 World Cup, the England team had a Kiwi security team, including a copper. And it was the copper who took the report from the mother of the maid and passed it on to his superiors, who then blew it up into a legal situation. Stuart Lancaster was smart enough to realise that in a world of camera phones and social media, where so many people are trying to catch you out, you need your own people on board: a crack, loyal team that is wise to people taking liberties.

Stuart got the RFU to hire a brilliant team of former Marines and Special Forces soldiers, who were absolutely on the ball. These blokes were the crème de la crème of the British military, the top 1 per cent, trained to spot anything unusual from a thousand yards, so drunk blokes trying to have a pop were small fry to them. One night, a few of the lads were out in Manchester and a young lad staggered out of a bar with sick all over his shoes. He looked at us, shouted something and I just laughed. Next thing I knew, security had folded this bloke in half and launched him into a metal fence. What I didn't know was that this bloke had run up behind me and tried to hit me on the back of the head.

These boys were like Ninjas. They'd sweep the team room to check for bugs and make sure no one had been in, patrol training pitches and carry out recces on bars and restaurants. On nights out, they were constantly stopping people trying to get in our faces, trying to put us in headlocks and take potentially compromising photos. They were our eyes and ears, so if anyone claimed we'd done something untoward, they'd say, 'Actually, no. This is what really happened …' Like the time some girl accused me of refusing to have a photo taken with her on Twitter (I accused her of lying, obviously) and they told the management she'd made the whole thing up to get some attention. They had seen first-hand me agreeing to have a photo with her and others.

I got quite friendly with the security boys and would play this game where I'd try to creep up behind them whatever they were doing, whether it was on patrol or sitting down quietly. I would get as close as I could and put one hand near their neck and shout, 'You're dead!' before they could react. I only managed to pull it off a couple of times, but I never let the blokes forget it. Every time I saw them, I'd say, 'Are you sure you were in the Special Forces? You're not getting them mixed up with the Territorial Army?' When Dylan Hartley tried to creep up on one of them on Bagshot high street, the bloke dropped to one knee, threw Dylan over his shoulder and grabbed him by the throat. Dylan was on his back, choking and mumbling, 'Sorry! Sorry! I was only joking. It's me, Dylan, Dylan Hartley!' The bloke realised just in time that it wasn't an enemy but in fact a player. He released his death grip and hauled Dylan up, saying, 'Don't ever fucking do that again,' before storming off, leaving Dylan rubbing his throat and wondering how he was going to explain the marks and blood-shot eyes when he got home.

God knows what the people of Bagshot must have thought when they witnessed the scene. It turns out this particular security guard had a touch of PTSD and was always on edge. Dylan never did it again and we all gave this guy a wide berth.

Eventually, I had to stop playing that game because my ankles creaked so much. I would get ten metres away from one of the guards and they would hear the clicking and say, 'Fucking hell, James, I heard you coming a mile off. You would be an awful soldier.'

I was always trying to get one over on people, and one of our conditioners is a hero of a bloke and a former Marine called David 'Tweety' Silvester. I crept up behind him in the dining room once and put my arm around his neck and said, 'Got you!' In one motion he ducked forward and threw me over his shoulder and onto my back before he said, 'No, I've got you.' The lads loved it. He had tossed 120 kg like it was nothing, and fully got me. I thought perhaps it was time to find another game.

Having got used to the best in the business, I was quite shocked by the security team on the 2017 Lions tour. What a motley crew they were. They'd stroll around giving it the thousand-yard stare – as if to say, 'You don't understand. You weren't there, man' – and were always going on about how hard they were working. But they were always turning up late or stuffing their faces with burgers and pizza. Then one day I found one of them asleep outside the team room, when he was supposed to be keeping watch. Obviously, I took a photo of him and sent it to all the lads, and he never heard the last of it.

Another time, I was in the gym in Christchurch when a fan started on one of my teammates. I ran over and dragged the fan off, before looking around to see where the security guy was. He was doing biceps curls in the mirror. Eventually, he said to me, 'What happened?' and I replied, 'Don't worry about it, mate. We dealt with it while you were sculpting your guns.' Then there was the time fans started streaming in and demanding autographs, photos and kit, and the security guy was practising his karate moves on a bag. By the time this bloke finally remembered why he was supposed to be there, we'd managed to get rid of them. I said to him, 'We've just quelled a potential riot, while you were karate chopping a fucking bag, you idiot!'

We ended up taking the piss out of the security boys so much that it got a bit needly between us. We'd be in the gym and I'd say to them, 'Lads, you aren't really security, you're more like stewards really. You'd be better off wearing hi-vis jackets. Actually, thinking about it, you're worse than stewards, you're more like fire marshals.' We wound them up so much that one of them kept staring at me, with a look of pure hatred in his eyes. I couldn't resist going up to him.

'You want to kill me, don't you?'

'Yeah,' he replied.

'Do you want to know why you won't?'

'Why?'

'Because you'd fuck it up and the police would arrest you within five minutes. You would forget to hide the body properly and leave fingerprints everywhere.'

When the tour manager John Spencer got roughed up in a restaurant, security were late on the scene again. We said to them, 'Brilliant. There's only one bloke who really needs looking after, our elderly tour manager, and you've let him get beaten up.' And even when they thought they'd got it right, they'd got it wrong. On the last night, we were in a bar, a woman asked one of our table for an autograph and this security bloke came out of nowhere and tackled her into the table. The two of them were lying on the floor, covered in bottles and glasses. After I'd helped the poor woman back to her feet, apologised and made sure she got the photo with the player she wanted, I eyeballed the security guy.

'What on earth did you think you were doing?'

'You said we weren't doing our job properly and to stop fans!'

'But she was hot and that lad is single. It's not the nice ones who politely ask for photos we want you to stop, it's the nightmare ones who look like something from *Hellraiser*.'

That security team reminded me of the two debt collectors, Barry and Glen, from *The League of Gentlemen*. Barry starts out all useless and timid, before Glen winds him up so much that he ends up stomping on an old lady in her hallway. I had wound up the security team so much that they had lost the plot and were taking everyone out. If they weren't such raters I would have felt sorry for them, but I wouldn't have let them secure a children's party let alone a Lions tour. They were lovely but as useful as a sunroof in a submarine.

When I was playing in Japan, I spent most of my spare time watching box sets (the internet connection over there was so fast, I could download an entire series in about four minutes). Anyway, I was watching the *X-Files* one evening and my then partner, who was visiting for a couple of weeks, was in the kitchen. I was on a particularly scary bit about a monster breaking into people's houses and eating them, when I got a strange feeling come over me that something was not right. I looked to my left and saw in between the bottom slats two eyes peering at me through my window blinds. I looked back at the TV screen, wondered if the *X-Files* was messing with my mind, before thinking, 'I definitely saw some fucking eyes!'

Having been more than a little bit spooked, I leapt up and started shouting, 'What the fuck are you doing?', which made my partner scream. In one stride I was at the windows and had wrenched open the blinds, ripped the French windows off their hinges and jumped straight through the mosquito net on the other side (I literally left an outline of my body, just like in a cartoon). Once outside, I saw this little bloke running off down the side of the house and going through the side gate, which he shut behind him. I gave chase and instead of opening the gate smashed through it, sending splinters and rotten wood everywhere. I caught up with this middle-aged Japanese bloke as he was trying to run out onto the main road. I tackled him to the floor and screamed, 'Who the fuck are you?!'

He was mumbling in Japanese and stunk of alcohol. I could not understand a word and he was trying to get away. I grabbed him by the shirt and started dragging him over to my team-mate Roy Kinikinilau's house, which was just around the corner from mine, as he spoke good Japanese, having been over there playing for so long. As I was dragging this guy he tried to break free a couple of times, so I gave him a few body shots to sharpen him up. I was livid that this perv had been watching me and my partner. After the third time, I realised he was trying to go back to get his shoes as they had fallen off. I told him to forget about them. When people get spooked, it's usually a case of fight or flight, and I was very much in fighting mood on this occasion.

It was about 11.30 p.m. when I knocked on the door, and when Roy's wife answered it she looked at me as if I'd lost my mind; there I was, red-faced and furious, with a tiny bleeding Japanese man stuffed under my arm. Roy carried out an interrogation and this bloke claimed he'd just been looking for his dog, which had chased a cat into my garden. I started mouthing off, telling Roy and his wife that this bloke was talking bollocks, there was no dog, and he was actually perving on me and my partner, and eventually Roy had to tell me to let go of him, as he was getting more irate and may or may not have started crying. And when I did, this bloke disappeared into thin air, like something from a Japanese horror movie.

You know how weird and scary Japanese horror movies are. And I was already living in an old house that looked like the place in *The Grudge* horror film (my bedroom was right under the exact style loft hatch they have in the movie, and I'd sometimes lie in bed expecting a head to appear through it). So when this bloke evaporated, I went into a state of panic. I was literally running around in circles, shouting, 'Where the fuck has he gone?!' I assumed by how quickly this guy had disappeared that he lived very close to me in one of the other pink houses, perhaps even the one attached to mine. I had never seen the occupants. Obviously, my partner was terrified and wanted to leave. I tried to calm her down, but without knowing who he was and where he went I spent the whole time looking out for further Japanese sex pests and telling her to calm down.

When I'd calmed down later that night, I became quite nervous about how the situation might pan out, because I knew a fair bit about the Japanese culture. Serious scandal is a big no-no in Japan. When I say 'scandal' I don't mean getting drunk on a night out and doing something silly. That is in fact all good. If you strip naked and start dancing on the tables it gets forgotten about the next day, unlike in England, where you would rib the victim endlessly. It was one of the benefits of being in Japan that no one ever talked about the night before. One evening, I was in a restaurant when this Japanese businessman walked over to my table, shouted, 'Go home, foreigner!', promptly passed out and smashed his face on the floor. I was properly concerned for this bloke because he'd hit the deck with a sickening crunch and there was blood pouring from his nose. But everyone else carried on as if nothing had happened, and I'm sure no one ever mentioned it to him again.

During my time in Japan, I saw guys in suits hanging out of bushes and upside down in bins, and you just knew that once they'd regained consciousness they'd brush themselves down and stroll into work, as if they'd been cosily tucked up in bed at 9 o'clock the previous evening. If you don't believe me, check out the Instagram page Shibuya Meltdown, which captures some of the bizarre things you see on a night out in Japan.

What I am talking about is proper scandal. When that happens there is no going back. If a player gets into trouble with the police, just look at what happened to George Smith or the late Jerry Collins. Jerry had it worse than most as he upset some proper gangsters and they chased him into a department store to kill him. He had to pick up a knife and get arrested just to get away from them. In Japan, not only is the player fired and sent home in disgrace, but the head coach has to step down, and the person who recruited that player has to step down too. It's a huge, huge deal. Honour in Japan comes before everything else. It was the one thing my agent Duncan Sandlant hammered home to me: do not get into proper trouble, do not fight, do not get arrested. If you do, it's game over.

I was worried that tackling a Japanese man to the floor, giving him a shoeing and dragging him around by his head would constitute a proper scandal. The issue was I had to tell the team manager, as when I surveyed the damage to my house I needed new French windows, new blinds, a new mosquito net and a new side gate as it was smashed beyond repair. There was no way I could cover this up.

So the day after the peeping Tom incident (or should that be peeping Tomohito?) I strolled into the changing room and started telling everyone about how I'd caught this pervert neighbour who had been looking through my window. The translators were all laughing and saying, 'Oh James, you're so funny,' because they thought I was making it all up. And I was saying, 'No, lads, you have to believe me. This actually happened. So you need to find this bloke and tell him not to do it again. I also need some new blinds, some new French windows, a new mosquito net and a new gate, because I smashed them all to pieces while chasing him.'

When the penny started to drop that I was telling the truth, you could see the panic on their faces, because they now realised they had a delicate situation on their hands. And I suspected one or two of them still thought I'd got drunk and imagined the whole thing. But after training the following day, club officials having done a bit of detective work, I paid this bloke a visit with a couple of translators and the team manager. As I had suspected, it was the house attached to mine. We knocked on the door of this little pink house and a middle-aged Japanese woman in a pink velour Juicy Couture tracksuit with a cigarette hanging from her lip answered. And she was stubbornly sticking to the line that her husband had chased their dog that was chasing a cat into my garden, was too scared to speak to me as his English was no good and decided to stare through my window instead. When I asked why he didn't ring the doorbell, she shrugged. I am not sure how looking through the window was going to help him get his non-existent dog. I asked the translators to ask these questions, but when she smiled I knew they weren't relaying my questions properly so I gave up. As far as the translators and the club were concerned, that was the case closed. It didn't matter that I knew – and they probably knew as well – that this bloke's story was bollocks. He was a drunk perv who wanted to look at a western girl; I knew it, they knew it and I'm sure his wife knew it. They were worried that digging deeper would just bring shame on him, me and everyone involved. I never saw the guy again and, in hindsight, I probably dodged a scandal. Everything was repaired and we never spoke of it again. It was like it never happened. But it did make me wonder what else they cover up in Japan.

PAUL DORAN-JONES:

'When sportspeople do speaking engagements, people have this weird idea that because they've bought a ticket for lunch or dinner, they can walk up to that person and do and say whatever they want. And that's particularly true with James.

'We were both at a dinner once, James did a talk and some bloke came up to him and slapped him across the face. Out of nowhere. He'd obviously had a few beers and was presumably thinking, "It's Hask, the Bantersaurus rex, he won't mind." But Hask did mind, obviously. He's always had a thing about people touching him on the head, so someone slapping him across the face was always going to go down particularly badly. On what planet did that bloke think that was acceptable behaviour? Jim had been quite jovial before that, but I saw his chin drop and it looked like he was going to iron *this bloke out. Luckily, I jumped in and managed to persuade him not to.*

'On the one hand, Jim has a classic rugby changing-room persona. He's larger than life and I love it. But when you strip all that back, there's an inner beauty most people don't get to see. The real Haskell is the one you see when he's interacting in a small group. That's when he's most comfortable. Put him in a larger group, and mix in members of the public, he's a different person.'

I always try to be myself, whoever I meet. But sometimes it's tricky because people say weird things and do weird stuff. Especially fans. That means I sometimes don't know how to act around them, can seem a bit cagey. I always stop for photos and autographs, but Chloe often says to me, 'You could have given them a bit more time.' But it's not easy when you have people striding up to you and saying, 'You're James Haskell. What are you doing here?' What can you say to that? Sometimes I'll say, 'Yes, I am,' and walk off. Then there are the fans who can't get a word out, so you're left standing there while they're staring at you. I don't really know how to deal with that either.

If someone is nice and normal to me, I'll be nice and normal back. And most of the people I meet at dinners and awards ceremonies are lovely. But I reined the networking in, because I realised that a lot of people in high-powered positions are really odd and dry. I once met an alcohol and Formula 1 tycoon who was as weird as they came. Everyone was really excited to meet him and hanging on his every word, but he had nothing to offer. And I thought, 'Do you know what? I can't be fucked with this.' If I can't be myself around someone, they're not worth bothering with. I'm not averse to a bit of brown-nosing, but I can't be doing it for too long. After a while, I've got two choices: either I walk away, or I'll end up calling them out on their bullshit.

I've definitely got angrier since I retired from rugby. I smashed up our Sky box the other day because I wanted to watch England in the European Championships and I couldn't get a connection. I'd just returned from walking the dog, my back was sore and I found myself getting increasingly angry. I wasn't even that bothered about watching the football, but it was England–Scotland, it was going to be a talking point and I wanted to be informed.

So there I was, on my hands and knees with the Sky box instructions, and Bertie the dog licking my face, and I just couldn't get this thing to connect. I tried about a million times. It involved me getting up and leaving the room, holding a button down in another room, then coming back and waiting for it to connect. The getting up and down was doing my head in; every time I got on the floor Bertie thought it was play time. It was also doing my back in. I did it about 20 times and then lost the plot. I always get fucked off with inanimate objects. If something won't work, it's getting a kicking. In the end, I started hammering this box with my fists and then smashed it on the floor until it turned into dust. I was like Basil Fawlty, when he smashes the shit out of his car with a branch. Once I'd done that, I grabbed Bertie, who looked slightly shocked and was sniffing and pawing at the crumbled Sky box in the corner of the room, I lit a cigar and went and watched the football in the pub. I sat right in the back, out of the way, smoking and still fuming about the box, and my back. I could tell people were deliberately giving me a wide berth. And when I got home, I plugged in an old Sky box and it fucking worked straightaway.

I'm also less able to let stupid stuff go. At least when it comes to people in authority, who think that wearing a hi-vis jacket makes them omnipotent. Then again, I was like that at school. If I thought a teacher was talking nonsense, I'd tell them. As a result, I got a reputation for being rude and cheeky. That never made sense to me – if you're not allowed to disagree with someone, you're living in a dictatorship (which is, let's face it, basically what most schools are). And while I was normally respectful of referees during my career, I was constantly having to bite my lip. And it got worse as I got older, especially if they were being pernickety or giving me a death stare. I'd think, 'You wouldn't look at me like that if there weren't millions of people watching.'

I recently turned up at a venue to do a talk and the woman in charge of the multi-storey car park told me I wasn't allowed in. I kept telling her they'd explicitly told me to park in the multi-storey, showed her the email on my phone, but she wasn't having it. After about ten minutes of reasoning and a big build-up of cars behind me, I lost it, because I was running late and supposed to be speaking in ten minutes. Predictably, she accused me of being rude and threatening, I called her an idiot and it escalated from there. Luckily, someone from the event came down, told the woman I had permission to park there, and this woman replied, 'Sorry, sir, I didn't realise he was allowed to park.' I just stared at her for a long time without saying anything. I was trying to imagine I could use some dark force and snatch the life from her. It was only when the client said, 'James, James,' and pulled my arm did it break my focus. The hi-vis wankers are everywhere and their sole mission is to destroy your morale and break your spirit. Don't let them do it. There is a special circle of hell reserved for them, where they have to spend at least a millennium queuing, but once they get to the front it's like a Sisyphean tragedy and they are taken to the back to start all over again, all the while getting a lecture on health and safety from a droning old curmudgeon.

The one thing this pandemic has done is make the scared more scared, the stupid more vocal and it's now a nit-picker's dream. 'Don't stand there, you aren't wearing a mask, why haven't you sanitised your hands, you aren't two metres,' etc., etc. It's hell on earth at the moment.

Chloe says I'm turning into Alan Partridge, in that I just hate the general public. I'm not sure that's completely accurate, but I do have a problem with people not letting me do things for no good reason. And I have spent a lot of time speaking with my therapist about accepting things as they are, rather than getting upset that things aren't how I want them to be. Someone else Chloe thinks I'm turning into is my dad. Every argument we have, she throws that at me: 'You never think you're wrong, like your dad never thinks he's wrong.' I say to her, 'I spent almost every day with him for the first 30 years of my life. Of course I'm turning into my dad!' I use the same phrases as my dad, such as 'That's very sweet,' or 'The problem is,' and 'Yes, yes, yes.' And I'm turning into him physically – we've got the same posture, and if I grow a beard the likeness is quite spooky. It also doesn't help that I'm losing my lid.

9

THE MOST CONFIDENT MAN IN THE ROOM?

KEN HOPKINS:

'*During James's two seasons in Wellington's first XV, he just kept getting bigger and stronger. So one day I said to him, "Hask, what are you on?" I was only joking, I didn't really think he'd been taking drugs, but he got very defensive and a little upset. He told me he was just looking after his body. He was a complex character and could be sensitive if you hit the mark with the right question.*

'*When players I've coached make it to the very top of the game, it does fill me with pride. I like to think I helped them get there, in some small way. James was a fine player who had a dream, and so many people have dreams that never come to fruition. So I was quite surprised by the last conversation I had with him. He seemed quite disappointed with his achievements, wondered if he could have done more. That made me a bit sad. So I said to him, "You need to look back on your career with pride, because you achieved everything you set out to do, won everything there was to win with Wasps, played 77 times for England, became a Lion." I've seen so many talented young sportsmen not have the careers they could have had, because they didn't have the right attitude. But James surpassed my expectations of him.'*

CHLOE MADELEY:

'James is one of the most insecure people I've ever met, which is hilariously funny, because he's so loud and brash and acts like he doesn't give a shit. He'll be the first to tell you how insecure he was throughout his rugby career – about whether he was good enough, whether he deserved to be in the England team, whether people liked him or not. That's why he saw three or four psychologists over the six years I was with him during his career.

'At one Six Nations dinner, Joe Marler was giving James loads of stick from another table. James kept biting, and Courtney Lawes said to me, 'Chloe, I keep telling James to be like me and let it go, but he can't do it.' James was getting so wound up, I could see his jaw clenching. He really cared that much. Here was this bloke who was supposed to be the most confident man in the room, showing that he most definitely wasn't.'

EDDIE JONES:

'Modern rugby has become very uniform, and a lot of players' personalities have been drummed out of them by the time they've graduated from academies. And while I wouldn't go as far as to say that James is one of the last rugby players with a personality, he's one of the last rugby players with the courage to be himself all the time, stick his neck out and not be liked. In that respect, he's probably the most courageous player of the professional era.'

It's weird when people say nice stuff about me, because it just didn't happen for most of my rugby career. I'm not sure I deserve what Eddie said about me, about probably being the most courageous player of the professional era – this is a man who literally lives and breathes rugby and bases so much on personality and character – but I will certainly take it from the great man. People probably think I prepped Eddie to say that about me, but I didn't!

To be honest, I don't really look at it as courage, I look at it as just being myself. Everything I did, I wanted to give it 100 per cent, whether it was training, playing games, giving interviews. And I just lived my life as I wanted to live it. On second thoughts, maybe it is courageous to do that, because so many people don't. And I suppose it did take courage to keep being written off and coming back stronger when others would have thrown in the towel.

But one of the downsides of desperately wanting to do so well and prove people wrong is that I'm sensitive to certain criticism. The problem is, the other lads know they'll get a bite. When someone is getting into me, I'll see Courtney Lawes smiling, because he knows I'm going to blow up at some point. It's almost like he's counting it down in his head. He'd always say to me, 'Why do you let it get to you? Just let it go, otherwise you're just giving them what they want.' But I can't, not when they're taking the piss. I always do it, I find it funny, because when I reflect I realise that's all they wanted and I have given it to them.

Throughout my rugby career, it didn't matter how quick-witted I was about anything else, if a teammate or coach criticised my skills, that was always difficult to take. If I had an Achilles' heel, that was it. You could come after me for anything, but they knew they would hit the spot if they got into me for that. When I was picked to play for England against the Barbarians, my Wasps teammate and All Blacks legend Craig Dowd called me up and said, 'Good luck, mate, make sure your hands don't let you down,' before putting the phone down. I thought wow, that's not quite the pre-match motivation I needed, but I'm sure it was coming from a good place. I think people assumed I was bulletproof.

DAN COLE:

'Haskell was very good at dishing it out, but it was easy to put him on the back foot by giving him shit about a certain aspect of his game. One of his big hang-ups was line-outs, because he was always up against Tom Croft and Courtney Lawes, blokes who were really good in the air, and Haskell wasn't that kind of player. Apparently, he'd send the England coaches videos of himself catching line-outs for Wasps, with the message: "Look, I can do it!"

'During one line-out session, Haskell didn't reach a couple of throws and started complaining about his knees. And Courtney Lawes, who is very blunt, said, "It's not your knees, mate, it's your hands. You can't catch." It was like someone had stuck a pin in Haskell, he deflated on the spot and had nothing to say back. Then, before the 2015 World Cup, he turned up wearing these massive Under Armour boots. Absolutely horrendous. The first line-out session, he was terrible, kept mistiming his jumps. So we kept saying to him, "Hask, it's your boots, they're too heavy." He was getting very wound up, kept blaming his dodgy knees again. But a few days later, Richard Wigglesworth, who was also sponsored by Under Armour, told us Haskell had got on the phone to *the company and told them to remove some weight from his boots.*

'Haskell could seem quite robotic, but I don't mean that in a bad way. It's just that he wasn't as naturally talented as some, so he drilled and drilled and drilled and grooved his skills so deep, so that maybe he didn't seem as fluent. But he had incredible drive to maximise his talents. It's difficult to think of someone who made more of his talent, and not many players could do what he did.'

I always had massive feet. Well, bigger than most. I have played with some lads with size 15s and 16s so I can't complain too much. I love Coley but he always took great delight in moaning about everything, including about my line-out jumping. In fact, everyone did given half the chance. It was odd, really, because for a while I was seen as a line-out forward. I did a lot of line-out stuff with Wasps, was used in finals and big games, and always delivered. Then the more time I spent with England, the more that area drifted away from my game, so I stopped really giving it that much attention. This perception developed that I couldn't jump and it became the narrative of my on-field play, which cost me a lot of England caps. I stopped being seen as a line-out forward and was relegated to chief lifter.

I always knew whether I would be in the starting XV when they handed out the line-out sheets on the Monday morning; if the 6 or 7 had any jumping roles and was involved in the shortened line-outs, I knew I was not going to be playing. The coaches would always say, 'Don't read anything into it,' which means, 'Always read something into it.' Don't get me wrong, I was no Courtney in the air but I was never as bad as they said. I was the perfect scapegoat. Someone does a shit lift, it's 'Fucking Hask'; someone overthrows it, the hooker goes,

'Hask is not quite jumping the same as the others.' I would just stand there and smile, thinking, 'You cunts.' I would jump and the lads would make these noises as if they were trying to lift a grand piano on their own. They would say, 'Fuck me, Hask, the amount you jump we could just about get a Rizla under your feet.' Or a player would come and check to make sure I wasn't wearing a weighted vest. All gags I had used on others, but then reversed onto me. Yes, by the end of my career when I weighed 120 kg I will admit that it took me a while to get the spring back. Ed Shirvington, the Wasps hooker, loved it when he threw me the ball at the back, because if I had to reach right back and up I would make all these noises, as mobility was not my strong suit. He called it the Haskell squeal. He'd say, 'All right, bud, going to make you squeal today.'

In the end, I made sure that line-outs be damned but that other areas of my game made it unavoidable to select me. And Coley's right, I did send videos of me catching the ball in line-outs to coaches. If I won a big line-out in a game, got a worldie of a take one-handed going backwards, went up and defended well or stole the ball, I would clip it up and send it over to the coaches. Just as a reminder that I could do it if they wanted me to. Why would you not? I was always going to challenge that unfair perception of me.

As an aside, I once sent a text bigging myself up to John Wells, just before the 2007 World Cup (which I didn't get selected for). Wellsy had said to me in a review after that Six Nations where I had made my debut, 'Hask, the problem with you is, you're all flash and no bash.' So after winning the Heineken Cup final with Wasps and nearly getting MOM off the bench, I sent Wellsy a message: 'Hi Wellsy, good luck for the tour, you should watch our game, I think I had all the flash and all the bash today.' We had also beaten up Wellsy's old team Leicester, who were always seen as the tough nuts of the Premiership. So I had double reason to message him. It turns out Wellsy was in a lift with a couple of players at the time, so obviously showed them. And one of them happened to be Ronnie Regan.

As I described in *What a Flanker*, me and Ronnie were always at each other. I used to say he had saggy knees, which he didn't take kindly to. He'd say to me, in his thick pirate accent, 'They're not saggy, they're scars.' And I'd reply, 'Well, you need to get your money back, and your surgeon needs his hands chopping off.' But Ronnie saw the text I'd sent to Wellsy as a chance for an amnesty. A couple of days later, he took me aside and said, ''Ere, Haskell, I've seen what you sent John Wells. If you don't get me, I won't get you.' That was the end of our little war, well, for that England camp anyway. We were back at each other's throats not long after that. I couldn't help it, he was such an easy target.

Under Armour used to send me a huge array of boots, some of them insane. They knew I would give anything a go and didn't mind being different. One pair went halfway up my calves, so that I looked like a superhero. And not a good one, more like Bananaman. When I turned up to training in them, the lads were roaring with laughter, they had never seen anything like them. The only time I had seen anyone come close was when Doz was asked to try this new range of boots that our agent Duncan sorted. They were so big they arrived in separate boxes. Doz reckons that after 20 minutes his back had gone as they were so heavy he couldn't run properly. All the Gloucester lads at the time were rolling on the floor laughing, as Doz had to pull out of the session. It must be a world first, being injured due to super-heavy boots. He was going to lob them away until one of his Fijian teammates approached him while no one was looking and asked if he could have them. Doz was never gladder to get rid of anything. It's good to know that somewhere in Fiji a person is running around in the equivalent of moon-landing boots and is super-happy about it.

Anyway, back to me and my crap boots. I was getting slaughtered by the lads, who were now refusing to try and lift me on the grounds that the boots were too awful and too heavy. Once again, all eyes were on me and not for the right reasons. Eddie Jones was strolling around with a big grin on his face and shouting, 'Look at the state of your fucking boots, Hask!' He asked if they came with a prescription. Eddie has a footwear fetish, remember. In the end, I had to call Under Armour and say, 'You've got to stop sending me all these funky boots. I'm a laughing stock, the heat I'm getting is unbearable! Just send me the regular ones.' But I'm not averse to a bit of mythologising, so for the purposes of this book I will say that I phoned Under Armour and said, 'These boots you've sent me are hampering my line-out jumping. Can you possibly remove a couple of grams?' I am not sure I was doing UA any favours as some of the stuff they sent was so off-key it would have put people off wearing it. The lads could not understand how Wiggy was walking around in these absolute fash numbers and I had special shoes on. It didn't matter who I worked with – and I was sponsored by them all, from Nike to Adidas and UA – I always managed to get the worst-looking clobber.

The weird thing is, I'm actually very self-deprecating about my rugby career. People are always telling me off for playing down my achievements, and Chloe tells me that by doing that I'm legitimising other people's piss-taking. Alex Payne has said the same thing to me: 'Hask, you have to stop doing yourself down about the career you have.' Even Ken Hopkins's comments about feeling I was disappointed not to have done more are true. I am never satisfied and it's something I know I must work on.

When talking myself down or making jokes about myself, I am essentially self-sabotaging, because I'm the one who gave them the joke to run with. I've made out I was a bit shit at rugby, when actually I wasn't. Yes, I was a meathead at times, but my hands were fine. Actually, I had good handling skills. But if I dropped a ball, people would say, 'God, there he goes again,' and it was me who paved the way for that criticism. Meanwhile, Dylan Hartley could drop three balls in a game and no one would say anything, because he didn't go around telling everyone what an average rugby player he was. I actually stuck a note on my laptop recently, reminding myself not to keep talking myself down when I do podcasts. But it's difficult to put the genie back in the bottle. For all my faults I am not great at talking myself up and have gone too far the other way.

When Stuart Lancaster took over from Martin Johnson, he made sure to check any motivational videos before they were shown. But even when they made sure to include clips of England players scoring amazing tries and putting in big hits, I'd come away from the viewing feeling demotivated, because me clearing out a ruck would have been my only 'highlight'. I even had to work on that stuff with my psychologist, because I had a massive chip on my shoulder; eventually I turned what I saw as negativity into fuel to perform better. People often talk about positivity being a good motivator, but I would disagree. I would say that you get more done through harnessing the power of negativity. So-and-so said I couldn't do it or would never make it, so I prove them wrong. They only want to show crap clips, so I will play every game like I am creating my own post-match showreel. That was something I started working on with Travis Allan, who I talked about in the first book. Every time I played, I wanted only big moments; it improved my game no end, made me let go of mistakes quicker and kept me content.

To be fair, it was the same at Wasps, and a lot of it was due to my own insecurities. From the age of 18, I never read a programme, because they kept getting my name or age or weight wrong, which made me think they couldn't have thought that much of me. Before the coaches put a highlights video on, I'd be thinking, 'Great, they're bound to show that try I scored against Harlequins or that break I made against Bath,' and I'd be really pissed off when they didn't. Instead of motivating me before a big game, it would mess with my head. So I just stopped worrying about any of this stuff and just got into a routine that focused only on the things that I could control. I have taken this thought process into every area of my life.

I remember being nominated for something at an awards ceremony and them showing some shit clips of me going on a bit of a trundle or a crap tackle. Even when they were trying to praise me, they were making me feel like I was ordinary. I used to mark these moments down in my phone notes as reminders and a little motivation for the next time I played. If a coach disrespected me, if a journo said I was gash or they didn't show good clips, it would all go in. I would then take them out one at a time to use pre-game. The only time I was happy at an awards ceremony was when I won Supporters' Player of the Season and Players' Player of the Season at Wasps. I was sitting there thinking, 'At last!' There is nothing better you can do. The fans love you and your teammates have voted for you. Those were the most important awards I ever won because they were voted for by the only people who really matter.

If things went well for me on a rugby field, I was the happiest person in the world. If things didn't go well, I wouldn't be able to stop thinking about the mistakes I'd made. That meant I forgot to reflect on some of the things I achieved, and instead of saying, 'Fuck me, that was good fun,' I was saying, 'Yeah, that was okay. We won the game, but I could have been a lot better.'

The ironic thing was, I spent most of my career not believing in myself while everyone assumed I thought I was the best thing since sliced bread. People rarely told me when I'd performed well, because they thought I was already too far up my own arse, so it was difficult for me to tell if I was any good or not. That's why I was so happy when former teammates and opponents started coming on the podcast and telling me what a good player and bloke they thought I was. I'd be sitting there thinking, 'God, I didn't know you thought that. You could have told me earlier, but better late than never.'

Being a good coach is about saying the right things, and it's very difficult to say the right thing to every player every time you interact with them. Coaches can't go around panicking about every interaction they have. But they need to know that how they talk to players is key. Just one bad interaction, the wrong words at the wrong time, might define a coach–player relationship forever. That's why being a parent is so hard, because every interaction you have with your kids can have a positive or negative impact. If you're having a bad day, don't take it out on your kids. Encourage them or tell them that it's okay to make mistakes, because that can shape how they are.

I'm sure Eddie Jones has made mistakes with how he's spoken to certain players, because everybody does. But he knew how to talk to me, just as Michael Cheika at Stade Français, Jamie Joseph at the Highlanders and Dai Young at Wasps knew how to talk to me. They didn't look at me and think, 'Jesus, this guy's a bit different, I don't really know how he's gonna fit in.' I had coaches like that, who had a set way of doing things and weren't willing or able to adapt. Instead, a coach like Eddie looked at me and thought, 'Yeah, this guy might be a bit different, but he can do good things for us, if we give him what he needs.'

When I was a youngster at Wasps, Shaun Edwards did so much to turn me into the player I became. But he could be brutal. He'd say to me, 'Hask, there's too many mistakes around you, kid,' and walk off. Or he'd say, 'Hask, if you can't pass the ball, just run.' And I'd be thinking, 'What does he mean? The whole point of rugby is being able to pass the ball, and he thinks I can't do it.' A lot of players often speak to the coaches to get some form of affirmation, but often it can cause more problems. You go to them thinking you will get a confidence boost when in fact you get your ego dented. I used to do this a lot but learned that it was more often not going to be as you wanted. You didn't need people to tell you that you had played well or badly, you knew intuitively.

Graham Rowntree, my long-time scrum coach and then head forwards coach with England, could never really get his head around how to manage me. We always got on and I have a lot of affection for Wig. He is a top guy and always means well, but you could see he was never sure how to get the best out of me and what the right tools were to use with me. I don't blame him, as once you understand the mentality of Leicester back in the day and the types of coaches and players around him, you understand his approach. It was the same for most of those England coaches back then and across the Premiership. When I told him I'd seen a psychologist and had for a long time, I think he kind of panicked, assuming I must have had issues, instead of seeing it as something that everyone should do as the mind is the most powerful tool at our disposal. Back then no one saw one, mental health was a myth, men were men and all that other crap. Our coaching staff at the time were all alpha males, so there was not a compassionate beta male among them who you could approach for a quiet chat if you needed help. That's why putting your coaching staff together is so important. Yes, you need a dictator, but you need approachable ones who can get more of a feel for mood and who the players can get a different energy from. You also need to make the coaches feel secure in their jobs because if they are looking after no. 1 then that does not engender a good atmosphere. I reckon I was the only one in the team talking to someone regularly about performance development, match prep, and how to deal with success and failure.

I'd ask Wig something on a specific bit of play, or when I was watching clips back with him about how I could improve this or that, or whether I should change things, and he'd reply, 'You're overthinking things, Hask. Don't worry about it.' That was not quite the answer I was looking for. I was expecting to be told, yes, you need to work on this and this is how I would do it. If it was just as simple as not worrying about it then life would be easy. I have a problem, don't worry about it. Problem solved.

I think he knew that I was hard on myself and probably got a bit down if I made mistakes so perhaps that was his way of helping me, but I always got the feeling he and the other coaches thought I was more fragile than I was. If you handled me right,

I would run through a wall for you and feel empowered. All I wanted was to be given help, told what I was doing well and what I needed to improve and how to do it. I'd then be on the training field until it got dark if need be, desperately trying to make myself better. The worst thing you could do to me was say you are crap, or you did that wrong and go away and work on it. That kind of feedback I would really struggle with.

I was recently talking to Tom Curry, the England and Lions flanker, about how great it must be to have a twin brother who's also a rugby player (like Tom, Ben plays for Sale). Whenever they needed to get better at something, they had a practice partner on standby. But when I got back from training and was concerned that a certain facet of my game wasn't up to scratch, I had to work on it then and there, but I didn't always have anyone to practise with. I'd sometimes have girlfriends passing me balls in the garden for hours, or if I needed to work on number eight stuff, I'd have them scrumming down with me and kicking the ball back and forth between us. I remember once wanting to work on my tackling but quickly realised that's not what girlfriends were for, as I tackled one of them a little bit too hard, she cried and was not happy. Classic me, I got a bit carried away and was so in the moment. It did not go down well. I look back and it all seems a bit mad, but I would have done anything to get better.

That was me taking my work home with me, because I couldn't stop thinking about the things I'd done wrong. Even when I thought I'd played well, I'd come out of the Monday review meeting thinking there were things I could have done better. When my girlfriend had finished passing me balls, I'd watch videos of other players in my position. It would be all-consuming, all I could think about. Looking back, I spent most of my career feeling down on myself.

When my Kiwi friend Travis watched one of my games and said, 'Mate, you're not going anywhere near the ball. It looks like you're worried about making mistakes,' I got quite defensive, but only because he'd touched a nerve. Deep down, I knew he was right. I thought, 'What a way to go through your career, playing within yourself because you're afraid of fucking up and people criticising you. Do you know what? You need to step up and put it all out there, start putting together a highlights reel.' It suddenly dawned on me that it was better to try and fail spectacularly than trundle along safely.

For a long time, there was a disconnect between my persona off the pitch and my performances on it. To many coaches and media pundits, I wasn't wholesome enough. It's not as if I was ever a trash-talker, like Conor McGregor, and it's not as if I was some kind of out-of-control sex person, like Tiger Woods. But I liked the sound of my own voice, which meant I was judged harshly by people. My entire career, I was haunted by people who thought there was only one way to be: like ex-England hooker Brian Moore, who seemed utterly convinced I was a wrong 'un, despite never having met me, and Martin Johnson, who once said to me, 'I'd love to have played against you so I could have filled you in,' and Stuart Lancaster, who couldn't get his head around doing all the things I did and still being able to be focused. But when Eddie Jones took over as England coach, he just got me.

After that disastrous 2015 World Cup, I thought, 'That's probably me done at international level. I won't get picked again.' It didn't help that I started our final game against Uruguay and didn't play particularly well, even fluffing a try-scoring opportunity. When I took part in the review, I wasn't scathing about the coaches. I said they'd worked hard, had the best intentions but hadn't got the selection quite right or focused enough on the players. And I honestly thought Stuart Lancaster and the rest were going to keep their jobs. I truly believe that none of them deserved to be treated and vilified the way they were. They are all good people who worked as hard as they could and tried to help the team win. Just look at how well each one of them has done since leaving England. Stuart Lancaster is back doing what he does brilliantly, which is coaching. He's no longer front of house and doesn't have the stresses and distractions that the England job brings. Ask any Leinster player – they say he's amazing on all fronts. Andy Farrell is Ireland coach and doing his thing with great skill as always. Graham Rowntree is loved by every team he works with – he is a great coach. However, it didn't work out for a number of reasons that I covered in my last book and don't need to be revisited here. Even when they all got binned and Eddie Jones came in, I still thought that was me done at the highest level.

When I was dropped by England or was not a starting fixture at club level for the first time in my career, there was a concern that I'd struggle being a squad man and not the centre of attention because it wouldn't hold the excitement I craved or I would be disruptive. I think that is part of the reason that Wasps never signed me for my final year, or at least the initial reason. The final nail was that the owner hated me and wanted me out, but the original reason was I don't think they thought I would deal with taking a huge pay cut or not being a starter. Jack Willis was coming through the ranks and looked like he was going to be a special player. I knew they were thinking this when Dai Young would say to me, 'Don't feel like you have to play in these Anglo-Welsh games,' because he thought it might be disrespectful to me. But I said to him, 'No, I want to play in every game possible. I want to perform and do everything I can for the team.' Of course I would take the chance to make a joke of it by saying that I thought the lads went on holiday at the club while we were on England duty. I'd never heard of the LV Cup (I assumed it was the Louis Vuitton Cup where we all got free bags) let alone the Anglo-Welsh Cup.

It was a shock to the system, but this was all just front. I would never think I was bigger than the team or playing in any game. It was fun playing all these games, working with all these fringe players and players on trial. I never thought I was above anything at club level, that's for sure. I proved this at Northampton where I was a fringe player and played in any game I could get my hands on. All I wanted to do was help the lads, be part of the team and play as much as I could to still get better and put my hand up for selection.

Wasps misjudged me and just showed they didn't understand me as a person. I would never have given up on fighting for my position, but as soon as a selection was made I would do everything to help my competition. I ended up taking a mega pay cut to play for Saints. At that stage it was never about money, but about playing well enough to make the England team.

If it had been the last time I played for England in 2015, I would have gone back to my club but not given up. Everything was all about trying to be the best, so while I was happy that I had done a lot for England, I was still going to fight for a place, even though I thought after 2015 that it wasn't going to happen. Whatever I do, however big or small, I always apply the same mentality. When I started DJing, I didn't just want to be performing at university gigs, I wanted to be performing in Ibiza. When I started writing books, I didn't just want to sell a few copies, I wanted to sell hundreds of thousands and become a bestselling author.

So imagine my surprise when Eddie called me up two weeks before the start of the 2016 Six Nations and told me I was in his squad and was going to start the first game. It was an unbelievable moment. I genuinely thought it was someone taking the piss. I was sitting on the bed, in a hotel in Scotland, before a Heineken Cup game. To be honest, I was surprised Eddie even remembered I existed.

As Eddie has already described, he'd tried to sign me when he was head coach of Saracens, and offered to double my money. I didn't want to leave Wasps at the time, because we were still winning things, but we had a good conversation and there were no hard feelings. Then, when I was playing in Japan, a good mate of mine, Richard Myerscough, who was a big cheese from Virgin at the time, took me out for lunch one day and I ended up sitting opposite Eddie, at a Trader Vic's of all places, in the posh part of Tokyo. And I remember thinking, 'I'm never going to work with Eddie Jones, it doesn't matter, just be yourself.' We had a good laugh, and now I know that I made a good impression on Eddie that day. Other coaches might have thought I was hard work, but Eddie liked that I didn't try to hide who I really was.

So, while I was shocked to receive that call from Eddie four or five years after that lunch in Tokyo, I shouldn't have been. I remember him saying to me, 'Listen, I really need your support in what I'm trying to do. I want you to be in my starting XV. I don't want you to overthink things. Just hit people and carry.' And then he put the phone down. No coach had ever phoned me, apart from Joe Lydon when he was in charge of the England sevens team. Even then, I thought it was a prank call. He said to me, 'James, Joe Lydon here, we're going to name you in the sevens squad.' And I replied, 'Fuck off, lads,' and hung up. Joe phoned straight back and said, 'No, really, this is Joe Lydon ...'

During my whole England career, I'd been on the periphery. I was never a Lawrence Dallaglio or a Maro Itoje, who were always the first name on the team sheet. The Leicester guys were always trying to find someone else to replace me. There were so many over the years, but I outlasted most of them. In 2010, they suddenly decided Leeds's Hendrie Fourie was the answer to all our back-row problems, because he was very good at competing for the ball and in one game in Australia against Australia A he tried to compete for the ball ten times, a record at the time. To be fair, out of the ten he did get four turnovers. The coaches were all very excited, Wellsy was positively vibrating with joy at how nuggety Hendrie was. He was also quiet, not brash, didn't have white boots, basically the perfect replacement for me. The coaches thought they had found England's answer to Richie McCaw. But Hendrie didn't last long, as it turns out you need more to your game than just competing on the ball. So they called me back in after making me travelling reserve for the first two games, which upset Stade and Max the owner, who then took half my monthly wages as punishment. I never got those back, by the way. I had it out with the club lawyers and everything, and they just told me to sue them – which would have cost me double what I'd have got back. You've got to love the French way of doing things. It was also the autumn internationals where they brought me back in for the South Africa game and Martin Johnson accused me of being a mole and leaking it to the press. Good times.

I'd get halfway through a Six Nations, while Tom Croft was injured, and as soon as Crofty was fit, come rain or shine, he'd be back in ahead of me. It didn't matter how I had played, I would get called into a room and told, 'Listen, we are going with Tom this week.' One year, I played in the first four games and played well but they then dropped me for Crofty for the last game, which was a Grand Slam decider against Wales and would have been my 50th cap. I got 10 minutes off the bench and we got humped. (I am more sad about that than most because I never got to lead my country out. I just got given my cap in a post-match ceremony after a huge loss. Not really the vibe or place you want to get it.) All the boys would laugh about it. I even started calling him 'Super Croft' as he could do no wrong. 'Don't worry, lads, everything will be all right, Crofty's back.' Wellsy loved this kind of chat, as did Wig, and he was always making jokes about it. Even when he wasn't coaching he would text me while I was in camp saying, 'You better watch out, Crofty is fit.' Crofty and I always got on well and we always had a good laugh about this stuff. As I have said before I never had problem with my competition; I was competitive but never a position hater. Crofty didn't pick the team and was a fantastic player who did things I could never do. Once the selection was made, I would help him all I could. It didn't mean I would stop taking the piss though. Super Croft was definitely a coaches' favourite.

In stark contrast, I went into that first camp with Eddie's England in 2016 thinking, 'This guy's backed me, I really need to repay him by showing him exactly what I can do.' And I played some of my best rugby in that Six Nations. At the end of meetings, Eddie would say, 'Hask, mate, what do you think?' And I'd be sitting there thinking, 'Oh my God, he actually wants to hear what I have to say.' I had over 50 England caps by this stage, so it made perfect sense to him that I knew what it meant to be part of a good team. He could see that I was desperate to be a leader and respected.

Eddie probably thought that by giving me that extra responsibility, it would make me slightly less selfish. I think that's why Dai Young made me captain of Wasps. He knew I was always working hard to be as good as I could be and was never disruptive. However, I was always eager to be in the midst of any nonsense that was going on and always getting stuck into youngsters. I handed out loads of nicknames that stuck forever, just off the top of my head. I wasn't a complete arsehole; if a bunch of youngsters were sitting around a table, I'd go and have a chat with them. But when you're captain, or the coach is asking for your input, you become more considerate of others and more aware of the consequences of your actions. You have to raise your standards and be aware you are setting an example. Just look at Ellis Genge and his development under Eddie Jones at England. He has grown into a real leader and someone Eddie can rely on. He is doing so well, and at the time of writing this he is Leicester captain. I reckon he could become England captain pretty soon. Sometimes the best leaders are not the media or coaches' favourite but a diamond in the rough.

On a related note, I interviewed a lad called Alfie Barbeary for my podcast recently. Definitely a future England player, Alfie was only 16 and being talked about as a future superstar when I first met him at Wasps. The other presenter asked him what his first memories of me were and he told this story. We were doing a scrum session before an Anglo-Welsh game when me and Guy Thompson started talking about Kevin Spacey, whose penchant for young men had just come out in the media. I looked at Alfie and apparently said, 'Kevin Spacey would have liked you, Alfie. You're young and tubby, just his type,' before walking straight off chuckling to myself. Then after the game Alfie was wearing white socks with black shoes, so I tried to get him to do a Michael Jackson moonwalk for the lads and kept shouting 'Hee! Hee!' at him in the post-match reception. The poor kid said once he realised that he brought the wrong socks to wear, he was trying to avoid anyone who would give him stick. Which meant avoiding me. He almost didn't go to the after-match function, and when he did who was the first person he should run into, but good old me. When he reminded me of this stuff, which I had completely forgotten about, I laughed out loud and felt a small pang of guilt, but I did say to him there was a silver lining. At least I was talking to him; most senior players wouldn't dare talk to a kid who was on trial from school.

Because Eddie gave me part-ownership of that England group, I never wanted to mess it up. That's a very different feeling to being on the edges. And that's why me and Eddie built such a good relationship. He never looked at me and thought, 'We'll break him to make him fit, keep hammering that square peg until it fits our round hole. And if he doesn't fit, so be it.' Instead, Eddie thought, 'He's obviously a square peg, so we'll have to make the hole square for him.' He just wanted me to be me, didn't give a shit about what I was doing in my spare time. In fact, he thought it was a good thing that I had other interests. As long as I trained the house down and played well, he loved it.

For years, people had been saying, 'Haskell's not an open-side flanker,' because I wasn't short and stocky, like Neil Back or Michael Hooper. So when Eddie picked me to play seven, it caused a bit of a stir in the media. And when Eddie pulled me aside for one of our first one-on-one chats at Pennyhill Park, I felt the need to sell myself to him. I reminded him I'd played seven for the Highlanders in New Zealand, that I'd held my own against Richie McCaw, and he launched into a big speech: 'Hask, mate, you're overthinking it. Don't fucking worry about these media people, they don't know what they are talking about and neither to do the fans. Don't fucking worry about any of it. All I want you to do is hit people really fucking hard and, if you get the ball, run really fucking hard with it. That's it. Don't worry about the breakdown, don't worry about trying to be like Richie McCaw – if the ball's there, go for it. But otherwise, I just need you to do what you do, and do it well. You have the physique of an Islander and hit as hard as an Islander. I'll take care of the fucking media if they ask stupid questions, you just fucking get on with the job I've asked you to do.' I was thinking, 'Fair enough. That's all I need to know.' That was Eddie empowering me, by getting me to do what I did best, rather than trying to do things that other people thought I should do.

When I started DJing, I didn't feel like I fitted in either. I wasn't 'cool' in the way most DJs are cool, because I was this giant in comparison to most DJs who played rugby. But quite a few people either started out as DJs before becoming famous in another field, or the other way around. Before he became an actor, Idris Elba was a DJ and still dips his toe in the scene, while the former basketball player Shaquille O'Neal now operates under the name DJ Diesel. Then there's the snooker legend Steve Davis, who plays weird, obscure techno and is well respected. He's even played Glastonbury a couple of times.

I remember my former DJ agent saying to me, 'Why did you get into this game?' I replied, 'Because I love the music. I enjoy the technology and learning a new skill. And I really enjoy the attention. It's like a perfect storm.' And this agent looked at me and said, 'Okay, but you won't make any money.'

'That's fine,' I replied, 'because it's not really about making money.'

'Good. Because you won't.'

Then this agent went off and booked me a gig that paid three grand. I mean, three grand for an hour's work is pretty good money, and that was my first job. Then this agent started saying, 'This is still going to be a difficult path for you to go down, but I suppose Steve Davis is doing all right.' I looked at him like he was mad and said, '*The* Steve Davis? The *snooker player* Steve Davis?' I couldn't get my head around it, but Steve Davis was like my canary down the mine. I thought, 'If Steve Davis can make a success of DJing, and he was famous for being the most boring man in Britain, surely I've got a chance.'

But while Steve Davis had been DJing on the radio for years before he started doing gigs, I was going into it virtually blind. And when I turned up for that first gig, I was all over the place. My hands were all shaky on the controls, any bravado soon evaporated, and I just wanted to crawl into a hole and die. It didn't matter how many times my DJ teacher told me I'd done fine and everyone had enjoyed themselves, all I wanted to do, after my hour was up, was to call Chloe and tell her I'd ruined everything and was probably finished as a DJ.

Whenever I mess up at something I've spent ages learning and want to be good at, it kills me. Luckily I have done so many gigs in front of thousands of people I don't get this anymore. I just hate to be embarrassed. I'll feel my ears burning, my cheeks going red and I'll be in a foul mood for ages afterwards. In stark contrast to my appearance on *Mastermind*, I was mortified by my appearance on the quiz show *Catchpoint*. Now *Catchpoint* isn't the most cerebral programme, it's basically answering a few questions and trying to catch balls falling from the ceiling. But after I dropped a couple, I was properly pissed off.

After the show, I was really down and Chloe couldn't understand why. She must have found it particularly weird because I'm always telling her off for doubting herself. She said to me, 'Babe, what's wrong with you? It's only a fun TV show. You threw yourself into it, you were funny. You just dropped a couple of balls.' And I replied, 'Yeah, but that was something I was supposed to be good at, and I fucked it up.' It was the complete opposite to my appearance on *Mastermind*. I even thought about asking them to cut my appearance. Thankfully, nobody really saw it, apart from my old Wasps and England teammate Andy Goode, who was calling me 'old shit hands' on social media. All those years working with psychologists, and I'm still riddled with self-doubt over certain things. The only difference now is my ability to shrug it all off and get back on the wagon of positivity; in the old days it would need a few days, but now it's a couple of hours. That's the thing to remember: you won't ever not have bad days, moments of doubt or feel shit. It's all about how quickly you can change focus and come back stronger.

10

I AM A PIG

CHLOE MADELEY:

'I was in a gym that we both used to train in and one of the guys posted a video of me lifting on Twitter. James saw it, slid into my DMs and said he'd love to take me out for a drink. I'm sure I wasn't the first, although I do hope I was the last. I said to the guys, "Is he a good man?" and they replied, "Definitely not, don't go near him." So I immediately deleted his message.

'I was sick to death of men and happily single for the first time in years. I was in one of those phases where I thought I'd be single for the rest of my life. And I soon learned that James had a similar reputation to Joey from Friends. He'd pursue women, sleep with them and then say, "Okay, I'm done now." He didn't want to commit or settle down, and I wasn't interested in that. At the time, I was thinking, "If I ever get into another relationship, it will be love at first sight and we'll get married almost straightaway."

'James could see that I'd read his message and not responded, so he posted a meme of SpongeBob SquarePants, looking lonely while drinking a cup of *coffee, and tagged me in it, with the message, "Waiting for you to get back to me." I quite liked that he put himself out there like that, so I went back into my DMs and sent him a message: "Listen, that was really sweet and funny, but I'm happily single and not interested." And he replied, "You've got the wrong end of the stick. I'd really like for you to be the female face of my supplement range." I thought, "Oh fuck, that's embarrassing, how egotistical of me." So we ended up meeting in a healthy-food café called Jak's in Chelsea.*

'I turned up in tracksuit bottoms and a hoodie, with no make-up. He had a stupid handlebar moustache, for Movember. I thought, "Eugh, classic rugby knob." We started talking and everything out of James's mouth was a one-liner or a meme, some of which he'd clearly read online. It made me cringe. I said to him, "You're the first rugby boy I've met since university, and your chat is no different to theirs. This is really embarrassing for you."

'After about ten minutes, it became quite clear that the stuff about me being the female face of his supplement range had been a ruse. And I'd shlepped all the way to Chelsea from north-west London. But then he suddenly started talking like a normal person. When I asked him about his rugby, he said he didn't want to talk about it, because that's all he spoke about with everyone else in his life. I found that really interesting, and I started to think, "This guy is actually quite funny, intelligent and articulate. This is quite good fun. I'd actually quite like to be friends with him."

'When it was time for me to go, James walked me back to my car, which was a little, beaten-up Ford Ka. When

he saw it, James said, "Whoa, really sorry, but someone seems to have stolen your car and replaced it with a piece of shit." I laughed and said, "You're actually quite funny," and he leaned in and gave me a light peck on the lips. When I got home, he'd sent me a text that said, "That was interesting …"

'I was staying with my parents that weekend. And when I woke up the following morning, my dad had the rugby on and there was James, playing for England. My God, I genuinely didn't know, because he hadn't told me. I said to my dad, "I went on a date with that guy last night." And he replied, "Wow, that's impressive," which he never normally says.

'I reckon that 80 per cent of the time, James is dead inside. I'll be thinking, "I don't understand. Have I married a complete psychopath?" Then he'll suddenly do something romantic that will completely blow my socks off.

'When he proposed, he went to ridiculous lengths. We had an insane few days away in Paris, with the best suite in the best hotel and everything taken care of. We both got Covid at about the same time, but he got over it before me. So when lockdown eased, he was out seeing his friends while I was stuck inside, feeling jealous. But when I finally recovered, he'd planned an evening at the Lanesborough Hotel, my favourite place in London.

'We didn't have to order anything, they just brought all my favourite food and wine to our table. He spent the whole night asking questions about me, my friends, my family and my work. That was really romantic because it wasn't really James and must have taken a real effort.

'And, to be fair to James, I wouldn't want romance all the time anyway. If the person I was with was more romantic than me, there'd be a problem.'

Chloe seems to think I'm an emotional cripple, with a serial killer's brain. I think what she really means is that I'm a very rational person. And when Chloe says that I'm dead inside, it probably just means she's feeling a bit neglected at that moment in time. But the truth is rather different!

She always goes on about the time I took her to Paris for a surprise and proposed to her out there, the subtext being that I've done nothing romantic since. She conveniently forgets her birthday trip, the spa trip, the expensive dinners, the little gifts. And in case you're thinking, 'James doth protest too much,' that isn't the case at all. If you tell me that I haven't done something, I will come back to you with a PowerPoint presentation, including pie charts and scatter plots, proving all the times I have actually done it. What I'm trying to say, in a polite way, is that Chloe is talking utter shit.

In fact, only recently she said to me, 'We never do anything romantic,' and I replied, 'I took you out for dinner the other night!' And you know what her response was? 'Yeah, apart from that.' And then I had to remind her about the bag I bought her and the fact I told her I loved her four times that morning. And you know what her response to that was? 'Yeah, but you didn't mean it ...'

I've spoken to therapists about this, and they've told me that if a partner starts using phrases like 'You've never' or 'You don't' or 'You won't', that's their emotion talking. They usually don't really mean that you never or don't or won't, it's just that they're feeling insecure and want to feel loved and heard. When it comes to arguing with Chloe, I try to tackle what she says point by point: 'Right, I've addressed that issue, now for the next one ...' But women will pivot mid-conversation, in a bid to throw you off. It's the arguing equivalent of someone tipping a chess board over when they're about to be check-mated. Do not fight irrationality with fact. You need to listen to what women are feeling, not what they are saying. It's taken me years to grasp this, and even now I'm still only a white belt.

I'm also very affectionate, very touchy-feely. I don't mind kissing Chloe in public, so that all my mates will tell us to get a room. Every time I see my dad, I give him a hug and a kiss on the cheek. Some of the Wasps boys thought that was weird, back in the day. Fraser Waters used to take the piss and would always jokingly say, 'Urgh, look at you necking your fucking dad.' I'd reply, 'Fraser, just because you still shake your fucking dad's hand and show no actual affection for each other doesn't make me odd.' Another teammate, who will remain nameless, was absolutely disgusted that I kissed my dad and he kept saying I was gay. It almost made him physically sick. I think his issue was his dad, who barely ever spoke to him and if he did it was to criticise him. He had the kind of father who would have sent him away to a boarding school until he came of age and then their first meeting would be at dinner on his 18th birthday. A real old-school parent.

There are some funny stories about that teammate and his family. One day at school, he was getting filled in by another kid in the playground and saw his brother running towards him. He thought his brother was going to save him, but he started filling him in as well. Then there was the time his partner met his parents for the first time. He dropped her off on his parents' doorstep and drove off, having given her the wrong names. When his dad answered the door, she said, 'Oh, hello, Terry,' and his dad slammed the door in her face. He was actually called John. When this teammate introduced her to his friends for the first time, he dropped her at the pub and went somewhere else for two hours. He said it was an experiment, to test if the relationship had any legs. This guy had typical Daddy issues and shockingly the relationship didn't last. What a surprise that was! (I did think about trying it with Chloe, just to see what would happen, but I bottled it.)

It's true that I don't get that excited or emotional about things. For example, Chloe was very excited about her brother's wedding and I didn't really give it a moment's thought until the actual day. It's not that I wasn't bothered about the wedding, it's just that I had lots of other stuff on. Chloe said to me, 'Why aren't you excited? You never get excited about anything.' And I replied, 'Actually, I'm doing my JCB digger course next week. I'm excited about that.' That didn't go down well.

Chloe will well up over the smallest thing, like a TV advert, and I'll be looking at her and thinking, 'I'm not really feeling anything. Maybe I'm dead inside.' I get teary after a big weekend of boozing, though. I'll stick a Harry Potter film on and be in pieces within five minutes. The post-booze comedown will get you. But the only stuff that makes me cry otherwise is injured animals, especially dogs; that movie *Marley & Me* almost emotionally crippled me for life. Also movies about underdogs or anything involving kids and parents. But even then, it will probably only be a single tear running down my cheek. Meanwhile, Chloe will be sobbing uncontrollably and almost strangling Bertie with hugs.

SUSIE HASKELL:

'One January morning, when James was seven, one of his teachers was looking out of his window and noticed him standing in the snow, wearing a short-sleeved shirt and

shorts. The teacher shouted, "James, what are you doing out there in the snow?"

'James replied, "Hush …"

"What are you listening to?"

"The silence."

'That's just one example of how sensitive James was as a child.

'If I was upset about anything, he'd be dreadfully upset as well. He and his brother always used to fight, as brothers do. And because I never knew who had started it, I usually decided that both would be punished. But one day, after a particularly turbulent episode between my two sons, James slipped a note under my bedroom door: "I no [sic] I am a pig." I still have that note.

'When James became a professional rugby player, we didn't want him to fritter his money away and waste his spare time. So my husband decided that the best thing would be for James to have a website, so that he could promote himself and learn about business. But that rugby banter can destroy people, especially if you're sensitive. They don't miss a trick, will pick up on anything, whether you've got a spot on your nose or your shoes are the wrong shade of brown. So James was very upset when his teammates were mocking him, calling him "The Brand". And they did evil things when his love life made the press, and put newspaper articles all over the changing room. He was devastated about a break-up, almost inconsolable, and what reaction did he get from his work-mates? Just a lot of mickey-taking.

'He's got great bravado, comes across as brash and full of himself. But the real James is a very emotionally intelligent, caring young man. He's remained friends with *some of those little chaps he was at school with when he was five or six. And he makes new friends wherever he goes. That tells you everything you need to know.'*

Hahahahaha. Oh my God, I think my mum must have been high when I interviewed her. What the fuck is she on about, listening to the sound of silence? I have never heard such crap in my life. I mean kids often do odd things, but I'm not sure this ever happened. At least we now know where I got my vivid imagination from. I think my mum is living in an alternative universe where I am some soft-centred person, or soft in the head from the sounds of it. Yes, I have some friends from school, but who doesn't? I'm not sure that qualifies me as a sensitive soul and they are most certainly not little boys anymore. As far as putting notes under her door, I was probably working some angle and trying to get one over on my brother, who was a nightmare and always getting away with stuff. But bless her, she wants me so badly to not be the loud, aggressive, slightly misogynist man that I am. If I do get cancelled, at least I know who to employ to help me with the PR rebuild: good old Susie Haskell.

Look, I'm never going to be the most emotionally intelligent person ever or the most sensitive bloke, but I am slightly deeper than a saucer and I care very much about certain things in my life. When Stuart Lancaster was in charge of England, he was very big on culture and would sometimes ask players to describe what playing for England meant to them. And on the 2014 tour of New Zealand, he asked me to speak in the changing room before the first Test at Eden Park. This was normally reserved for new players getting their first camp, but as I had only played once before for Stuart he thought he would give me the opportunity to share what the shirt meant to me.

Players tended to speak about making their parents proud and the thrill they got from putting on the shirt, that sort of stuff, but I spoke about the effect Matt Hampson's injury had had on me and how it was about making the most of whatever talent you had; how lucky I was to be there when others did not get that chance.

I was on the pitch, taking part in an England Under-21s training session, when Matt suffered his terrible injury – a scrum collapsed and he never walked again, having severed his spinal cord. It was only the quick thinking of referee and paramedic Tony Spreadbury, who stabilised Matt's neck, that saved his life. So I spoke about how that incident had shaped my whole approach to life; how you never know if or when it's all going to be taken away from you; how inspirational Matt had been since the incident; and how I had a responsibility to make the most of what talent I had. I'd made notes on my phone, and I could see some of the lads looking at each other as if to say, 'Oh God, get ready for another Haskell performance.' But it was important that I articulated my thoughts properly, and I ended up getting quite choked up.

It wasn't just speaking about Matt that made me emotional, it was also the fact that it was the first time an England coach had asked me to put into words what playing for England meant to me. And I'd already won 50 international caps. I think some of my teammates were a bit taken aback; they couldn't understand how this bloke who was always fucking about and taking the piss was now almost in tears. Graham Rowntree said to me afterwards, 'You got a bit emotional there. Are you all right?' Graham probably didn't know that men could cry. In fact, if anyone had started crying in that Leicester team Graham played for, they probably would have been sacked on the spot and chucked out of the window.

That wasn't the only time I got a bit emotional before an England game. On the 2012 tour of South Africa, I was recalled to the team for the third Test in Port Elizabeth, having thought I'd never play for England again, following the 2011 World Cup debacle. I said to the lads, 'Listen, never take playing for your country for granted. It feels like I've been out of this changing room forever, and I thought I'd never get back here. You have to make the most of these moments, leave nothing out there, put a big performance in, want it more than them, because you might not have many more of these moments, if any. You always have to play as if there is no tomorrow, because at international level there often isn't.' I could see that my words had touched home with the lads and they told me as much after the game, saying I motivated them. No sooner had I finished than Graham Rowntree, in an attempt to get the lads further fired up, started ranting and raving and then kicked out at a large plastic box, putting a big hole in it and getting his foot stuck. He tried to keep his cool, stay on track, all the while trying to shake this box off his foot that would not for love nor money come off. Now we were suddenly all trying not to piss ourselves laughing.

We managed to draw that third Test 14–14, breaking a run of nine straight defeats by the Springboks. It was a huge moment for a young squad (that was the game where I made 34-odd tackles, had one of my best games for England ever, and one journalist gave me 4 out of 10, citing defensive frailties on my part for the low score). As I mentioned, some of the lads felt I had spoken well and that this was just what was needed. The feedback from the coaches was not quite as nice. They were surprised that I was speaking up when I was new to the team and hadn't earned any respect yet and if anything was too emotional. I had 45 caps, not sure how many you need to be able to speak. I was dropped soon after that into the Saxons and only found this out from a Sky news bulletin.

When the Lions squad was selected for the 2021 tour of South Africa, I was quite sad about it. It's not as if I was in the running – I'd already been retired for two years – but it made me fear my own mortality. While I'm limping around my house in pain, young, fitter blokes would be putting their bodies on the line for the Lions. Some of them were old teammates, and I know what a magical adventure a Lions tour is. Plus, everyone was talking about it all the time, which didn't help. It was jealousy, really, wanting what they had. It seemed so close, yet so far away, and I'd never experience it again.

I couldn't watch any rugby straight after retiring. I found the fact that I didn't finish on my own terms very hard. I'm not a quitter, and I'd had to bow out mid-season. That didn't sit at all well with me. I had a ticket for the World Cup final between England and South Africa, could have watched it with the lads in the stand, but watched it in a bar in Tokyo with my fellow podcasters Mike Tindall and Alex Payne, and with Chloe instead. I worried how I'd react if we won, or if we lost, and thought my emotions might overwhelm me if I was in the stand. If we won, which I wanted them to do, I would be sad for myself and happy for them, wishing I was part of it but couldn't be, because if I did I'd get accused of stolen valour – or doing a John Terry, as it's known. But if we lost, I wouldn't know what to say or do. So I thought it was safer to be with mates some way away.

Former teammates who weren't in the squad told me they didn't want England to win, because they weren't part of it. You'd be surprised how common that was, as well as 'position haters', players who resented the people they were competing with for a place in the team. I was never like that. The way I saw it, it was out of our hands anyway. Wanting England to lose, just because you'd been left out, seemed odd to me. And whoever got picked deserved it, end of story. If I didn't get picked, I'd always go straight to whoever did, shake their hand, say, 'Congrats, mate, well done. How can I help you this week?' I would do it every time without fail. Ideally, they'd do the same thing for me if I got picked ahead of them at some point in the future. We didn't have to be best buddies, but we had to respect each other for the sake of the team.

When you're a professional sportsperson, you are defined by your physical prowess. With me, it was my size and my power, and suddenly I couldn't even run anymore and was hobbling around the house like an old man. It was like someone had clicked their fingers and I was no longer the person I'd been. To be honest, I'm finding my limitations quite upsetting at the moment, which is probably why I've been getting increasingly irritable.

Not only were Chloe's parents celebrities, she herself also went to one of those alternative, progressive schools. If they didn't fancy lessons, or they were 'having a bad day', they'd be allowed to go off and take pictures of flowers or lie down in the sun. She'd also call all her teachers by their first names. At my schools, no one ever called me anything but 'Haskell'. If I'd told a teacher I was having a bad day and wanted to go for a walk, they'd have told me to shut up, given me six minus house points and ordered me to clean the headmaster's car.

I've been around boys and men my whole life, so the chances of me being particularly progressive on certain issues were always going to be slim. Rugby union is an elite sport and all about winning, so any weak links are spotted from a thousand yards and ripped out immediately. If a player isn't good enough, it's a case of, 'Get better or fuck off.' And if they don't get better, they're told their contract is being torn up and they're booted out of the door, without even a 'good luck with the rest of your life'.

It's a ruthless environment, so I find any environment that's not as professional as I'm used to difficult to deal with. That's why Chloe's always saying I think I'm better than everyone else. I'll say to her, 'Well, not everyone, but I'm definitely better than some.' She will always roll her eyes and say, 'You are not,' and walk off. My whole life has been defined by success and failure; it was never about just giving things a go, being a good sport and being mediocre.

People are always going on about the importance of building resilience nowadays, but kids have never been more coddled. We live in an age where kids call the shots, what they say goes and parents forcing their kids to do things they don't want to do is frowned upon. A mate of mine who is equally exasperated by all this recently told me that his kid was invited to a friend's house but didn't want to go, because he was worried they'd give him something he didn't like for tea. He could not believe it and was annoyed that his wife was pandering to all this. He caught her writing to the mate's parents, explaining that their kid wouldn't be eating. He stopped her and said no way are you going to send that. If the kid is invited for tea, tea is what he will have. I did check that his kid wasn't vegan or allergic to something. And my mate replied, 'No, he just doesn't like spicy food and gets all worried about it.' We both laughed, as firstly, who was serving vindaloo up for a kids' tea, and how different things are for the younger generation. Luckily, my mate was having none of this, and told his kid and wife he should just be polite and eat whatever he's given and was '100 per cent going'. But how many parents would pander to this and have sent the message? That's why we have a load of young people who can't cope with the smallest bit of pressure or discomfort. If I had tried to not go because of being fearful of food, my mum would have clipped me around the ear and just dumped me on my mate's doorstep. Then if she had heard I was being fussy, she would have made me sit there until I finished my plate whether it was at our house or someone else's. Do you remember when parents used to ask other parents how their kid was and did they behave, and if you were a dick they would be told you were awful and you would get a hiding from your parents? I'm not sure that happens now, in case there is some huge offence caused.

There seems to be a desire nowadays to medically diagnose and stick labels on everything, which has the effect of watering everything down. Take anxiety. I know people who have had anxiety; it's being up all night with heart palpitations and being unable to function. It's a serious disorder. Now, everyone seems to be anxious, but what most of them mean is that they're nervous or apprehensive. And being nervous or apprehensive about stuff is the most natural thing in the world. We all get nervous before doing something for the first time, it's natural. We all get nervous meeting new people. Again, it's normal. It doesn't mean I have performance anxiety or social anxiety. It means I am fucking nervous, end of story.

It's the same with depression. Depression is a terrible thing, absolutely shocking for the person who has it and those close to them. I've seen it up close and it's not pretty. But nowadays, a lot of people mix up depression with sadness or having a bad day. It's great that we're bringing up kids to be more in tune with their emotions than previous generations. But too many people forget that life is a constant competition, whether it's trying to do well in exams, get a good job, earn enough money to live a comfortable life, find a mate. And I suspect diagnosing emotions as medical problems and slapping labels on perfectly normal feelings is making kids weaker, not more resilient. The secret to life is being comfortable with being uncomfortable, not never being made to feel bad or to avoid struggling and all the associated emotions that go with it.

The more people claim to have depression or anxiety or stress, the more it cheapens the experiences of people who actually have those conditions. Once upon a time, the only people suffering from stress were A&E nurses, paramedics or City traders who were up all night taking cocaine and getting two hours' sleep, before spending the next 12 hours screaming down the phone at people. For them, stress meant being burnt out at 45, with their personal life in tatters. I'd never belittle people with real mental illness, but now people say they're stressed when they have to work late or someone doesn't like a video they posted on social media. It's just not the same thing.

Another thing that bugs me is that some stuff that's supposed to be progressive doesn't strike me as progressive at all. I was standing in a queue in a supermarket recently, behind a woman and what appeared to be her daughter, with plaited hair. Another woman said to her, 'Your daughter's got lovely hair.' And this kid's mum replied, 'That's a boy. I suppose you're not bringing your children up gender neutral?' I honestly almost stuck my oar in, which I'm sure wouldn't have gone down very well. I was thinking, 'I don't understand this. It's not about bringing up your kid "gender neutral", it's simply a case of not foisting old-fashioned gender rules on them.' So don't buy your daughter an apron and a broom and your son a calcula-tor and a suit. Don't buy your daughter a mop and bucket and your son some boxing gloves. In other words, let them do what they want to do, regardless of gender. But a boy with plaited hair is still a boy, just as a girl who likes trucks is still a girl.

My mate's son loves the movie *Frozen* and is always wandering around the house in a dress. Who cares! My mate's not like Billy Elliot's dad – 'Take that fucking dress off, you poof!' He lets his kid wear whatever he wants. But my mate knows that just because his son likes *Frozen* and wearing a dress occasionally, that doesn't mean he's a girl, and it doesn't mean he's 'gender neutral'. It just means he's a boy who likes wearing dresses occasionally. I've been known to roll up to parties in a dress! It had nothing to do with my sexuality or gender identity, it was just because I fancied wearing a dress that night.

The problem with giving children too much agency is that they don't know what they're doing – because they're children. At the time of writing, I'm 36, and I still don't know what I'm doing or exactly who I want to be. Let them explore their identities, let them mess around with gender if they want to. But people have been doing that for decades anyway – that's why we have the word 'tomboy'. But now, so many people in society view these kids who gender bend and think they're actually the opposite sex as special. And when kids see classmates getting special treatment, they want a piece of it. That's how kids work, that's how life works. Most people want to be part of something special.

Chloe is obsessed with this idea that I'm still, and always will be, a little lost boy. When we got Bertie the dog, it was as if Chloe fell in love. She kept saying, 'I can't imagine life without him. There was such a big hole in my life that I didn't even know was there.' The first time she came out with this stuff I said to her, 'I knew the hole was there, because you were trying to make me fill it all the time!' So now, poor Bertie gets shoved in this hole instead. Chloe cuddles and strokes him so much I reckon he's going to go bald soon. Sometimes, he'll wriggle out of her clutches, come and sit next to me and sigh. I'll say to him, 'Is she bothering you again?' And he'll give me a sad look that definitely translates as, 'Yes.' At least that's the story I'm going with.

Chloe goes to extraordinary lengths to try to work me out. One day, she came bouncing into the house and said, 'Babe, I've just been talking to a friend ...' As soon as I hear that, I think, 'Fuck, I really don't want to hear this,' but I usually just smile instead. It turned out she and her mate had done this test and become convinced I had narcissistic personality disorder.

Chloe spent the next half an hour character-assassinating me, but doing it with a big smile on her face, as if this was her greatest ever discovery. She kept saying, 'Babe, you tick all the boxes,' and I'd reply, 'Well, some of it sounds like me and some of it doesn't.' Then she said, 'Don't worry, I've got histrionic personality disorder,' as if that was supposed to make me feel better. I ended up talking about it with my therapist. I said to him, 'Look, Chloe thinks I'm a potential serial killer. Can we just go through it to make sure I'm not? Because if I am, we might have to address it.' After a few sessions the therapist decided I wasn't a serial killer, which was something of a relief.

And you know what? Compared to some people I meet, I'm a model of tact and sensitivity. I was at a video game launch once and got introduced to a young athlete and his dad. This athlete later came out as gay, but at the time was still firmly in the closet, even though it was pretty obvious where things were heading. So there we were, making banal small talk, when I turned to the kid and said, 'Do you like playing video games?' and he shyly said, 'Yes, I like playing video games.'

Then I turned to this kid's dad and said, 'Do you like playing video games, Mr Smith?' Mr Smith paused and said, 'No, I like playing with fannies.' As he said that, he did a fanny-fingering action. I was lost for words as he had done it not only in front of his son but in front of the CEO of Electronic Arts Inc., Europe. What do you say to that? All I could muster was, 'Well, don't we all, Mr Smith, don't we all,' before wandering off. It was only a few years later, when his son came out, that I thought, 'No wonder it took him so long.' Can you imagine the conversations they must have had?

'Dad, I'm gay.'

'That's good, son. I'm very happy as well.'

'No. I mean I love men.'

'Yes, son, I love men as well. Your Uncle Roger, Granddad George …'

'I want to have sex with men.'

'You've lost me there, lad. What do you mean have sex with men? You mean women, don't you?'

11

GETTING CANCELLED

ALEX PAYNE:

'Just after we started in business together, James said to me, "You have to realise that if you play with me, you're playing with fire." He might even have said, "If you play with me, you'll get sued." So I've always known what I was dealing with, and I've ended up being led down alleys I wouldn't necessarily have chosen to go down. But for every catastrophe that comes James's way, there are three or four things he does brilliantly.

'When the idea of a podcast was put to me, they asked who I'd like to do it with. James was the only person on the list, because I knew he'd give the listeners something no one else could. Rugby is a game built on beer and funny stories, but that's been lost in the last ten years or so. Everyone is trying to behave a bit better, make the sport more accessible and inclusive. So when someone as big, brash and noisy as Hask walks into that world, screaming and shouting and telling stories that supposedly don't fit into that world anymore, people love it. He's intoxicating to listen to, listeners get swept up in it and want a piece of it. No one can question how *professional and committed James was to the sport, but he's also a Saturday-night car crash. The reason our podcast is a success is fundamentally down to him.*

'Hask is unique, a bit of a throwback, because he doesn't worry about the consequences. He genuinely does just chuck it out there and deal with it later. And he finds it very difficult to turn the other cheek. He's used to an environment in which alpha males thrive, that's what made him an international sportsman. But that's not the real world, especially not in 2021.

'The fact that James lives a very full-on, boisterous existence, and is such a big, loud presence opens him up to criticism and occasional calls for him to be cancelled. It was Churchill who said it was good to have enemies, because it means you've stood up for something in your life. But to have longevity, James needs to soften. I think he knows that, but we keep seeing him flip back to that alpha male caricature every now and again.

'I always say that I'm just sitting in James's sidecar, hanging on for dear life while he's driving the bike at 150 mph. We'll often joke that The Good, The Bad & The Rugby *will end like the final scene in* Thelma & Louise, *where they drive off a cliff. But that's part of its appeal, you're never quite sure if each show will be the last. And that's what I signed up for. He's taught me that there's no point in whingeing about it, it's best just to cling on and see where we end up. It's Planet Haskell and I'm just living on it.'*

When I get involved in spats on social media, I'm not saying things for my benefit, I'm saying things to make people laugh (and because I quite enjoy outraging the people who don't find me funny). But I've got a self-destructive streak, even if it's an unconscious one. If I'm doing something for one of my sponsors, I might suggest changing things up, seeing if we can do things better. Creative types who make adverts and other content aren't used to being challenged, but I like pushing back as far as I can and seeing people panic.

I am often getting asked to do appearances, present or interview people for various brands and companies. I recently did something where I was to interview staff at a rugby club who had been helped out with a full club makeover. The producer would say to me, 'Can you get them to say this: "NatWest has given us a platform to be financially sustainable for the future."' And I couldn't resist replying, 'Sorry, how the hell am I going to get them to say that? It's the most unnatural thing ever. Who goes around saying, "NatWest has given us a platform to be financially sustainable for the future?"' The producer would say, 'I didn't write it!' and to be fair to him, he didn't. But I just couldn't get my head around the fact that a load of creative and PR types had sat around a table, brainstorming ideas for days on end (and getting paid very well for it, no doubt), and that's the best they could come up with. People are always going on about 'authenticity' nowadays, about 'being your true self', but nothing about the advertising industry is authentic. It's just a load of creative types justifying their jobs.

I recently did an advert for Amazon, where they dressed me up as a delivery driver, stuck me in one of their vans and had me getting into all sorts of amusing scrapes. I was dropping boxes and getting lost and basically behaving like Frank Spencer, but after they'd filmed it someone got in touch and said, 'It's a bit too serious. We're a little bit concerned that people might think James actually works for Amazon.' Most people would just let that slide, but I replied, 'Sorry, what are you talking about? It's like an episode of *Some Mothers Do 'Ave 'Em*. It's quite obviously a joke! Why would anyone think I was now working as a delivery driver for Amazon?' Luckily, saner minds at Amazon prevailed and we created some great content that went down a storm. I am excited to see them working once again in rugby, as streaming services are the way to go. They have all the money and can help grow rugby tenfold, and it was great that Amazon let us be ourselves and make funny content that promoted them and rugby.

It's almost like people feel they need to say something when asked. They can't just leave it, because if they leave it people think they are not doing their job. Compliance teams at huge corporations can be tricky time and time again; you start with a great idea and what's left at the end is this sanitised, vanilla, all things to all men mess. They have to make sure that no one gets offended, which is impossible, but they don't realise that. You can't please everyone, so why try? The sooner people stop worrying about the vocal minority getting their knickers in a twist over something stupid the better the world will be. Social media should not dictate policy on anything. Ever.

I'm also a bit confused as to where the boundaries are. One company said to my agent recently, 'We'd love to work with James, we think he's great, but he's got to stop swearing at people on social media.' When my agent told me this, I said, 'But surely you replied with, "You have a guy working for you who allegedly got caught doing a tonne of coke and shagging a load of prostitutes."' That appears slightly worse to do than calling the odd troll a cunt. At least now I know where the line is with this company: coke = okay, swearing = unemployment. Funny enough the agent did not bring it up, as he rightly felt it wouldn't have helped my cause. If I had been there I would have 100 per cent mentioned it just to see the guy squirm.

I'm never going to conform completely, and if that means I can't do certain things, that's fine. Even companies I work with at the moment don't really want me to be me. It's not personal, it's how everyone is treated. They'll say, 'We want to work with you because we love what you're about.' But I'll do an advert for them and they'll put me on a very short lead. The director will start out by telling me to say something in my own words, and then say, 'No, not those words. Could you say it in these words?' I'll be thinking, 'Why didn't you just ask me to say that in the first place? Why the pretence?' So we want you to be organic and yourself, but do it this way and act completely differently to how you actually are. It always makes me smile, but there is no point fighting it. It's the world we live in.

I recorded another advert, and they came back to me and said, 'Sorry, it's too funny for our brand.' How can something be too funny? What's the point in hiring me because they like what I'm about, and then telling me to pretend to be someone I'm not? It's the fear factor that social media has created, and it's only going to get worse.

Companies and organisations just seem shit scared of anyone having a strong opinion. It winds me up, makes me want to rail against it. Most people are too busy getting on with their lives, but there is a very loud minority who have got nothing better to do than moan and complain about anything that doesn't fit in with their view of the world. These people are just so sensitive about everything and intent on erasing anything that happens to offend them.

Chloe thinks I lack self-control, because I often do and say stuff that makes life harder for me. She's right, I often can't shut up when staying schtum would be the more sensible option. I've got a photo of the England squad on my wall, which was never published. Every single player is smiling or laughing, because I've just shouted something daft, as one of the lads standing behind me was trying to give me a combover while commenting on my ever-receding hairline. I told him to get fucked and then the photographer Dave Rogers told me to be serious, so I jokingly told him to get fucked and take the photo, followed by giving him the middle finger. He of course captured this moment and it's amazing, I look at it every day and it makes me smile. It's exactly what I have talked about before, the lads getting me to bite, which I did, and then me replying and making them all laugh. Even Tom Wood, who you can see in the photo and who never wanted to find anything I said funny, has got a smirk on his face. This picture encapsulates what I brought to the team. I wasn't a bad man. I always made those around me laugh whether they wanted to or not, and I did things my way in my style.

When Eddie Jones took over as head coach, Canterbury took over from Nike as our kit supplier. The photoshoot for the kit was a bit of a shambles because they hadn't planned it properly. We were being driven backwards and forwards, the lads were moaning, everyone was standing around on their feet for ages, and we had a game that weekend. I ended up shouting, 'Bring back Nike!' All the lads found it amusing, but someone from Canterbury complained. The media man took me aside and said, 'Look, they didn't appreciate you saying that stuff about Nike.'

I couldn't believe that someone had been offended. It's not like I was calling Canterbury shit on my Instagram account; I was just having a bit of a joke during a photoshoot, giving them a bit of a ribbing because they hadn't organised things properly. It's not as if I was being disruptive – they still got all the shots and footage they wanted. And I was quite happy to do the extras they asked for. But that day was me in a nutshell, with most people coming away from it thinking I'd been entertaining company, and a couple of people coming away from it thinking I was a complete arsehole and never to be trusted.

It irritates me when potential business partners tell me that while they can see my point of view they can't be associated with someone who behaves like that. But when I'm in a slightly more empathetic mood I can see where these companies are coming from. People want an easy life, and it's simply a lot less hassle working with someone vanilla who's going to say all the right things. I'll work my bollocks off for sponsors, go above and beyond, but the perception is that there is a risk I will fuck up. I can imagine the board meeting: 'Yes, James is certainly an interesting guy and will probably attract a lot of custom. But can we be sure he isn't going to shoot someone or flatten someone in his digger?'

DYLAN HARTLEY:

'James openly admits he's not everyone's cup of tea, or he'll say he's like Marmite. He's pretty self-deprecating like that. Having spent so much time with him, I know he's a very intelligent, caring, sensitive guy. But I can see why people think he's not much more than a loud, brash rugby lad. He's got a big mouth and a personality that rubs people up the wrong way. When you live life like James, have a big social media following and have opinions on things, some people will take against you. That comes with the territory.

'But at some point, you've just got to think, "Fuck it, why am I pandering to people? I shouldn't have to be

making excuses for who I am." He's got a great wife, family and friends, who like him for who he is.

'I've got stories like Hask, but I'd never put them in a book. But Hask is savvy, knows that by sharing his experiences, telling stories – which he loves doing – they'll sell. The game has changed, in that there aren't as many characters around anymore. There are still a few behind closed doors, but it's not an attractive prospect for a player to display his full personality in public, let people know exactly who they are and what they get up to. The kind of stories Hask tells aren't supposed to happen in professional sport, and aren't good for a team's brand. That's why they aren't making many rugby players like Hask nowadays. In fact, I'd say he's one of the last of a dying breed.'

They say the definition of insanity is doing the same thing over and over again and expecting different results. I'm not quite that bad, because I don't do *exactly* the same thing over and over again – I make slightly different mistakes each time. However, the results are usually the same, namely a load of flak from the media and public, as well as lost sponsorship deals and other potential sponsors not wanting to touch me with a bargepole. As Dylan says, I do like being me and to be honest I will always try to get better, but I will not be acting any different. I like me. I might act smarter, but I won't change who I am at my core.

I never really mean or want to escalate things and cause a drama; it just seems to happen. I'm like my dad that way. I am capable of putting my hand up and admitting I've done something wrong. I'm not as proud as people think and I always want to be a better person, which is connected to my constant need to develop. But for a long time I just couldn't understand how people could be so fragile and hypocritical. If someone called me a dickhead, then I thought they should be strong enough to take whatever I fired back at them. Why should I have to be the bigger man? Why should those people feel like they could carry on getting away with insulting people? If I upset someone who thought I'd overstepped the mark and been heinously offensive, so be it.

However, I recently had another epiphany, which made me realise that I need to choose my battles more wisely, however upset or angry I am. The first rule of doing that was never, ever reply to people on social media. You will never win and I haven't since. The watershed moment was something that happened to me recently, which caused all sorts of drama. It all started when I was taking our dog Bertie for a walk. I'd just entered this field while talking to a mate on the phone, when I noticed this bug-eyed old bloke staring at me from his garden. Then he sidled up beside me and said, 'Taking the dog for a walk?'

'Yes,' I replied.

'A couple of sheep were killed here recently. Attacked. By a dog.'

'Oh, that's awful.'

I could tell he wasn't going to stop mithering me, so I told my mate to hold on a minute while I found out what this bloke wanted.

ME: 'Sorry, mate, is there anything you need?'
BLOKE: 'Are you going to put that dog on a lead?'
ME: 'Why do I need to put my dog on a lead?'
BLOKE: 'Because of the sheep.'
ME: 'What sheep?'
BLOKE: 'There could be sheep.'

ME: 'There aren't any sheep and I won't be putting Bert
      on a lead.'

He cocked his head and gave me a disappointed look, before
pulling out his phone and filming me, so I said to him, 'Listen,
mate, however much you want to have this conversation, it's
not going to happen.'

With that, I started walking off. I knew the field was empty
because I'd been there the day before. It was on the top of a
hill, so I could see for miles around, and literally every square
inch of land was sheep-free. And I knew what the law said: if
there is livestock in a field, you must keep your dog on a lead
– but there's no legal requirement to have your dog on a lead
if there is no livestock in a field and if it's not a certain time of
the year or there are no specific local by-laws. I was also on a
public footpath. He was just being a jobsworth.

So there I was, about 30 minutes into the walk at the bottom
of a field getting Bertie to do a bit of retrieval work, when I
saw this woman walking towards me from over yonder. It was
like a slow death: 2,000 metres, 1,000 metres, she was getting
closer and I just knew what she wanted to do. I thought to
myself, 'Please say she's not coming to give me a dressing
down.' I could feel myself tensing up, because I don't cope very
well with jobsworths, as you've probably worked out already.
I tried my best to get away from this woman, but she was
marching so fast – basically speed walking – that she eventually caught up with me.

WOMAN: 'Can I have a word?'
ME: 'Listen, if you've walked all that way to tell me the
      same thing that old guy told me, you've wasted your
      time. I'm just trying to walk my dog in peace.'

WOMAN: 'Let me explain why you need to put your dog
on a lead.'

ME: 'I know, he already told me, some sheep got killed
by a dog.'

WOMAN: 'Exactly. Which is why you need to put your
dog on a lead.'

ME: 'No, I don't. Can you see any animals?'

WOMAN: 'That's not the point.'

ME: 'Yes it is. There aren't any sheep for miles, are
there? Just please leave me alone!'

WOMAN: 'There might not be any sheep today but what
about next time?'

ME: 'Then next time I will put a lead on or not come in
here.'

WOMAN: 'That's not good enough.'

This woman wouldn't leave me alone. We had a bit of back
and forth and she ended up calling me the rudest person she'd
ever met, before storming off. Bertie didn't know what was
going on and thought she had come to play, so was running
around her and got in the way as she was trying to close a gate.

'Is your dog coming or not?'

I said, 'Sorry, love, he is staying with me as he has all these
imaginary sheep to maul.'

With that she bustled off, as only an angry horsey woman
can do.

To be honest, I was more amused than annoyed, and filmed
myself telling the story. But almost the second I posted the
video on Instagram, I started getting hammered by trolls
pretending to be farmers, going on about livestock and
attacks by dogs being a serious issue. I never said it wasn't, I
just pointed out how ridiculous it was that people would be

telling me to put my dog on a lead in a field with no animals in it. The point was more about old people needing things to do and the fact that officious people were everywhere. But it soon escalated into a classic case of people only hearing what they wanted to hear; as far as they were concerned, I was a fucking idiot who was putting farmers' livelihoods at risk, whose dog was running wild, attacking livestock and should be shot.

One woman sent me a picture of a bleeding sheep and called me a dick, and in the end I thought, 'I'm not having this. I'll do some funny responses, like James Blunt does when he's under attack on Twitter. Maybe that will defuse the situation.' That didn't quite work out as planned. In fact, it was a textbook case of how quickly a situation can spiral out of control on social media.

If I'm having a debate in person, I'm not particularly confrontational because more often than not you can walk away. But if someone starts having a go at me online, I get very angry and upset quite easily. And I'm getting worse, to the extent that Chloe reckons I've got brain damage from too many whacks on the head. And it doesn't matter if they're women, because the idea that they can say horrible things about me and I'm not allowed to go back at them because of their sex just seems like hypocrisy. So I fired back at the woman who'd sent me a picture of a bleeding sheep and called me a dick, only for another woman to accuse me of bullying her. I said, 'But she called me a dick!' And another woman popped up and said, 'You've got little dick energy.' Why do women always target my genitalia? How do they know how small it is? I replied to the you-have-got-little-dick-energy woman with, 'You have average bird banter,' which again seemed to make things worse. One rule for them and one for me.

I was in the pub by now, so thought this was all a bit of a giggle. I probably stepped over the mark when one women said, 'I am not a farmer but I can see you are a dick,' and I responded, 'Well, I am not a gynaecologist but I can see you are a cunt.' I shouldn't have done that, however funny I found it and everyone else did. I was only giving as good as I was getting. But then some bloke piled in with, 'You're a fucking cunt, mate, a misogynist who likes abusing women. I'd shoot you and your dog.' At that point I thought, 'Hang on a minute, this is getting a bit silly …' That was the first of about 20 death threats, calls for me and my dog to be shot, men asking to fight me. It appeared that every woman in the farming world came out, they called me everything and especially focused on me having a little dick and being a woman-beater. I kept having to check that there wasn't a picture of my dick on the internet they were referencing. Again, they said they were farmers, but they appeared just to be trolls, using farming as an excuse.

Apparently, a woman can call you anything they like in 2021, but if you respond it becomes about gender. They want to have free rein to insult you, but if you say it back you are attacking women and being a brute. The narrative then became all about me versus farmers. I love farmers, I have done lots to help them and have many friends who farm. This was just about angry trolls who wanted to get me for no reason, it had nothing to do with the amazing farmers who are so much a part of Britain's make-up. I showed a video of how well Bertie was trained, and they then accused me of damaging arable land and that everyone always says their dog is not a killer until he mauls a sheep. The fact that Bertie is always around sheep and doesn't care or ever chase them somehow escaped their attention. They smelt blood and wanted to cancel me. This was a good old-fashioned social media pile-on.

One minute I was happily walking my dog in an empty field, the next people were telling me I should be shot for killing sheep, destroying farmers' livelihoods and abusing women. How the hell did this happen? Suddenly, my timeline was full of people accusing me of worrying cows so much that their calves had to be aborted, and blinding new-born calves with Bertie's dog shit. I was even called a racist, after telling one woman that she sounded like Borat. And it didn't matter how many times I said, 'Hang on a minute. I was walking my dog in an empty field! Bertie didn't attack anyone or anything!', the abuse kept getting worse. All that mattered was that people felt offended, even if most people knew I hadn't actually done what I was being accused of.

Eventually, I posted that clip of Alan Partridge having a row with a farmer, after he'd trod in a rather large cowpat and made some comments about intensive farming: 'If you see a lovely field with a family having a picnic, and there's a nice pond in it, you fill in the pond with concrete, you plough the family into the field, you blow up the tree and use the leaves to make a dress for your wife, who's also your brother.'

Then I put a funny filter on my face (it made me look like I'd had my lips blown up, like Pete Burns) and recorded another video, describing in grisly but tongue-in-cheek detail exactly what I'd do to a farmer if he shot my dog. It was meant as a joke, but people started accusing me of threatening to kill farmers. It was like that scene from *The Life of Brian* when Brian is preaching in the street and people in the crowd keep misunderstanding him.

'What are you worrying about?'

'I'm worried about what you've got against birds.'

'I haven't got anything against birds. Consider the lilies.'

'He's having a go at the flowers now ...'

It was a full-blown crisis, the anatomy of a social media shitshow. After about an hour of this, and having blocked literally hundreds of people (some of them called things like 'The Friendly Shepherdess', who were far from friendly), I decided to switch my phone off. I thought it would soon blow over, but the following day I got a phone call from a sponsor who said, 'Look, farmers and women are a big part of our brand. We're dropping you.' I tried to explain that I hadn't done anything wrong, that I'd simply responded to being attacked, but they weren't having it.

It turned out that a female journalist had sent emails to all my sponsors and pretty much everyone I did business with, accusing me of making light of the epidemic of mental illness and suicide among the farming community during the Covid pandemic. She sent this picture of 30 pairs of empty wellington boots, saying this is how many farmers have taken their lives recently, would you like to comment on James's contribution to this. So I'd gone from replying to people's abuse to apparently making people kill themselves. That's when I was like, 'Wow, they really are trying to cancel me. This has got serious.' What made it even worse was the National Sheep Association then released a statement about the affair and said dog owners not respecting sheep was a huge issue. Then the National Farmers Union released a statement. I honestly couldn't believe it. Out of nothing, and I mean nothing, we had a national disaster on our hands.

Luckily, except for that one sponsor everyone else stuck by me and understood the truth. I'm glad that the sponsor dropped me as I don't want to be with weak companies who do anything to save face instead of making a stand. For every five people who complained, there were 5,000 who saw what I was saying as amusing, funny and just me responding to being trolled. They also understood that nothing had happened.

It probably didn't help that a few weeks before 'Farmergate', I'd got involved in another quite explosive row on Instagram. On that occasion, I'd posted some pictures on social media, showing how I'd managed to transform my body in eight weeks (I'd got too heavy during lockdown), and some personal trainer and former rugby player had had a go at me for faking them.

This personal trainer said, 'You're an influencer. How dare you post these fictional pictures. It's all down to the lighting.' I'd lost that weight by working my bollocks off, and I don't consider myself to be an influencer anyway, so I was livid. But having called the guy out, he then accused me of messing with people's mental health. That was too much. Again, I said some things I shouldn't have, and the *Daily Mail* ran a story with the headline, 'James Haskell launches foul-mouthed attack on personal trainer'.

Anyway, about eight other sponsors told me I couldn't go around calling people every name under the sun, whatever the provocation, and I had no choice but to admit I'd been in the wrong. That was a big wake-up call. I was costing myself money, and as you all know from reading this book, I love earning money, so I decided I wouldn't respond to anyone ever again. I'd just have to take the bending of the truth, abuse and death threats, because getting involved in rows with strangers online never fixed anything. The only person I was doing over by firing back was me. I thought I was being funny – for every complaint, I was getting loads of laughing emojis and thumbs up, which are like a drug – but I was demeaning myself. And I did feel bad that I'd dragged farmers into it, because it wasn't farmers who'd asked me to put my dog on a lead in the first place, it was small-minded trolls trying to fight me.

By getting involved in social media spats, I was taking far bigger risks than people not in the public eye. It didn't matter what anyone said to me, I'd be the one who made headlines and got judged, not the people who attacked me in the first place. As Chloe kept reminding me, 'If you work in the public eye, you can't go round swearing at people.' And as Jonathan Swift once said, 'Falsehood flies, and truth comes limping after it.' And he said that 300 years before social media was invented. But I was less bothered about my reputation than the fact I was doing myself out of money, which is the definition of stupid.

Actually, there was a funny postscript to Farmergate (there usually is, which makes it all seem worthwhile). A few weeks after it all kicked off, my dad called me and said, 'I've just seen a press release that says you're hosting the National Potato Industry Awards.' He was right, I was. What a strange life I lead. Then my dad said, 'Are you sure you should go? I'm worried it's a set-up, that they're luring you down there and you're going to get filled in by a bunch of potato farmers, out for revenge.' I told him not to talk such nonsense, that it had been booked months before Farmergate. But it did start playing on my mind. I imagined them dropping a cow on top of me, like irate farmers did with Alan Partridge, before chopping me up and putting me in bags of oven chips. As it turned out, I got cancelled anyway. My speaking agent called me some months later and said to me, 'You know that National Potato Industry Awards you were hosting, they have just called and said they can't use you as you are now hated by all UK farmers.' He didn't know about the story so I had to explain it all again. At least my agent saw the funny side. I called my dad up and told him, as he had been asking me, I'd say at least once a week for months, if I was still doing it. Bless him, he was so worried I was walking like a lamb to the slaughter. According to my agent, the organiser did say that if it blew over, maybe I could come back next year and host. My reply? 'Fuck 'em, give them Joe Marler's number …'

CHLOE MADELEY:

'James will often say to me, "Don't you think I'm in the right?" And I'll have to reply, "Quite honestly, I don't." From day one, I've never lied to him, tried to comfort him by telling him he's right. Instead, I'll tell him to leave things alone and walk away, if I think that's the best course of action.

'I think that's one of the things he likes about me, because it makes him feel like he's got a bit of a safety net. He knows he's a bulldozer, personality-wise. He's very outspoken and in your face, like his dad. So he needs honest feedback from at least a few people in his life. But he still can't help overstepping the mark sometimes, like that Instagram row he had with farmers. Instead of thinking, "I'm a former England rugby player who wants to work in the media, with hundreds of thousands of followers, maybe I should step away from this," he started trolling them back.

'James has always had a strange relationship with social media, for as long as I've known him. We'd been dating for a short while when I went to Austria for a couple of months, to film the Channel 4 show The Jump. *Before I left, I said, "I need to know if I'm in a relationship or not. Is me going away going to be a problem?" And James replied, "No. Get ready for when I have to go away for two months with England. Let's give it a go, let's be exclusive."*

'Somehow the press got hold of the fact we were now in a relationship, but when I returned from Austria I suddenly realised that James was following every porn star imaginable on Twitter and Instagram. It was like he had some pathological habit. I said to him, "James, I don't mind if you watch porn. Most people watch porn, at least from our generation. But the press now know that you're dating Richard and Judy's daughter. And if I can see that you've been following and liking all these porn stars, everyone else can see it. And it's only a matter of time before the press pick up on it."

'James's response was, "Social media isn't like real life. Why do you care?" We almost broke up over it. How could he say "social media isn't real" when we met on it? He even got Dozzer involved, to try to convince me that social media wasn't real. It was like they were trying to gaslight me. Luckily, I'm not an idiot. This argument went on for days, and in the end I had to change tack. I said to him, "Forget about the fact the press could get hold of the story, it's just really disrespectful to me. You must be able to see that!" In the end, I gave him an ultimatum: stop following porn stars, or I'm out.

'The day after that row with the farmers, James got paid a lot of money for a job which basically consisted of hanging out with Peter Crouch at Wembley. When he got home, he said to me, "How come they can say what they like to me and I can't say it back to them?" And I replied, "Because when you're being paid to hang out with Peter Crouch at Wembley, the trade-off is that you can't act like a bog-standard nutter on the internet. You must understand this."

'Because I grew up with celebrity, I understand more than most that you have to act a certain way in public. When you're in a privileged position like that, doing an exciting job with lots of perks that millions of people would kill to do, you can't just act how you'd like to, you have to rein things in. Maybe if I hadn't been made aware of that growing up, I'd have thought, "Yeah, fuck 'em, James," and watched his media career implode.'

Chloe's being a bit disingenuous, because it's not as if I was interacting with porn stars, sending them messages or leaving comments like 'Cor, I'd love to have a go on that!' I was just following them on Instagram. As far as I was concerned, it was no different to looking at women in bikinis in *FHM* magazine, because it's not like porn stars can do their thing on Instagram. Looking at attractive women is not the same as cheating. And these porn stars had millions of followers. It's not like I was making personal contact with Dusty Debbie who lives down the road and once appeared in *Razzle* magazine with a cucumber, it was a tad more removed and impersonal than that.

I just thought it was a bit weird that she'd been checking up on who I was following on social media, and I didn't understand why anyone else would care. Plus, on the odd occasion I looked at her Instagram profile, it would be full of blokes with their tops off, showing off their muscles. Chloe's excuse would be that they were big in the health and fitness industry, so I'd reply, 'Well, those girls are big in the porn industry.' In the end, I had to concede the argument and ended up unfollowing every woman on the list. I couldn't agree that I'd done anything wrong, but I really needed to minimise the stress levels.

Chloe says I'm rugby's answer to Donald Trump, so narcissistic that I genuinely think I know better than anyone else. The way I see it, I'm quite prepared to hear a counter argument, whatever the topic might be, and I don't mind being wrong. During my rugby career, I was always one to hold my hand up whenever I made mistakes. But some stuff I just don't think I'm wrong about. It's like that famous Brian Clough quote, when he was asked what he'd say if someone came to him and told him he'd got something wrong: 'Well, I ask him which way he thinks it should be done, we get down to it, and then we talk about it for 20 minutes and then we decide I was right.'

Having said that, Chloe is far more intelligent than me and has become an important sounding board for me, because she's naturally a far more careful person than I am. So when I'm going off about something, instead of doing something rash, I'll say to Chloe, 'This person has done this, can I react in this way?' And more often than not, she'll reply, 'No, don't do that, that wouldn't be right.' I still make mistakes and pile into things when I shouldn't, like with Farmergate, but only when I forget to confer with Chloe first.

Chloe will make me think about a situation in a completely different way to how I was thinking about it before, and often had some very enlightening views when it came to my rugby. During and after the 2021 Six Nations, the England boys had some terrible abuse thrown their way, some of the worst I'd seen. And Chloe said to me, 'How dare these fans claim to care more about the England rugby team than the actual players? How dare they think they're more upset?' I'd never thought about it like that, but she was right. When you play for England, you put your heart and soul into it. Nobody wants to play badly, and it really hurts when you do. After a game, fans get to go back to their normal lives, but playing rugby for England is our normal life. So the idea that fans – or indeed the media – care more than us is ridiculous.

Not only does Chloe make me see things from a different perspective, she's also made me more compassionate and empathetic. I'll storm through the door and start telling her about some spat I've had on social media, assuming she'll agree with me, but instead she'll say, 'They might be a wanker, but you can't go around calling them that on a public forum. You could have beaten them with intelligence, but you've descended to their level and become as simple as them.' I'll storm out into the garden in a huff, but after thinking things over for ten minutes I'll normally conclude that Chloe was bang on.

There are plenty of people on social media who claim to be kind but are actually far bigger arseholes than me. Look at the American model Chrissy Teigen: she spent years calling people out for not meeting her very high standards of 'compassion, empathy and humanity', and then it came out that she was one of the vilest trolls of all – she once told a fellow celebrity to kill herself. Don't preach perfection if you have more skeletons in your closet than Fred West.

But not being true to yourself is never a good idea. I tried it when I was playing for England, because people kept saying to me, 'Life would be easier if you weren't so full-on.' But it didn't work. After a while, those same people were saying to me, 'Are you all right? The lads are a bit worried about you. You haven't been your usual self, you seem a bit down.' I'd think, 'I was just giving you what you asked for, which was quiet and retiring. And now it turns out you don't like that version either!' I'd had that my entire life. At school, teachers would say to me, 'Try toning things down a bit.' And then a few weeks later they'd say, 'Is something wrong? Try being yourself again. But not too much ...'

It was only when Eddie Jones took over as head coach that I was able to be who I really am, and I was a better player for it. But it's just so difficult to be authentic nowadays. Whatever you say, someone will pop up and claim it's problematic and making them feel uncomfortable. Everything is so sanitised, everywhere there are people telling you not to say this and not to say that. I think there will be a backlash eventually because people still want authenticity and character, but it's going to get worse before it gets better.

Sometimes it's so ridiculous it's funny, like the time I put up a post about my love of coffee. I had people saying to me, 'Have you not thought about the farmers in developing countries who don't get a fair price for their beans?' Or, 'I think tea's more ethical.' I was thinking, 'How has this happened? I just said I liked coffee, and now I'm under attack.' It's like that Ricky Gervais skit, when he talks about someone going into a town square, seeing an advert for guitar lessons and saying, 'But I don't fucking want guitar lessons!', before phoning the number and telling the teacher in person. As Ricky says, 'Fine, it's not for you. Just walk away. Don't worry about it!'

How arrogant do you have to be to think that people having different interests or disagreeing with you is a problem? How arrogant do you have to be to think that people who disagree with you are lesser human beings, immoral even? I've got no problem with people disagreeing with me, but I do have a problem with people insulting me, telling me I'm a terrible person for thinking differently to them. I don't understand why they feel the need to point out our differences at all. What happened to tolerance? Why do so many people take things personally? Once upon a time, if you had a dodgy meal at a restaurant, you just didn't go back. You might have made a discreet complaint, told the waiter that the food was cold, but you didn't go on social media and start slagging the restaurant off and try to bring their business to its knees.

PAUL DORAN-JONES:

'Am I worried about James getting cancelled? Yes. He just gets himself involved in so many unnecessary situations, especially on social media. When Farmergate happened, he said to me, "Doz, you need to have a look at this. What do you think?" I replied, "Jim, I don't need to look at it to know that you've brought it on yourself. Why are you oxygenating random idiots? Why are you fanning the flames? How do you even have time to do this?"

'Celebrity and social media are not my worlds, but I understand that if you're in those worlds, and you're earning money from having a profile, you have to feed it. You have to open the door to your life, your relationships, your opinions, and people will walk straight through that door and clatter you. And that's exactly what happens to James, over and over again.

'James is usually articulate and quick enough to get himself out of tricky situations, but not always. And while he tries to take advice on board, he'll just go and do the same thing a couple of weeks later. But part of me admires James for digging in and sticking up for himself. And I don't think he'll ever stop having social media spats, because he knows that for every person he offends, he amuses someone else. And his point would be, "If you don't like it, don't follow me." And that's how it should be. I actually think the culture is the problem, not James. We live in pretty mad times. People need to stop *complaining about everything and telling people they're wrong.*

'There are so many great rugby players around nowadays, but most of them are vanilla. Rugby was always supposed to be about characters, fun and stories, but it was noticeable towards the end of both our careers that this kind of stuff was on its way out. The USP of rugby was disappearing. And if you take away the colour from rugby, I'm not sure what you've got left, because the product on the field isn't always the greatest. In contrast, James is just an interesting bloke and never shies away from a conversation, whatever it's about. He's not afraid to call someone out, never takes the middle ground, never gives a bland answer, says exactly what he thinks. And if you don't like it, tough. In this current climate, that's quite dangerous, but it's also really refreshing.'

Everyone who knows me seems to be worried I'll get myself cancelled. *I'm* still worried I'll get myself cancelled, become the definition of self-sabotage, because I'm not sure how long I'll be able to bite my lip for. If I'm sitting at a table with ten other people and I say something that makes nine people laugh and one person cry, I consider that a win. That was my attitude during Farmergate and every other spat I've had. I just like making people laugh. But that's a dangerous game nowadays, because all that seems to count is the opinion of that one person who's crying. I should add that I'm not talking about bullying, which is something else completely. I'm talking about people taking offence to something I just happen to say, which isn't even directed at them.

There are things that people should get cancelled for, like racism, homophobia, sexual assault and paedophilia. But if I got cancelled for calling someone a wanker on social media, because they said they wanted to kill me, I'd just become even noisier. Because once you've been cancelled, there's no way back anyway. That said, I certainly don't have any plans to be some kind of free-speech martyr, like Laurence Fox. Unlike Laurence, who's torpedoed his own career by refusing to shut up about things, I'm not on some moral crusade. To be honest, I just like money too much. As much as I love doing lots of different things, the best part of any job is getting paid (my favourite two words are 'paid invoice'). And I'd rather tone it down and have a few quid than keep shouting my mouth off and be poor. Also, I don't really care about any of it. I am never fighting for a cause, I am just fighting against trolls and morons, while trying to make people laugh.

There are so many nice people out there, so why get bogged down rowing with stupid, negative people? You're never going to win. As Mark Twain was supposed to have said, 'Never argue with stupid people, they will drag you down to their level and then beat you with experience.' So while I haven't given up highlighting bullshit, I have realised that I have to let some of it slide. I'm always going to have an opinion on things, but the days of arguing with idiots on social media are over. I think that's the right balance, because it means staying authentic without shooting myself in both feet.

ALEX PAYNE:

'If James has had an epiphany, it's the slowest epiphany known to man. He's been going around epiphany roundabout for the best part of ten years. I don't really worry about it, although I'm sure other people who are in business with him do. And I do hope he takes the right exit eventually.'

Luckily, if I do say or do something really stupid and get cancelled, I've got something up my sleeve. Having got my digger licence at JCB, I am now qualified to operate any machine up to 100 tonnes. Even if I don't get cancelled, if there's another pandemic, or some other catastrophe that necessitates a lockdown, I can now work through it, instead of kicking my heels in the house. And who doesn't love driving around in giant pieces of machinery?

That was a very funny week down at the JCB Golf and Country Club in Uttoxeter for my digger course. I'd walk into the clubhouse at four o'clock every day, happy as Larry, having been digging holes and trenches and filling dumper trucks all day. Most people were there on corporate golf days and there was me, walking about in my Timberland boots with flakes of dried clay leaving a Hansel and Gretel-style trail wherever I went. I only realised this after it was too late and asked for a pan and brush to clean it up. I was also wearing muddy track-suit bottoms while everyone else was smartly dressed. I could see the golfers looking my way and whispering to each other, probably saying, 'Is that fucking James Haskell sitting in the corner? What the hell is he doing here?'

That course was some of the most fun I've ever had. Parts of it were like being on a school trip, like the fact they gave me a packed lunch every day, consisting of a ham and cheese sand-wich, a Scotch egg, a bag of crisps, a Dairy Milk, an apple and a can of Coke. And I loved slumming it in the quarry with the other guys, listening to their stories and hearing what it's like to be part of the famed JCB Dancing Diggers, doing shows all around the world for thousands of people. The way a couple of the lads spoke, you'd have thought they were the Harlem Globetrotters, with a girl in every port. My instructors Ben and Tom, who were doing the actual teaching, were stifling laughs over all these stories of women throwing themselves at the Dancing Digger boys. It was just like being in a rugby changing room, and I was loving it. They did point out after we had left, 'Who the hell do they think they're kidding? The only people interested in diggers are 60-year-old men and five-year-old boys.' Honestly, I had such a good time. I was able to switch off and relax. Everyone looked after me so well and I spent the whole time either working hard or laughing. Perfection.

I won't bore you with the details, but it was very technical stuff and you had to be quite dextrous to pull some of the manoeuvres off. But there was also a lot of mucking about, so much that I spent a lot of time pissing myself laughing. The JCB film crew wanted to make out I was a complete amateur at the start of the week, which wasn't actually true, because I'd been driving diggers for a while already. But I happily played along, doing my best Frank Spencer impersonation, skittling cones, running stuff over, getting told off for drinking and digging. And the idea was that by the end of the week I'd be an expert. Meanwhile, Frank, the guy in charge, an owner of Operator Training, the testing school, and father of Ben, kept interfering when we were filming (as he kept saying, 'Sorry to interrupt and talk about myself again, but that is my favourite topic.' He had me pissing myself all week; he is such a legend and the best in the business on a machine). While I was doing my theory test, he suggested dropping the clipboard on the desk in a menacing way, to add some drama to the occasion. Then, whenever he spoke, he seemed to develop this James Bond villain voice. Ben kept bollocking him and said, 'Speak normally, Frank. No, you don't sound like that normally.' Frank was faux upset when his lines got cut out and his acting suggestions ignored. He would have stormed off to his trailer, if he'd had one. It was so funny to be a part of. I was lucky they were all such good people and made my time with Operator Training and JCB so much fun. Plus they tolerated me acting like a kid in a sweet shop.

As there was millions of pounds worth of kit flying around the place, I was constantly asking, 'Can I have a go on that?' And they always said yes. I drove diggers, bulldozers, huge dumpers and tractors, and reversed a 50-tonne front shovel around a course. I wouldn't say I was an expert by the end of the week, but it turned out I'd found something I was naturally good at. All the team had the patience of saints. They did have to keep checking I was 36 and not in fact 12. They had never seen someone so excited to be there.

I got 50 out of 50 in my health and safety test, 215 out of 215 in my theory and one minor in the practical. And two of my most prized possessions are now the hi-vis vest and helmet presented to me by Murphy, the massive London construction company, who were on a visit to the JCB quarry at the same time. They have pride of place in my study, along with some of my old rugby gear. I came away from that course thinking, 'Bollocks to everything else, I honestly want to go and work on a building site.' I'm definitely going back to do my dumper truck and classic JCB 180 tests.

Working heavy machinery has become my new obsession, which I'm sure a lot of people reading this will find a little bit weird. But it makes perfect sense. Like I said when Chloe asked why I was getting my licence, 'It's very relaxing, and I've been obsessed with digging since I was a kid.' On that JCB course, I was back to being that little boy, pestering the builders in my mum and dad's garden (and not about their porn stash), or that annoying kid from *Home Alone*, wanting to know how everything worked. I loved the fact that I was learning skills, then having to execute and be judged on them.

Chloe came round to my point of view eventually. As she said, 'A building company doesn't care if you've been cancelled, they'd probably still hire you if you murdered someone. They hire pretty much anyone apart from nonces.' I have done many daft things in my life and will probably do many more. But there is one thing I'm certain of: murder and noncery will never be on the menu.

So now that we've reached the end, what conclusions can we draw from this Haskovery™? Well, I think it's fair to say I am a dickhead but a good dickhead. The world is changing, and while I'm still around I like to think there is a place for people with opinions who want to be themselves. We need to keep fighting the good fight against those who moan for moaning's sake. We need to make sure that social media and the very loud people on it don't change our way of life too much. Don't believe everything that you read or see online, though we all do it and half the time we don't have the facts. Stay strong, applaud hard work and remember that sport is just a game. Laugh every day if you can, and don't be scared to leap in and give things a try. The worst thing that can happen is you get an amazing story to tell your mates.

Life is for living; it's not about the end, it's about the journey. I have had the most interesting and fun adventure for the last 36 years, with many lows but millions more highs. I have laughed, I have cried and I have made others do the same. I'm not sure that we've solved anything with *Ruck Me*, but what we have learned is that my mum thinks I'm amazing, my friends and work colleagues like me, my wife thinks I'm Donald Trump, and I need to call Ollie Phillips more often.

ACKNOWLEDGEMENTS

Behind any great book – and this is a great book, even if I do say so myself – you need to thank all the people who made it possible. My fellow writer Ben Dirs: once again you have pulled it out the bag. I know it was touch and go as to whether you would be able to do this book – I appreciate your moving heaven and earth to finish your other projects so we could work together again. At the start of any conversations around *Ruck Me*, I said it's you or it doesn't happen until you can do it.

Next I need to thank Oliver Malcolm: who knew from some Instagram stalking on his part that we would have one *Sunday Times* bestseller and two more books in the works, including *Ruck Me*? Thank you for your support and your belief. I am sorry I always ignore your demands for word counts and the length of social media content. You always take it in good humour, even though I know you would like to shout at me.

Thank you to Holly and the rest of the team at HarperCollins: once again you made this a dream process and are super-easy to work with. You are professional and always smash it.

To Lucy: thank you for all your help with the PR and making sure we got the book in front of all the right people. Also thank you for helping me sign over 3.5k books in three hours. No mean feat.

I would also like to say thank you to Laurence Mowbray, the brains behind the *What a Flanker* podcast. I know who you are, even if nobody else does.

Thank you to my agent Clare: once again you have sorted me the best deal and always been there for some sage advice and to put out any fires.

Thank you to all my mates, teammates and coaches who were interviewed for this book. You were honest – if anything, too honest at times – and you helped shape this book into what it is. I really appreciate all the support, love and friendship you have given me over the years. I regard all of you as mates and if you need someone to slag you off for your own books then please feel free to call me.

To my parents: you always gave me everything to succeed and pushed me to be the best version of myself. Mum, thank you so much for fighting my corner and for being part of this book. I am not sure you were ever talking about me – perhaps a long-lost brother I didn't know I had – but at least we know who to call in if I need some good PR and talking up. I love you both more than anything.

To Chloe, my rock, my guidance counsellor, my best friend and at times my carer. You are an amazing person who makes me better every day. I am sorry about causing so much drama, but at least we got another book out of it. You are amazing in every way and I would be lost without you. You make me smile and always try to laugh at my jokes, when you – in your own words – think I am rugby's answer to Donald Trump.

Lastly, I want to thank you the reader. Without you there would be no books and no life after rugby. I know I am hard to take sometimes, but as you will have learned from *Ruck Me*, I am a pretty simple person who wants to enjoy this journey we call life to the fullest and have as much fun as possible doing so. If I've made you smile, then good; if I've offended you, then good. As long as it wasn't indifference, I am happy.